the Blue Castle

The Original Manuscript

L. M. Montgomery

Edited and Annotated
by **Carolyn Strom Collins**

NIMBUS
PUBLISHING
— NIMBUS.CA —

Nimbus Publishing Limited
3660 Strawberry Hill Street, Halifax, NS, B3K 5A9
(902) 455-4286 nimbus.ca

Printed and bound in Canada
NB1682

The Anderson Muskoka Series Postcard on the cover is provided courtesy of the Toronto Public Library.
Design: Jenn Embree
Cover design: Heather Bryan
Editor: Marianne Ward
Editor for press: Claire Bennet

Nimbus Publishing is based in Kjipuktuk, Mi'kma'ki, the traditional territory of the Mi'kmaq People.

Library and Archives Canada Cataloguing in Publication

Title: The blue castle : the original manuscript / L. M. Montgomery ; edited by Carolyn Strom Collins.
Names: Montgomery, L. M. (Lucy Maud), 1874-1942, author. | Collins, Carolyn Strom, editor.
Description: Includes bibliographical references.
Identifiers: Canadiana (print) 20230596800 | Canadiana (ebook) 20230596819 | ISBN 9781774712757 (softcover) | ISBN 9781774712948 (EPUB)
Subjects: LCSH: Montgomery, L. M. (Lucy Maud), 1874-1942. Blue castle. | LCSH: Montgomery, L. M. (Lucy Maud), 1874-1942. Blue castle—Criticism, Textual.
Classification: LCC PS8526.O55 B5 2024 | DDC C813/.52—dc23

Nimbus Publishing acknowledges the financial support for its publishing activities from the Government of Canada, the Canada Council for the Arts, and from the Province of Nova Scotia. We are pleased to work in partnership with the Province of Nova Scotia to develop and promote our creative industries for the benefit of all Nova Scotians.

TABLE *of* CONTENTS

Introduction

L. M. Montgomery: A Biographical Sketch

L. M. Montgomery, author of *Anne of Green Gables, The Blue Castle,* and many other novels, stories, poems, and essays, was born in Prince Edward Island, Canada, on November 30, 1874. She began writing journal entries and poems at an early age. Her first publication, the poem "On Cape Leforce," was published November 26, 1890, just before she turned sixteen. Her best-known novel, *Anne of Green Gables,* was published in 1908. More titles followed and in the summer of 1926, her eleventh novel, *The Blue Castle,* was published.

Montgomery grew up in Cavendish, PEI. She lived with her grandparents, Alexander and Lucy Macneill, after her mother died in 1876. Her father left her in the care of her grandparents when he left PEI for Saskatchewan. In 1890, accompanied by her grandfather Sen. Donald Montgomery, she travelled by train to Prince Albert, Saskatchewan, to live with her father and his new family. However, she and her stepmother didn't get along, and young Maud returned to Prince Edward Island the next year. She attended Prince of Wales College from September 1893 to June 1894 and began a teaching career, teaching in three PEI schools over three years. When her grandfather Macneill died in 1898, she returned to Cavendish to care for her grandmother for the next thirteen years.

In 1906, Montgomery became engaged to marry the Rev. Ewan Macdonald. They married after grandmother Macneill died in 1911. After a long honeymoon in Scotland and England, the Macdonalds made their home in Leaskdale, Ontario. Montgomery continued to write while helping Ewan in his ministry and becoming a mother to sons Chester and Stuart. They lived in Leaskdale for fifteen years and moved to Norval, Ontario, in 1926, a few months before *The Blue Castle* was published. After ten years in Norval, the Macdonalds retired to a new home in the Swansea suburb of Toronto. Montgomery died there in April 1942.

The Setting for *The Blue Castle*

A two-week vacation in the Muskoka area of Ontario, a visit to a rustic cabin on the shores of Lake Muskoka, and memories of her early years in Cavendish, Prince Edward Island—all of these experiences L. M. Montgomery wove into her novel *The Blue Castle*.

She wrote to George B. Macmillan, one of her correspondents: "I loved Muskoka so much that for once I forsook my dear Island and laid the scene in Ontario" (from *My Dear Mr. M.*). Indeed, *The Blue Castle* is Montgomery's only novel not set wholly or in part in Prince Edward Island, where she was born and spent most of her early life. (*Jane of Lantern Hill*, published in 1937, is set in both Prince Edward Island and Ontario.)

The Macdonald family's trip to Bala, Ontario, in 1922 was the primary inspiration for *The Blue Castle*. In *Lucy Maud Montgomery and Bala*, Jack Hutton and Linda Jackson-Hutton identified the locations that Montgomery used for the novel. "Deerwood" is actually the town of Bala; "Lake Mistawis" is Lake Muskoka; "Port Laurence" is Gravenhurst; Roaring Abel's house and Barney's island are north of Bala as is "Chidley Corners," which is based on Glen Orchard. Jack and Linda have lived in Bala for many years and own Bala's Museum with Memories of Lucy Maud Montgomery. Their book is invaluable in understanding Montgomery's fascination with the Muskoka area.

L. M. Montgomery's Trip to Bala

The Huttons believe Montgomery and her family decided to spend two weeks in Bala in the summer of 1922 because they had an invitation to visit Rev. John Mustard's rustic cottage on Lake Muskoka. They visited the Mustards at their cottage on July 29. They discovered that John Mustard and his son Gordon had built the cottage themselves on a remote spot on the shores of Dudley Bay in Lake Muskoka, across from Acton Island. There are two smaller islands in the bay, as well. It is reasonable to assume that the Mustards' cottage was a model for the home of *The Blue Castle*'s Barney Snaith and that one of the small islands

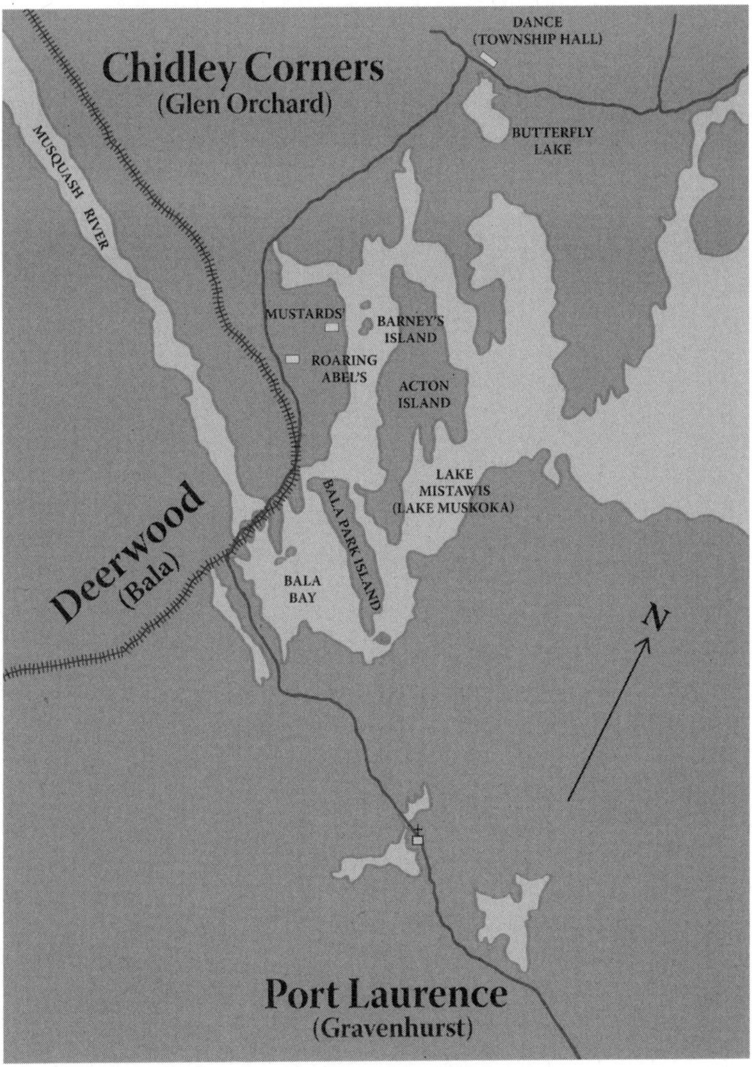
DANCE
(TOWNSHIP HALL)
Chidley Corners
(Glen Orchard)
BUTTERFLY
LAKE
MUSQUASH RIVER
MUSTARDS'
BARNEY'S
ISLAND
ROARING
ABEL'S
ACTON
ISLAND
LAKE
MISTAWIS
(LAKE MUSKOKA)
BALA PARK ISLAND
Deerwood
(Bala)
BALA
BAY
N
Port Laurence
(Gravenhurst)

This map is based on one drawn by Linda Jackson-Hutton for *Lucy Maud Montgomery and Bala* (USED WITH PERMISSION).

must have been chosen by Montgomery as his. It also seems reasonable to suggest that John Mustard may have been, at least in part, a model for the character of Barney Snaith. Mustard's love of the natural world and his self-sufficiency in the woods surrounding the cottage strongly resemble some of Barney's characteristics. (Other men have been suggested as partial models for Barney, as well: John Stirling, minister in Cavendish; Bliss Carmen, Canadian poet; Rev. Edwin Smith, a friend of the Macdonalds; even Irish playwright George Bernard Shaw. See Elizabeth Waterston's *Magic Island*.)

John Mustard had been Montgomery's teacher in Prince Albert, Saskatchewan, in 1890–91, and had courted her, finally asking her to marry him. She flatly refused and never expected to see him again. However, Mustard eventually became a well-known Presbyterian minister, living with his family in the Toronto area for many years. His and Montgomery's paths crossed occasionally due to her husband's affiliation with Presbyterian churches in Ontario. (For more on Montgomery and John Mustard see her journal entries, especially from 1890–91, and "John Mustard: A closer look at the first man to ask Maud to marry him" in *Lucy Maud Montgomery and Bala*.)

Writing *The Blue Castle*

L. M. Montgomery began writing *The Blue Castle* early in 1924, two years after she and her family had vacationed in the "cottage country" of Ontario. She writes in her journal entry of April 10, 1924, that she "did some work on a book I'm trying to write, *The Blue Castle*, but couldn't get in the proper mood." This had changed by November 27, when she noted, "I am finding much pleasure writing my new book *The Blue Castle*." She finished it a few months later, writing on February 8, 1925, that "On Wednesday [February 4] I finished a novel, *The Blue Castle*—a little comedy for adults. I have enjoyed writing it very much. It seemed a refuge from the cares and worries of my real world. I shall still have a good bit of work revising it."

According to her journal entries of February 19 and 26, she spent the next few weeks revising the manuscript and getting it "ready to be typed." She wrote that "an undercurrent of unrest and depression" was making it difficult to enjoy the process.

Finally, on March 10, 1925, she wrote that she had "finished revising *The Blue Castle* and have it ready to be typed. I am sorry it is done. It has been for several months a daily escape from a world of intolerable realities." These "intolerable realities" included worrying over the Church Union question, her husband Ewan Macdonald's severe melancholia, her own tendency to depression during the winter months, local church problems, and lawsuits with her original publisher, L. C. Page and Company of Boston.

In late December of 1925, Ewan received a call to become minister of two churches in Norval and Union, Ontario, adding to Maud's feeling of sadness at having to leave Leaskdale where they had lived for nearly fifteen years. By mid-February 1926, they had moved to the manse in Norval where they would spend the next ten years.

Publishing *The Blue Castle*

The Blue Castle was published in August 1926. Montgomery received her first copy on August 5 and was rather disappointed in the look of it. She wrote that "It has a make-up different from all my other books. Not so pretty. A plain cover." The next edition featured a sketch of a turreted castle high on a cliff; most editions published since 1926 include a castle on the cover.

Although the dedication is not included in the manuscript, Montgomery dedicated the novel to her long-time correspondent, Ephraim Weber. However, the first edition did not include the dedication. It was not until the next edition was produced that the dedication was printed: "To Mr. Ephraim Weber, M.A., Who understands the architecture of Blue Castles."

When Weber questioned her about the meaning, Montgomery explained that "I merely meant that I thought you, like most people of the house of Joseph, understood 'how fair the realm imagination opens to the view' and knew, too, how much more beautiful and satisfying our own secret 'Blue Castles' are to any mansion we may build or have built for us in 'real life'" (from *After Green Gables: L. M. Montgomery's Letters to Ephraim Weber, 1916–1941*).

The Manuscript (and Its Transcription)

L. M. Montgomery kept her manuscript of *The Blue Castle* with her all her life, along with most of the manuscripts for her other novels. Fifteen of those manuscripts are now kept in the permanent collection of the Confederation Centre in Charlottetown, Prince Edward Island. (The *Rilla of Ingleside* manuscript is kept in the L. M. Montgomery Collection at Guelph University in Guelph, Ontario; typescript versions of *The Blythes are Quoted* are kept at Guelph University and at McMaster University, in Hamilton, Ontario.)

The paper on which *The Blue Castle* is written looks to be ordinary ledger paper, torn into pieces about 21.7 cm (a little less than 8.5 inches) by 17.0 cm (about 6.66 inches). The manuscript is 3.7 cm (about 1.5 inches) thick. (These measurements are based on Rea Wilmshurst's description of the manuscript in *Lucy Maud Montgomery: A Preliminary Bibliography*.) The paper is thinner than most ledger or notebook paper used today.

The manuscript is in two sections: the first is the main body of the novel; the second contains Montgomery's "Notes," additions to the text that were to be added to the main body when the manuscript was typed.

At first glance, it appears that the main body contains 516 pages, as that is the number on the final page. However, on closer inspection, we see that Montgomery renumbered or misnumbered some of the pages. The first six pages of the manuscript are numbered 1a–4a, and 3b–4b; Montgomery rewrote the original pages 1 and 2, extending them to just over three pages, which she numbered 1a–4a; pages 3b and 4b seem to be her original pages 3 and 4. After page 4b, she continues with the original page 5. Next there are pages 40a–49a, 40b–46b, 45c–46c, 47b–49b; after page 53, there are 54a–54b, and pages 55 and 56 are combined onto one page. After page 118, there are pages 119a–119b; pages 123 and 124 are combined onto one page as are pages 155 and 156. Page 192b follows page 192; after page 223, there are pages 224a–224b; after page 233, there are pages 234a–234b; pages 352–354 are combined onto one page; after page 414, there are pages 415a–415b. This results in the actual number of pages in the main body totaling 531.

As for the Notes pages, it appears that they number 228, the number on the last Notes page; but due to Montgomery's numbering page 51 as "51–57," page 25 as "25/26" and page 127 as "127 & 128," the actual count is 220. Thus, the entire number of pages in the manuscript comes to 751 (not 744).

The Notes pages were completely rewritten as Montgomery readied the manuscript for typing. She begins with "Note A" on her newly written first page (page 1a). But by the time she gets to page 3b (originally page 3), we see that she began to rework the original notes to put them in order. The first note on page 3b started as "N," but Montgomery struck that out and made it note "B." On that same page, note C started out as "Y3" before Montgomery reorganized the notes. The first notes she wrote are not in any kind of numerical order, indicating that she must have made many passes through the manuscript before finally renumbering them. But for the most part, the reorganized notes follow her usual numbering system: notes A–Z, then A1–Z1, and so on through Note Y14, with some of the notes being added into the manuscript later and out of the usual order.

Montgomery was not one to waste paper. Even after she was able to afford the luxury of writing on one side, she wrote on both sides of the pages in her manuscripts. She frequently used the backs of published stories and poems, even bills and invoices, as manuscript pages. For instance, the first 296 pages of her manuscript for *Anne of Green Gables* were written on the reverse sides of some of her stories and poems; the remaining pages were written on both sides of clean paper. (See *Anne of Green Gables: The Original Manuscript*.)

The manuscript for *The Blue Castle* was written on both sides of clean pages, except for three leaves. One of these (after manuscript page 386) was left blank; two (manuscript pages 129 and 130) were written on the backs of a two-part poem entitled "The Difference – 1. The Man" and "The Difference – 2. The Woman." ("The Difference," parts one and two, was published in *Brief Stories* in September 1925.)

After photographing each page of Montgomery's manuscript for *The Blue Castle*, I began transcribing the main body and Montgomery's additional notes, inserting the notes into the transcribed pages as closely as possible to the places Montgomery had indicated they should go. I also added some annotations to further explain some of the vocabulary, allusions, and other items in the form of editor's notes. In this book, Montgomery's notes appear alongside the text where she intended them to be inserted, marked by the note number she gave them. My own notes and annotations also appear alongside the main text.

In order to point out the differences between the original manuscript and the published version, I used the first edition of *The Blue Castle* published by the Frederick A. Stokes Company (New York, 1926); this edition was published simultaneously by McClelland and Stewart (Toronto, 1926). The text in these two editions is identical, according to *Lucy Maud Montgomery: A Preliminary Bibliography* by Russell, Russell, and Wilmshurst.

Montgomery wrote so quickly that she did not always insert punctuation—periods, commas, hyphens, or other marks. Where Montgomery neglected to write the necessary punctuation and left out the occasional word (or the occasional letter, in the case of misspellings), her publisher added them. Those additions to the original manuscript are shown here in square brackets. Montgomery made liberal use of dashes. Where they "should" be em dashes, I've used em dashes, but where they "should" be a semicolon or some other punctuation, I have left them as is. There are a few spelling errors in the original manuscript; where necessary, these have been explained in the notations throughout the text. There is also text (including pieces of punctuation) in the original manuscript that does not appear in the published version; those instances are marked with a strike-through to indicate a deletion by Montgomery or a double strike-through to indicate a deletion by the publisher.

Throughout *The Blue Castle* manuscript there are about eighty words and phrases circled in pencil. It is my view that the typist circled them in order to ask Montgomery for clarification about them at some point. In some cases, the circled words are so faint that it may have been difficult for the typist to read them; in other cases, Montgomery's handwriting is not easy to decipher. A few words, such as "empery" and "jamfry," were probably unfamiliar to the typist and needed explanation. (The circled words are indicated in this book with a grey highlight.) Chapter numbers were out of order and needed to be checked. In any case, these issues were addressed and clarified for submitting to the original publisher. (I have numbered the chapters in this book to reflect the final numbers used in the original published version. Readers can see Montgomery's original numbers in the scans that accompany the printed text.) Unfortunately, the typescript for *The Blue Castle* has been lost, so it cannot be compared to the manuscript.

Revising the Manuscript

Perhaps the most obvious revisions in the manuscript are changes in characters' names. Montgomery had first called her main character Miranda throughout the manuscript. However, she decided to change her name to Valancy when revising the manuscript, so "Miranda" is struck out in nearly every case and "Valancy" is written above it. I have left "Miranda" in the few places that Montgomery did not strike it out. By the time Montgomery revised (or rewrote) the first pages, she had decided to call her Valancy, so she did not write Miranda in those pages; we first see the change on page 3b in the manuscript (her original page 3). In the published version, Valancy is used throughout.

Why might Montgomery have chosen to rename her main character? In *Lucy Maud Montgomery and Bala*, Jack Hutton and Linda Jackson-Hutton suggest that Montgomery decided that calling her Miranda was inadvisable as it was the name of the main character in

Charles G. D. Roberts's book *The Heart of the Ancient Wood* (1902), a volume Montgomery owned and read. Why did she then choose the unusual name Valancy as a replacement? Perhaps it was a nod to well-known Canadian poet Isabella Valancy Crawford (1846–1887), as suggested to the Huttons by Yuka Kajihara-Nolan, librarian at the Osborne Collection of Early Children's Books in Toronto.

There are 218 references to "Valancy" in Montgomery's Notes section. However, "Miranda" appears in only about a dozen notes. Montgomery wrote "Miranda" with no strikeouts in notes N, T, K3, and Q6; but elsewhere in those same notes, she also refers to her as Valancy. There are eight notes (Q6, S6, Y6, Y7, X8, Z10, J11, and Z11) in which she strikes "Miranda" and writes "Valancy."

Several other name changes are evident in the manuscript: at first, Valancy's mother is referred to as Mrs. Stirling; on page 15 of the manuscript, Montgomery begins calling her Mrs. George (as in "Mrs. George Stirling"), but in later edits, she strikes out "George" and changes it to "Mrs. Frederick." (In the Notes pages, she is Mrs. Frederick only.) Mrs. Stirling's maiden name was originally Barraclough, but that was changed to Wansbarra in the published version. Roaring Abel was first called Roaring Sandy (changed to "Abel" on page 52 of the manuscript). Dr. Redfern was called Dr. Shortreed, then Dr. Goodwin (in note Z). Montgomery appears to have settled on Shortreed at first but then changed it to Redfern throughout the manuscript during her revision period. Barney's cat Jigglesqueak was renamed Banjo in the published version but not in the manuscript.

Passages from Montgomery's own essays on the seasons, which are attributed to John Foster in *The Blue Castle*, were used in several chapters, with minor alterations. These essays—"Spring in the Woods," "The Woods in Summer," and "The Woods in Winter"—were written in Cavendish and first published in *Canadian Magazine* in May, September, and December 1911. (Montgomery did not use material from "The Woods in Autumn" since she had used a great deal from it in other books, especially *The Golden Road* [1913].)

In revising the manuscript, Montgomery seems to have gone through it several times. In the first pass or two, she used a black pen to strike out words or sentences, add "Notes" designations, and number the pages. In the later edits, she used a red pen or pencil for strikeouts, renaming characters, updating the "Notes" designations, etc.

Literary Allusions

There are literary allusions throughout the manuscript. These have been identified in the annotations on the pages on which they appear. Biblical allusions are quoted from the King James Version as that is the one Montgomery would have known.

The Great War Question

It is curious that The Great War (the First World War) is not mentioned in *The Blue Castle*, even though Montgomery was obsessed with it in her journals and letters during the years 1914 to 1918. In chapter 28 of the novel, Barney gives his age as thirty-five years. If we assume that Montgomery set the novel in the years she was writing it (1924–25), Barney's birth year would have been about 1890 and he would have been ages twenty-four to twenty-eight during the war years. (The average age of Canadian soldiers in the Great War was twenty-six, according to the *Canadian Encyclopedia*.) Instead of enlisting as thousands of Canadians did, Barney was travelling. He had left home eleven years earlier (c. 1913–14), according to Dr. Redfern (chapter XXVIII), and had made his way to the Klondike, then travelled all over the world during the war years. He would have arrived in the Muskoka area about 1918, just before the war ended.

The Blue Castle on Stage

Montgomery writes in her journal on March 14, 1927, that "a theatrical manager in New York has purchased an option on the Blue Castle and wants to bring out a play from it if it can be managed." Alas, according to her journal entry of June 17, 1927, it couldn't. The manager had run into difficulties and was not able to go ahead with the project. In summer of 1934, Montgomery signed a contract for another stage production of *The Blue Castle*, but nothing seems to have come from that, either.

Nonetheless, at least two successful efforts have been made to put *The Blue Castle* on the stage. In 1982, *The Blue Castle* was produced as a musical in Poland. In 1992, actor, writer, and Prince Edward Islander Hank Stinson debuted *The Blue Castle: A Musical Love Story*. It has been produced several times for stages in Prince Edward Island and Ontario. A movie based on *The Blue Castle* is in process from Cinegryphon Entertainment.

Reviews of The Blue Castle

"Natural, although Unusual"; "A Pleasant Tonic"; "Creator of 'Anne' Sees Muskoka"; "A Dainty and Fragrant Concoction"; "Valancy's Revolt"— these are a few of the titles of reviews published at the time *The Blue Castle* was published. L. M. Montgomery kept reviews of her books in scrapbooks that are now housed in the University of Guelph Library. Twenty reviews of *The Blue Castle* can be seen in Benjamin Lefebvre's collection of reviews of Montgomery's novels in *The L. M. Montgomery Reader: Volume Three: A Legacy in Review*.

The Blue Castle Serialized

After *The Blue Castle* was published in 1926, it appeared in serial form in the *Dundee Courier* newspaper (Angus, Scotland) from March 10 to April 13, 1927, and on April 3, 1927, it appeared in the *Cleveland Plain Dealer's* Sunday magazine section. It was published as a serial in *Canadian Countryman* magazine from August 27, 1927, to January 14, 1928.

The Blue Castle and Plagiarism

In 1987, well-known Australian author Colleen McCullough (*The Thorn Birds*, etc.) published her novel *The Ladies of Missalonghi*. Before long, Montgomery readers were commenting that it was so close to *The Blue Castle* that McCullough may have plagiarized it. McCullough denied it but admitted she may have read *The Blue Castle* some years before. According to Kate Macdonald Butler, one of the heirs of L. M. Montgomery, "the lawyer for the heirs of L. M. Montgomery communicated with Colleen McCullough's agent and the dispute was settled amicably."

In Conclusion

Many readers of L. M. Montgomery's works consider *The Blue Castle* their favourite of her novels, even though *Anne of Green Gables* is her best-known work. Written for a more mature audience, *The Blue Castle* explores several topics that were considered somewhat radical in its day (for example, independent women and the scandal of babies born out of wedlock), but most of today's readers surely find that Montgomery's approach to these issues is both refreshing and sympathetic. *The Blue Castle* certainly has lasting appeal, and my hope is that scholars and fans of L. M. Montgomery will enjoy seeing the original manuscript and how it evolved.

Reader's Guide to Symbols and Notes

Montgomery's handwritten manuscript is compared throughout to the Frederick A. Stokes (New York) first edition of *The Blue Castle*, published in 1926.

* Carets (^example^) indicates the text between each caret is an addition from Montgomery.

* Note A, B, C, etc., indicate a longer addition from Montgomery.

* Strikethrough (~~example~~) indicates a deletion from Montgomery.

* Square brackets ([ ]) enclose words (or a space) inserted by the publisher of the first edition.

* A double strike-through (~~example~~) indicates a deletion from the publisher.

* ℂ indicates the start of a new paragraph.

* Underlined text (<u>example</u>) was underlined by Montgomery in the handwritten version; typically this translated to italics in the published version.

* Superscript numbers (example[1] example[2]) indicate a corresponding note from the editor, usually explaining a slight difference between the handwritten manuscript and the first published edition.

* Highlighted text (example) represents text that the typist had circled.

the *Blue Castle*

The Original Manuscript

The Blue Castle.

by

L. M. Montgomery.

I

If it had not rained on a certain May morning Valancy Stirling's whole life would have been entirely different. But it did rain and you shall hear what happened to her because of it.

Valancy wakened early in the lifeless, hopeless hour just preceding dawn. She had not slept very well. One does not sleep well, sometimes, when one is twenty-nine

1a[1]

The Blue Castle.

By

L. M. Montgomery

I.

If it had not rained on a certain May morning Valancy Stirling's whole life would have been entirely different. NOTE A But it did rain and you shall hear what happened to her because of it.

Valancy wakened early in the lifeless, hopeless hour just preceding dawn. She had not slept very well. One does not sleep well, sometimes, when one is twenty[-]nine[2] on the morrow, and unmarried, in a community and connection where the unmarried are simply those who have failed to get a man. ~~Deewooo~~ ❰ Deerwood and the Stirlings had long since relegated Valancy to hopeless old maidenhood. But Valancy herself had never quite relinquished a certain pitiful, shamed[,] little hope that Romance would come her way yet—never, until this wet, horrible morning, when she wakened to the fact that she was twenty[-]nine and unsought by any man.

Ay, there lay the sting. Valancy did not mind so much being an old maid. After all, she thought, being an

1: Montgomery re-wrote the first two pages of the manuscript, re-numbering them 1a–4a. See page 6 for more information on page numbers in the manuscript.

NOTE A: She would have gone, with the rest of her clan, to Aunt Wellington's engagement picnic and Dr. Trent would have gone to Montreal.

2: Montgomery did not always hyphenate "twenty-nine" or other compound numbers; they are all hyphenated in the published version.

old maid couldn't possibly be as dreadful as being married to an Uncle Wellington or an Uncle Benjamin, or even an Uncle Herbert. What hurt her was that she had never had a chance to be anything but an old maid. No man had ever desired her.

The tears came into her eyes as she lay there alone in the faintly graying[3] darkness. She dared not let herself cry as hard as she wanted to[,] for two reasons. She was afraid that crying might bring on another attack of that pain around the heart. She had had a spell of it after she had got into bed—rather worse than any she had had yet. And she was afraid her mother would notice her red eyes at breakfast and keep at her with minute, persistent, mosquito-like questions regarding the cause thereof.

"Suppose," thought ~~Miranda~~ Valancy[4] with a ghastly grin, "I answered with the plain truth 'I ~~was~~ ^am^ crying because I ~~am not~~ ^cannot get^ married.' How horrified mother would be—though she is ashamed every day of her life of her old maid daughter." ^But of course[5] appearances should be kept up~~."~~^ ~~NOTE N~~ NOTE B

The thought of her mother's expression made ~~Miranda~~ Valancy laugh—for she had a sense of humor nobody in her clan suspected. ~~NOTE Y3~~ NOTE C But ~~the~~ ^her^ laughter was very superficial and presently she lay there, a huddled, futile little figure, listening to the rain pouring down outside and watching, with a sick distaste, the chill, merciless light creeping into her ugly, ~~sordid room~~ ^sordid room.^

She knew the ugliness of that room by heart—knew it and hated it. The yellow-painted ^floors^ ~~rugless floor~~, ~~NOTE O19~~ NOTE D ~~the hideous dark-red paper~~

3: "Graying" is spelled "greying" (and "gray" is spelled "grey") here and throughout in the published version.

4: This is the first time we see Montgomery write (and later cross out) her original name for Valancy: Miranda. This was on page 3b of the manuscript.

5: In the published version, "But of course" begins a new paragraph with no quotations marks around the sentence.

NOTE B: "It is not," Valancy could hear her mother's prim, dictatorial voice asserting, "it is not ~~maidenly~~ to think about ~~men.~~"

NOTE C: For that matter there were a good many things about Valancy that nobody suspected[.]

NOTE D: with one hideous, "hooked" rug by the bed, with a grotesque "hooked" dog on it, always grinning at her when she awoke; the ~~hideous~~ faded, dark red paper; the ceiling discolored[6] by old leaks and crossed by cracks; the narrow, pinched, little washstand; the brown paper lambrequin[7] with purple roses on it; the spotted old looking-glass with the crack across it, propped up on the inadequate dressing table; the jar of ancient potpourri made by her mother in her mythical honeymoon; the shell-covered box, with one burst~~ed~~ corner , which Cousin ~~Stick~~ STICKLES[8]

had made in her equally mythical girlhood; the beaded pincushion with half its bead fringe gone; the one stiff, yellow chair; the faded old mottoes, "Gone but not forgotten," worked in colored yarns about Great-Grandmother Stirling's grim old face; the ~~pict~~ old photographs of ancient relatives long banished from the rooms below. There were only two pictures that were not of relatives. One, an old chromo of a puppy sitting on a rainy door= step. That picture always made Valancy unhappy. That forlorn little dog crouched on the door-step in the driving rain! Why didn't some[ ]one open the door and let him in? The other picture was a faded, passe-partouted[9] engraving of Queen

~~NOTE G19~~ ~~the narrow, pinched little wash stand,~~ the
spotted old looking-glass ~~propped up on the table
with the crack across it,~~ propped up on the inadequate dressing table, ~~NOTE C~~ ~~the one stiff yellow chair,~~
~~NOTE V3~~ ~~the pictures of~~ ^of ancient relatives^ ~~long
banished from the rooms below. Of ancient relatives
in wide-ma.~~ ~~NOTE R9~~ ~~The only pictures that was not
a relative was a faded passe-partouted engraving
of Queen~~ Louise ^coming down ~~her~~ a stairway^[10]
which Aunt Wellington had ^lavishly^ given her
on her tenth birthday. For ~~nine~~ nineteen years she
had looked at it and hated it, ~~though she never dared
to remove it~~ beautiful, smug, self-satisfied Queen
Louise. But she never dared destroy it or remove it.
Mother and Cousin Stickles would have been aghast.
~~NOTE F~~ NOTE E

Every room in the house was ugly, of course. But
downstairs appearances were kept up somewhat.
There was no money for rooms nobody ever saw.
~~Miranda~~ Valancy sometimes felt that she could have
done something for her room herself, even without
money, if she were permitted. But ^her^ mother
had negatived every timid suggestion and ~~Miranda~~
Valancy did not persist[.] ~~Miranda~~ Valancy never persisted. She was afraid to. ~~her~~ Her mother could not
brook opposition. Mrs. Stirling would sulk for days if
offended, with the air of an ~~outraged~~ insulted duchess.
~~And after all, what did it matter?~~ ~~NOTE X3 NOTE T~~
NOTE F

~~of~~ if a room, which you ~~just~~ used ^for nothing
except^ sleeping ^and dressing^ in, was ugly?[11] | NOTE
G ~~Her room in ¶~~ ^But her room[12] in^ the Blue Castle[13]
was everything a room should be.

~~Miranda,~~ Valancy, so cowed and subdued and
overridden and snubbed in real life, was wont to
let herself go rather splendidly in her day-dreams.
Nobody in the Stirling clan, or its ramifications,
suspected this, ^least of all her mother & Cousin
Stickles.^ They never knew that ~~Miranda~~ Valancy
had two homes—the ugly red brick box of a house,

6: All instances of "color" are
spelled "colour" throughout
the published version.

7: lambrequin = a decorative
frieze added to the edge
of a mantle or top of a
window

8: "STICKLES" is written
in capitals, apparently to
make the spelling clear to
the typist; Montgomery
used this method in several
other places later in the
manuscript.

9: passe-partout = in this
case, an embossed mat
framing the engraving

10: Queen Louise of
Prussia (1776–1810)
was called "The Venus
of Mecklenburg." *Queen
Louise Descending Staircase*
was painted by Angelo Asti
(1847–1903).

NOTE E: —or, as Valancy
irreverently expressed it in
her thoughts, would have
had a fit.

NOTE F: The only thing ~~she~~
Valancy liked about her
room was that she could be
alone there at night to cry
if she wanted to.
    But, after all, what did it
matter?

11: "Was" is corrected to
"were" in the published
version.

NOTE G: Valancy was never
permitted to stay alone in
her room for any other purpose. People who wanted to
be alone, so Mrs. Frederick
Stirling and cousin Stickles
believed, could only want to
be alone for some sinister
purpose.

12: Although Montgomery
indicates this sentence
should begin a new para-
graph, it continues the
existing paragraph in the
published version.

13: This is the first mention of
Valancy's "Blue Castle" in
the novel.

on ~~Elee~~ Elm Street[,] and the Blue Castle in Spain.[14] ~~Miranda~~ Valancy had lived spiritually in the Blue Castle ever since she could remember. She had been a very tiny child when she found herself possessed of it. Always, when she shut her eyes, she could see it plainly, ~~the that~~ with its turrets and banners on the pine-clad mountain height, wrapped in its faint, blue loveliness, against the ~~sunset~~ moonlit sunset skies of a fair and unknown land. Everything wonderful and beautiful was in that castle.~~r~~ Jewels that queens might have worn; robes of moonlight and fire; couches of roses and gold, ~~NOTE W3~~ NOTE H halls of mirrors that reflected only ~~lovel~~ handsome knights and lovely women—herself the loveliest of all, for whose glance men died. ~~NOTE M9~~ NOTE I Most, if not all of the Stirlings would have died of horror if they had known ^half^ the things Miranda did in her Blue Castle. ~~NOTE H4~~ NOTE J

But, on this morning of her day of fate, ~~Miranda~~ Valancy could not find ~~refuge in~~ the key of her Blue Castle. Reality pressed ~~too~~ on her too hardly, barking at her heels like a maddening little dog. She was twenty[-]nine, lonely, undesired, ill-favored—the only homely girl in a handsome clan, with no past and no future. As far as she could look back, life was drab and colorless, with not one single crimson or purple spot anywhere. As far as she could look forward it seemed certain to be just the same. ~~NOTE P9~~ NOTE K The moment when a woman ~~rel~~ realizes[15] that she has <u>nothing</u>[16] to live for—neither love, duty, purpose or hope—holds for her the bitterness of death.

14: "Castle in Spain" is a reference to daydreaming, fantasizing, "building castles in the air." The phrase first appeared in "The Romance of the Rose," a poem written in France in the thirteenth century that gained popularity in Europe in the Middle Ages: "Thou shalt make castles then in Spaine, And dreame of joy, all but in vaine."

NOTE H: long flights of shallow marble steps, with great white urns, and slender, mist-clad maidens going up and down them; courts, marble-pillared[,] where shimmering fountains fell and nightingales sang among the myrtles.

NOTE I: All that supported her through the boredom of her days was the hope of going on a dream spree at night.

NOTE J: ⟨For one thing she had quite a few lovers in it. Oh, only one at a time. One who wooed her with all the romantic ardor of the age of chivalry and won her after long devotion and many deeds of derring do, and was wedded to her with pomp and circumstance in the great, banner-hung chapel of the Blue Castle. ~~At her~~ At twelve, this lover was a fair lad with golden curls and heavenly blue eyes. At fifteen, he was tall and dark and pale but still necessarily handsome. At twenty, he was ascetic, dreamy, spiritual. At twenty[-]five, he had a clean-cut jaw, slightly grim, and a face strong & rugged rather than handsome. Valancy never grew older than twenty[-]five in her Blue Castle but recently – very recently, her hero had reddish, tawny hair, a twisted smile & a mysterious past.

I don't say Valancy deliberately murdered these lovers as she outgrew them. One simply faded away as another came. Things are very convenient in this respect in Blue Castles.

NOTE K: until she was nothing but a solitary, little, withered leaf clinging to a wintry bough.

15: "Realizes" is spelled "realises" in the published version, here and throughout.

16: "Nothing" is not underlined or italicized in the published version.

"~~And~~ ^NOTE NM^ I may have to live eighty years," thought ~~Miranda~~ Valancy in a kind of panic. "We're all horribly long-lived. It sickens me to think of it."

She was glad it was raining—or rather, she was drearily satisfied that it was raining. There would be no picnic that day. This annual picnic, whereby Aunt and Uncle Wellington—one always thought of them in that succession—inevitably celebrated their engagement at a picnic thirty years before, had been, of late years, a veritable nightmare to ~~Miranda~~ Valancy. By an ~~unpish~~ impish co-incidence it ~~came~~ was the same day as her birthday and[,] after she had passed twenty-five[,] nobody let her forget it. NOTE M14

~~Miranda Valancy~~ knew exactly[17] what every[ ] one would say to her at the

~~Section I.~~

picnic. Uncle Wellington ~~NOTE H~~ NOTE M would say to her in a pig's whisper, "Not thinking of getting married yet, my dear?" and then go off into the ~~perfect~~ bellow of laughter with which he invariably concluded his dull remarks ~~NOTE K~~ NOTE N ⁋ Aunt Alberta, enormously fat, ~~NOTE O9~~ NOTE O who ~~would~~ could never forget that she had been a great beauty in her youth, would condole with ~~Miranda~~ Valancy on her sallow skin—

"I don't know why all the girls of to-day[18] are so sunburned. When I was a girl my skin was roses and cream. I was ~~considered~~ counted the prettiest girl in Canada, my dear."

Perhaps Uncle Herbert wouldn't say anything—or perhaps he would remark jocularly,

"How fat you're getting, Doss!"

And[19] then everybody would laugh over the ^excessively humorous^ idea of poor, ~~thin~~ ^scrawny,^ little Doss getting fat.

^Handsome, solemn^ Uncle James, whom Miranda disliked ~~and~~ but respected ~~NOTE L~~ NOTE P would probably remark in[21] ~~his dry, sarcastic fashion,~~ the owl-like sarcasm that had won him his

NOTE L: "And I just have to go on living because I can't stop.

NOTE M14: Much as she hated going to the picnic it ^would^ never [have] occurred to her to rebel against it. There seemed to be nothing of the revolutionary in her nature. And she knew exactly

17: Montgomery did not strike "knew exactly" here even though she wrote it in NOTE M14.

NOTE M: whom she disliked and despised even though he fulfilled the highest Stirling aspiration, "marrying money,"

NOTE N: Aunt Wellington, of whom Miranda ~~feared abjectly~~ stood in abject awe, would tell her about ~~Olive's~~ OLIVE's new chiffon dress and Cecil's last devoted letter. Valancy would have to look as pleased & interested as if the dress & letter had been hers or else Aunt Wellington would be offended. And Valancy had long ago decided that she would rather offend God than Aunt Wellington, because God might forgive her but Aunt Wellington never would.

NOTE O: with an amiable habit of always referring to her husband as "he," as if he were the only male creature in the world,

18: In the published version, "to-day" is spelled "today" here and throughout.

19: In the published version, "And" does not begin a new paragraph here but continues on the line above after "Doss!"

NOTE P: because he was reputed to be very clever & was therefore the clan uncle—brains being none too plentiful in the Stirling clan—[20]

20: "Clan" is changed to "connection" in the published version.

21: "In" is changed to "with" in the published version.

NOTE Q: Aunt Isabel prided herself on saying what she thought but didn't like it so well when other people said what <u>they</u> thought to <u>her</u>. Valancy never said what <u>she</u> thought.

22: George the Fourth (1762–1830) was King of England from 1820 to 1830. His younger brother was Prince Edward (1767–1820), for whom Prince Edward Island was named.

NOTE R: —really First Cousin Gladys once removed, according to the strict way in which the Stirlings tabulated relationship—a tall, thin lady who admitted she had a secretive disposition,

reputation, "I suppose you're busy with your hope-chest these days?"

And Uncle ~~Benjamin~~ Benjamin would ask some of his abominable ~~riddles~~ conundrums, between wheezy chuckles, and answer them himself.

"What is the difference ~~bee~~ between Doss and a mouse?

~~One~~ ["]The mouse wishes to harm the cheese and Doss wishes to charm the he's."

~~Miranda~~ Valancy had heard him ask that ~~riddle~~ riddle fifty times and every time she wanted to throw something at him. But she never did. In the first place ~~throwing things was simply not done in the Stirling clan;~~ ^the Stirlings simply did not throw things;^ in the second place, Uncle Benjamin was a wealthy ~~old bachelor~~ ^and childless old widower^ and ~~Miranda~~ Valancy had been brought up in the fear and admonition of his money. If she offended him he would cut her out of his will—supposing she were in it. ~~Miranda~~ Valancy did not want to be cut out of Uncle Benjamin's will. She had been poor all her life and knew the ^galling^ bitterness of it. So she endured his riddles and even smiled ~~twisted lit~~ tortured little smiles over them.

Aunt Isabel, downright and disagreeable as an east wind, would criticize her in some way—~~Miranda~~ Valancy could not predict just how, for Aunt Isabel ~~never~~ never repeated a criticism—she found something new with which to jab you every time. ~~NOTE U3~~ NOTE Q

Cousin Georgiana—named after her great-great-grandmother who had been named after George the Fourth[22]—~~would recount dolorously the names of all those~~ relatives and friends who had died since the last picnic and wonder "which of us will be the first to go next." ¶ ~~And capable, patronizing~~ ^Oppressively competent[,]^ Aunt Mildred would talk endlessly of her husband and ^her odious prodigies of^ babies to ~~Miranda~~ Valancy, because ~~Miranda~~ Valancy would be the only one she could find to put up with it. ~~And Olive~~ For the same reason[,] Cousin Gladys ~~NOTE M~~ NOTE R would describe minutely the tortures of her neuritis. And Olive, ~~NOTE J~~

~~handsome~~ who had everything ~~Miranda~~ Valancy had not—beauty, popularity, love,—would show off her beauty and ~~presunme~~ presume on her popularity and flaunt her diamond insignia of love in Miranda's dazzled, envious eyes. ~~NOTE Q~~ NOTE T

Oh, yes, ~~Miranda~~ Valancy knew exactly what the picnic would be like and she blessed the rain that had saved her from it. There would be no picnic this year. ~~Aunt~~ If Aunt Wellington could not ~~ceb~~ celebrate on the sacred day itself she would have no celebration at all. Thank whatever gods there ~~be~~ ^were^ for that.[24]

Since there would be no ~~pirnic~~ picnic ~~Miranda~~ Valancy made up her mind that, if the rain held up in the afternoon, she would go up to the library and get another of John Foster's books. ~~Miranda~~ Valancy was never allowed to read novels, but John Foster's books were not novels. They were "nature books"—so the librarian told Mrs. ~~George Stirle~~ Frederick Stirling—"all about the woods and birds and bugs and things like that, you know." So ~~Miranda~~ Valancy was allowed to read them—under protest, for it was only too evident that she enjoyed them too much. ~~A book that was enjoyable.~~ It was permissible, ~~or~~ even laudable, to read to improve your mind ^and your religion,^ but a book that was enjoyable was dangerous. ~~Miranda~~ Valancy did not know whether her mind was being improved or not, but she felt vaguely that if she had come across John Foster's books years ago life might have been ^a^ different ^thing^ for her. They seemed to her to ~~set open the door~~ ^yield glimpses^ of a world into which she might once have entered, though the door was forever barred to her now. It was only within the last year that John Foster's books had been in the Deerwood library, though the librarian told ~~Miranda~~ Valancy that he had been a well-known writer for several years.

~~"His books are so popular we can't keep them in at all," she said.~~

"Where does he live,"[25] ~~Miranda~~ Valancy had asked.

"Nobody knows. From his books he must be a Canadian[,] but no more information can be had. His

NOTE S: the wonder girl of the whole Stirling clan,

NOTE T: ⁋ There would be none of all this today. And there would be no packing up of teaspoons. The packing up was ~~all~~ always left for Miranda and Cousin Stickles. And once, six years ago, a silver teaspoon from Aunt Wellington's wedding set had been lost. Valancy never heard the last of that silver teaspoon. Its ghost appeared Banquo-like[23] at every subsequent family feast.

23: Banquo is a character in Shakespeare's *Macbeth*. Macbeth orders him murdered, and his ghost appears to Macbeth at a banquet to remind him of his treachery.

24: Likely from the 1875 poem "Invictus" by William Ernest Henley (1849–1903). The line in the poem reads "I thank whatever gods may be For my unconquerable soul."

25: In the published version, the comma after "live" is replaced with a question mark.

26: "Limbo" here means "oblivion."

27: "Tantalizing" is spelled "tantalising" in the published version.

NOTE U: and the palpitations were becoming annoying, not to speak of an occasional dizzy moment & a queer shortness of breath.

28: Montgomery had drawn a short line here, then added "Laurence" later, which is evident from the smaller letters written to fit the space. In the published version, "Laurence" is spelled "Lawrence."

publishers won't say a word. Quite likely John Foster is a nom=de=plume. His books are so popular we can't keep them in at all, though I really can't see what people find in them to rave over."

"I think they're wonderful," said ~~Miranda~~ Valancy timidly.

"Oh – well –" Miss Clarkson smiled in a patronizing fashion that relegated ~~Miranda's~~ Valancy's opinion to limbo,[26] "I can't say I care much for bugs myself. But certainly Foster seems to know all there is to know about them."

Miranda didn't know whether she cared much for bugs ~~herself~~ either. It was not John Foster's uncanny knowledge of wild creatures ^& insect life^ that enthralled her. She could hardly say what it was—some tantalizing[27] lure of a mystery never revealed – some hint of a great secret just a little further on – some faint, elusive echo of lonely, forgotten things—John Foster's magic was indefinable.

Yes, she would get a new Foster book. It was a month since she had ~~the last one,~~ ^Thistle Harvest,^ so surely mother could not object. ~~Miranda~~ Valancy had read it four times—she knew whole passages off by heart.

And – she almost thought she would go and see Dr. ~~Frent~~ Trent about that queer pain around the heart. It had come ~~so~~ rather often lately[,]; NOTE U But ~~dared~~ ^could^ she go to see him without telling any[ ]one? It was a most daring thought. ~~Nobody~~ None of the Stirlings ever consulted a doctor without holding a family ~~conclave~~ ^council^ and getting Uncle James' approval. ~~Then, they went to Dr. Penbroco Marot~~ Ambrose Marsh of Port _____ ^Laurence^,[28] who had married Secondcousin Adelaide Stirling.

But ~~Miranda~~ Valancy ~~hated~~ ^disliked^ Dr. Ambrose Marsh. And[,] besides, she could not get to Port ~~Ci~~ Laurence, ~~ten 15~~ fifteen miles away, without being taken there. She did not want any[ ]one to know about her heart. There would be such a fuss made and every member of the family would come down and talk it over and ~~advise~~ advise her and caution her and warn her and tell her horrible tales of great-aunts and cousins forty times removed who had been "just like that" and "dropped dead" without a moment's warning, my dear." ~~NOTE M NOTE O~~ NOTE V ❦ ^~~No, Miranda~~ Valancy felt that she couldn't tell anybody unless she had to. ~~Very likely~~ ^~~She felt grateful~~^ ^She felt quite sure^ there was nothing at all seriously wrong with her heart and no need of all the pother that would ensue if she mentioned it. She would just slip up quietly and see Dr. Trent that very day. ~~NOTE C~~ NOTE W ❦ Dr. Trent was a gruff, outspoken, ^absent-minded^ old fellow[,] but he was a recognized[31] authority on heart disease, ~~He did nothing in an old the way of general practice. He had come to Deerwood a few years bef back~~ ^even if he were only ~~an old~~ a general practitioner in^ out-of-the-world Deerwood. Dr. Trent was over seventy and there had been rumors that he meant to retire soon. None of the Stirling clan had ever gone to him since he had told Cousin Gladys, ten years before, that her neuritis was all imaginary ^and that she enjoyed it.^ You couldn't patronize a doctor ~~that~~ who insulted your first-cousins-once-removed like that. ~~NOTE P~~ NOTE X But ~~Miranda~~ Valancy, between the devil of disloyalty to clan and the deep sea of fuss and clatter and advice[,] thought she would take a chance with the devil.

NOTE V: Aunt Isabel would remember that she had always said Doss looked like a girl who would have heart trouble—"so pinched and peaked always;" ¥ and Uncle Wellington would take it as a personal insult, when "no Stirling ever had heart disease before;" and Georgiana would forbode in perfectly audible asides that "poor, dear, little Doss isn't long for this world, I'm afraid;" and Cousin Gladys would say, "Why, my heart has been like that for years," in a tone that implied no one else had any business ever to have a heart; and Olive – Olive would merely look beautiful and superior & disgustingly healthy, as if to say, "Why all this fuss over a faded superfluity like Doss when you have me?"[29]

29: In the published version, this sentence does not begin a new paragraph but continues in the previous one.

NOTE W: As for his bill, she had the two hundred dollars[30] that her father had put in the bank for her the day she was born. She was never allowed to use even the interest of this[,] but she would secretly take out enough to pay Dr. Trent.

30: When Montgomery was writing *The Blue Castle* in 1924–25, $200 (Canadian) would have been the equivalent of about $3,400 today.

31: "Recognized" is spelled "recognised" here and elsewhere in the published version.

NOTE X: Not to mention that he was a Presbyterian when all the Stirlings went to the Anglican church.[32]

32: In the published version, this phrase is added to the previous sentence with a long dash substituted for the period after "removed like that," and "Not" is not capitalized.

2, and that she enjoyed itself enormously. You couldn't patronize a doctor that who insulted
your first - cousins - once - removed -
like that. But Valancy, between
the devil of disloyalty to clan and
the deep sea of fuss and clatter
and advice thought she would take
a chance with the devil.

II.

When she heard the clock in the
hall below strike half past seven
Valancy.

When Cousin Stickles knocked at
her door Valancy knew it was half
past seven and she must get
up. As long as she could remember
Cousin Stickles had knocked at
her door at half past seven. Cousin
Stickles and Mrs, George Frederick
Stirling had been
up since seven but Valancy was
allowed to lie a bed half an hour

II.

~~When she heard the clock in the hall below strike~~
~~half past seven Miranda~~

When Cousin Stickles knocked at her door[,]
~~Miranda~~ Valancy knew it was half[-]past seven and she
must get up. As long as she could remember[,] Cousin
Stickles had knocked at her door at half past seven.
Cousin Stickles and Mrs. ^~~George~~ Frederick^ Stirling
had been up since seven but ~~Miranda~~ Valancy was allowed to lie a=bed a half an hour longer because of a
family tradition that she was delicate. ~~Miranda~~ Valancy
got up, though she hated getting up more this morning
than ever she had before. What was there to get up for?
Another dreary day like all the days that had ~~gone before~~
^preceded it,^ full of meaningless little tasks, ^joyless
and unimportant,^ that benefitted nobody. But if she did
not get up at once she would not be ready for breakfast at
eight o'clock. Hard and fast times for meals were the rule
in Mrs. Stirling's household. Breakfast at eight, dinner at
one, supper at six, year in and year out. No excuses for
being late were ever tolerated. So up ~~Miranda~~ Valancy
got, shivering.

The room was bitterly cold with the raw, penetrating
~~cold~~ ^chill^ of a wet May morning. The house would
be cold all day. It was one of Mrs. ^~~George~~^ ~~Stirlings~~
^Frederick's^ rules that no fires were necessary after the
~~first~~ ^~~Th th~~ twenty[-]fourth^ of May. Meals were cooked
on the little oil[-]stove in the back porch. And though
May might be icy and October frost-bitten, no fires were
lighted until the ~~first of November~~ ^~~21ˢᵗ of October~~ ^
^twenty-first of October^ of[1] the calendar. On the first

1: "Of" is changed to "by"
in the published version.

25

2: Valancy's undergarments probably consisted of drawers, corset, camisole, and a long petticoat.

NOTE Y: thick, black stockings & rubber heeled boots.

NOTE Z: always lustreless despite the fact that she gave it one hundred strokes of the brush, neither more nor less, every night of her life & faithfully rubbed ~~Shortreed Goodwin's~~ ^Redfern's^[3] Hair Vigor into its[4] roots;

3: This is the first mention of "Redfern" in the novel.

4: "Its" is changed to "the" in the published version.

NOTE A1: that always fell open a trifle over little pointed, white teeth,

---

~~of November 21st~~ ^21ˢᵗ of October^ ^twenty-first of October^ Mrs. ~~Stirling~~ ^George^ ^Stirling^ ^Frederick^ began cooking over the kitchen range and lighted a fire in the sitting-room stove in the evenings. It was whispered about in the connection that the late ~~Mr.~~ ^George Frederick^ Stirling had caught the cold which resulted in his death during ~~Miranda's~~ Valancy's first year of life because Mrs. ~~Stirling~~ ^George Frederick^ would not ~~light~~ ^have^ a fire on the ~~31ˢᵗ~~ ^20ᵗʰ twentieth^ of October. She lighted it the next day—but that was a day too late for ~~George~~ ^Frederick^ Stirling.

~~Miranda looked at herself in her leprous mirror with distaste. Surely her narrow white face was narrower and whiter than ever, her straight black hair straighter and more lustreless. It was short and thin, too – Miranda thought of Olive's masses of rich wavy golden-brown hair.~~

~~Miranda~~ Valancy took off and hung up in the closet her nightdress of coarse unbleached cotton, with high neck and long, tight sleeves. She put on undergarments[2] of a ~~smirl~~ similar nature, ~~and~~ a dress of ~~gray~~ ^brown^ gingham, ᴺᴼᵀᴱ ʸ

Of late ~~she~~ years she had fallen into the habit of doing her hair with the shade of the window by the looking[-]glass ~~pelled~~ pulled down. The lines on her face did not show so plainly then. But this morning, she jerked the shade to the very top and looked at herself in the leprous mirror with a passionate determination to ~~face the worst~~ see herself as the world saw her.

The result was rather dreadful. Even a beauty would have found that harsh, unsoftened side light trying. ~~Miranda~~ Valancy saw straight black hair, short and thin, ~~ᴺᴼᵀᴱ ᵀ⁹~~ ᴺᴼᵀᴱ ᶻ more lustreless than ever in its morning roughness; ~~a very thin, flat-breasted little fig~~ fine, straight, black brows; a nose she had always felt was much too small even for her small, three cornered white face; a ~~large~~ ^small,^ pale mouth, ᴺᴼᵀᴱ ᴬ¹ ~~little pointed white teeth~~, a figure thin and flat-breasted, rather below the average height. She had somehow escaped the family high cheekbones, and her dark-brown eyes, too soft and shadowy to be black, had a slant that was almost Oriental. Apart from her eyes she was neither pretty nor ~~pl~~ ugly—just insignificant looking, she concluded bitterly. ~~And~~ How plain the lines around her eyes and mouth were in that merciless light.[5] And never had her narrow, white face looked so narrow and so white.

~~"My face is ineffectual"~~

She did her hair in a pompadour.[6] Pompadours had ~~long~~ long gone out of fashion[,] ~~and~~ but they had been in when ~~Miranda~~ Valancy first put her hair up and Aunt Wellington had decreed[7] that she must always wear her hair so.

"It is the _only_ way that becomes you. Your face is so small that you _must_ add height to it ~~by hair~~ by a pompadour effect," said Aunt Wellington, who always enunciated commonplaces as if uttering profound and important truths. ~~It had such an effect on Miranda, that she never dared~~ ^that she never dared^ ~~--who had secret hankerings Miranda~~ ^𝕮^ Valancy had hankered to do her hair ~~in puffs above the ears and~~ ^pulled low on^ her forehead, with puffs above the ears, as Olive was wearing it.[8] But Aunt Wellington's dictum had such an ~~effort~~ ^effect^ on her that she never dared change her style of hair⸗dressing again. But then, there were so many things ~~Miranda~~ Valancy never dared do.

~~NOTE H~~ NOTE B1

~~"All my life I've been afraid of something,"~~ ~~she thought bitterly.~~ 𝕮 And ~~she~~ I always will be—I know it – I can't help it." I don't know what it would be like not to be afraid of something." 𝕮 Afraid of her mother's sulky fits – afraid of offending Uncle Benjamin – afraid of becoming a target for Aunt Wellington's contempt – afraid of Aunt ~~Isabell's~~ Isabel's biting comments, – afraid of Uncle ~~Herbert's~~ ^James'^ disapproval, ~~–afraid of poverty in her old age,~~ afraid of offending the whole clan's opinions and prejudices ^NOTE W^ NOTE C1 afraid of poverty in her old age. Fear – fear – fear—she could never escape from it. It ~~boore~~ bound her and enmeshed her like a spider's web of steel. Only in her Blue Castle could she find temporary release. And this morning ~~Meid Miranda~~ Valancy

5: The period after "light" is replaced by an exclamation point in the published version.

6: A "pompadour" hairstyle involves piling the hair on top of the head to create height and volume.

7: "Decreed" is changed to "decided" in the published version.

8: "It" is changed to "hers" in the published version.

NOTE B1: 𝕮 All her life she had been afraid of something, she thought bitterly. From the very dawn of recollection[,] when she had been so horribly afraid of the big, black bear that lived, so Cousin Stickles told her, in the closet under the stairs[.]

NOTE C1: – afraid of not keeping up appearances – afraid to say what she really thought of anything –

NOTE D1: ══ the ragged fence, the ~~terrible~~ tumble[-]down old carriage[-]shop in the next lot, plastered with crude, violently colored advertisements;[9]

9: Advertising signs on buildings began to appear in the late 1800s.

NOTE E1: especially the beastly advertisement, "Keep that schoolgirl complexion." Valancy had kept her schoolgirl complexion. That was just the trouble.

NOTE F1: She was one of the people whom life always passes by. There was no altering that fact. In this mood Valancy went down to breakfast.

could not believe she had a Blue Castle. She would never be able to find it again. Twenty-nine, ~~in~~ unmarried, undesired—what had she to do with the ^fairy-like^ chatelaine of the Blue Castle? She would cut such childish nonsense out of her life forever and face ~~facts~~ ^reality^ unflinchingly.

She turned from her unfriendly mirror and looked out. The ugliness of the view always struck her like a blow; ~~in~~ NOTE D1 ~~the ragged fence, the tumbledown old building~~ ^carriage shop ~~in the next lot~~^ ~~plastered with~~ ^crude, violently colored^ ~~hideous advertisements~~, the grimy railway station beyond, with the awful derelicts that were always hanging around it even at this early hour. In the pouring rain everything looked worse than usual ~~NOTE Y3~~ NOTE E1 There was not a gleam of beauty anywhere—"~~just~~ exactly like my life," thought ~~Miranda drearily~~ Valancy ^drearily.^ Her ^brief^ bitterness had passed. She accepted facts as resignedly as she had always accepted them.

~~NOTE U~~ NOTE F1 ~~She was~~ ^was of those people whom life always passes by^ ~~an old maid; life was ended for her—indeed, it had never begun. There was no~~ ~~That was all there was to it. Nothing could~~

~~In this mood Mira Miranda went down to breakfast.~~

III.

Breakfast was always the same. Oatmeal porridge, which ~~Miranda~~ Valancy loathed, toast and tea, and one teaspoonful of marmalade. Mrs. ~~Stirling George~~ Frederick thought two teaspoons extravagant[—]but that did not matter to ~~Miranda~~ Valancy who hated marmalade, ^too.^ The chilly, gloomy little dining[-]room was chillier and gloomier than usual; the rain streamed down outside the window; departed Stirlings in atrocious gilt frames, ^wider than the pictures,^ glowered down from the walls. And yet, Cousin Stickles wished ~~Miranda~~ Valancy many happy returns of the day!

"Sit up straight, Doss," ~~said her mother~~ was all her mother said.

~~Miranda~~ Valancy sat up straight. She talked to her mother and Cousin Stickles of the things they always talked of. She never wondered what would happen if she ~~asked or said some of the things she thought~~ ^tried to talk of something else.^ She knew. Therefore she never ~~asked or said them.~~ ^did it.^

Mrs. ~~Stirling George~~ Frederick was offended with Providence for sending a rainy day when she wanted to go to a picnic, so she ate her breakfast in a sulky silence for which ~~Miranda~~ Valancy was rather grateful. But Christine ^CHRISTINE^ Stickles whined ~~and~~ endlessly on as usual, complaining about everything – the weather, the leak in the pantry, the price of oatmeal and butter—~~Miranda~~ Valancy felt at once she had buttered her toast too lavishly—the epidemic of ~~measles~~ mumps[1] in Deerwood.

"Doss will be sure to ketch them," she foreboded.

1: A vaccine for mumps became available in 1948, and a more effective one was licensed in 1967. Today, the vaccine for mumps is combined with vaccines for measles and rubella. Known as the MMR vaccine, it is routinely given to children over a year old.

2: A vaccine for whooping cough was developed in 1926; a vaccine for chicken pox began being developed as early as 1875 but did not become licensed and commonly used until the 1990s. A vaccine for the common cold has not yet been developed.

NOTE G1: with its odd, out-land tang. It was always a wonder to Valancy that the Stirlings had allowed her to be so christened. She had been told that her ~~grandf~~ maternal grandfather, old Amos Barraclough[3], had chosen the name for her. Her father had tacked on the Jane by way of civilizing it[,] & the whole connection got out of the difficulty by nicknaming her. ^Doss.^[4]

3: In the published version, "Barraclough" is changed to "Wansbarra" here and throughout. This may have been due to the Macdonalds becoming friends with the prestigious Barraclough family when they moved to Norval, Ontario, in February of 1926, six months before *The Blue Castle* was published.

4: In the published version, there is no period after "nicknaming her." "Doss" is written in red in the manuscript, which indicates it was added later.

"Doss must not go where she is likely to catch ~~mea-sles~~ ^mumps,"^ said Mrs. ~~Stirling~~ Frederick shortly.

~~Miranda~~ Valancy had never had ~~measles~~ mumps – or whooping cough – or chicken pox – ^or measles –^ or anything she should have had—nothing but horrible colds every winter[2]. Doss's winter colds ~~near~~ were a sort of tradition in the family. Nothing, it seemed[,] could prevent her ~~catching~~ ^from catching^ them. Mrs. ~~Stirling George~~ Frederick and Cousin Stickles did their heroic best. One winter they kept ~~Miranda~~ Valancy housed up from November to May in the warm sitting[-]room. She was not even allowed to go to church. And ~~Miranda~~ Valancy took cold after cold and ended up with ~~bronchitas~~ bronchitis in June.

"None of <u>my</u> family were ever like that," said Mrs. ~~Stirling George~~ Frederick, implying that it must be a Stirling tendency.

"The Stirlings seldom take colds," said Cousin Stickles resentfully. <u>She</u> had been a Stirling."

"I think," said Mrs. ~~Stirling George~~ Frederick, "that if a person makes up her mind <u>not</u> to ~~take~~ ^have^ cold[s] she ~~won't~~ will not have colds."

So that was the trouble. It was all ~~Miranda's~~ Valancy's own fault.

But on this particular morning ~~Miranda's~~ Valancy's unbearable grievance was that she was called Doss. She had endured it for twenty[-]nine years and all at once she felt she ~~couldn't~~ could not endure it any longer. Her full name was ~~Miranda~~ Valancy Jane ~~Stirling~~. ~~Miranda~~ Valancy Jane was rather terrible[,] but she liked ~~Miranda~~ Valancy[,] NOTE ZI NOTE G1 ~~although all the Stirlings called her Doss – her baby nickname~~. She never got ~~Miranda~~ Valancy from any[ ]one but outsiders.

"Mother," she said timidly, "would you mind calling me ~~Miranda~~ Valancy after this? Doss seems so – so – I don't like it."

Mrs. ~~Stirling George~~ Frederick looked at her daughter in astonishment. She wore glasses with enormously strong lenses that gave her eyes a peculiarly disagreeable appearance.

"What is the matter with Doss?"

"It – seems so childish," faltered ~~Miranda~~ Valancy.

~~"Oh,"~~ NOTE H1 ~~Mrs. Stirling George smiled. Mrs. Stirling ^Mrs. Stirling George^ had been a Markley & the Markley smile ^ Mrs. Stirling George had been a Markley ^Barraclough^ & the Markley ^Barraclough^ smile was not an asset.^~~ "I see. Well, it should suit <u>you</u> then. You are childish enough in all conscience, my dear child."

"I am twenty[-]nine," said ~~Miranda~~ ^the dear child^ desperately.

"I wouldn't proclaim it ~~to all the world~~ ^from the housetops^ if I were you, dear," said Mrs. ~~Stirling George~~ Frederick. "Twenty[-]nine! <u>I</u> had been married nine years when I was twenty[-]nine."

"<u>I</u> was married at seventeen," said Cousin Stickles proudly.

~~Miranda~~ Valancy looked at them ~~for~~ furtively. Mrs. ~~Stirling George~~ Frederick, except for those terrible glasses, ~~NOTE K9~~ NOTE I1 was not ill-looking. At twenty she might have been quite pretty. But Cousin Stickles! And yet ~~Cousin~~ Christine Stickles had once been desirable in ~~some one~~ ^some^ man's eyes. Miranda felt that Cousin Stickles, ~~NOTE P1~~ NOTE J1 ~~gray, wrinkled, bent, withered, uncomely, with a mole on her nose and another on her chin had yet this advantage over her. = this right to look down on her. It~~

It rained all the forenoon without cessation. NOTE K1 ~~Miranda sewed on a gingham apron. Miranda hated sewing. ℂ After dinner~~ ^At noon^ it stopped raining[,] ~~but it was not~~ the sun did not come out until three. Then ~~Miranda~~ Valancy timidly said she thought she would go up town.

"What do you want to go uptown for?" demanded her mother.

"I want to get a book from the library."

"You got a book from the library only last week."

"No, ~~Really~~ it was four weeks."

"Four weeks. Nonsense!"

"Really it was, mother."

NOTE H1: "Oh!" Mrs. Frederick had been a Barraclough and the Barraclough smile was not an asset[.]

NOTE I1: and the hooked nose that made her look more like a parrot than a parrot itself could look,

NOTE J1: with her broad, flat, wrinkled face, a ~~XXXX~~[5] mole right on the end of her dumpy nose, bristling hairs on her chin, wrinkled yellow neck, pale, protruding eyes, and thin[,] puckered mouth, had yet this advantage over her – this right to look down on her. And even yet Cousin Stickles was necessary to Mrs. Frederick. Valancy wondered pitifully what it would be like to be wanted by some[ ]one – needed by some[ ]one. No one in the whole world needed her, or would miss anything from life if she dropped suddenly out of it. She was a disappointment to her mother. No one loved her. She had never so much as had a girl friend.

"I haven't even a gift for friendship," she had once admitted to herself pitifully.

"Doss," you haven't eaten your crusts," said Mrs. Frederick rebukingly.

5: Unreadable, crossed out

NOTE K1: Valancy pieced a quilt. Valancy hated piecing quilts. And there was no need of it. The house was full of quilts. There were three big chests, packed with quilts, in the attic. *(continued on next page)*

NOTE K1 *continued*: Mrs. Frederick had begun storing away quilts when Valancy was seventeen and she kept on storing them, though it did not ~~now~~ seem likely that Valancy would ever need them. But Valancy must be at work; and fancy work materials were too expensive. Idleness was a cardinal sin in the Stirling household. When Valancy had been a child she had been made to write down every night, in a small, hated, black notebook, all the minutes she had spent in idleness that day. On Sundays her mother made ~~the~~ her tot them up and pray over them.

On this particular forenoon of this day of destiny Valancy spent only ten minutes in idleness. At least, Mrs. Frederick and Cousin Stickles would have called it idleness. She went to her room to get a better thimble and she opened Thistle Harvest guiltily at random. "The woods are so human," wrote John Foster, "that to know them we must live with them. An occasional saunter through them, keeping to the well[-]trodden paths[,] will never admit us to their intimacy. If we wish to be friends we must seek them out and win them by ~~frequent, reverent visits at~~ all hours; by morning, by noon, and by night; and at all seasons, in spring, in summer, in autumn, in winter. Otherwise we can never really know them and any ~~pretience~~ pretence we

may make to the contrary will never impose on them. They have their own effective way of keeping aliens at a distance & shutting their hearts to mere casual sight=seers. It is of no use to seek the woods from any motive except sheer love of them; they will find us out at once and hide all their sweet, old-world secrets from us. But if they know we come to them because we love them they will be very kind to us & give us such treasures of beauty & delight as are not bought or sold in any market[-]place. For the woods, when they give at all, give unstintedly and hold nothing back from their true worshippers. We must go to them lovingly, humbly, patiently, watchfully, and we shall learn what poignant loveliness lurks in the wild places & silent intervals, lying under starshine & sunset, what cadences of unearthly music are harped on aged pine fir boughs or crooned in copses of fir, what delicate savors exhale from mosses & ferns in sunny corners or on damp brooklands, what dreams & myths & legends of an older time haunt them.[6] Then the immortal heart of the woods will beat against ours & its subtle life will steal into our veins & make ~~us its own forever, so that~~ no matter where we go or how widely we wander we shall yet be drawn back to the forest to find our most enduring kinship."

"Doss," called her mother from the hall below, "What are you doing all by yourself in that room?"

Valancy dropped Thistle Harvest like a hot coal & fled downstairs to her patches; but she felt the strange exhilaration of spirit that always came momentarily to her when she dipped into one of John Foster's books. Valancy did not know much about woods – except the haunted groves of oak & pine around her Blue Castle. But she had always secretly hankered after them & a Foster book about ~~the~~ woods was the next best thing to the woods themselves.

6: Most of this paragraph, through "haunt them," was taken from Montgomery's essay "Spring in the Woods" (*Canadian Magazine*, May 1911), the first of four essays on the seasons. A few changes from this essay occur here: "near" is omitted from the original phrase "if we wish to be near friends"; and "treasure" was used in the original essay instead of "treasures" in the phrase "such treasures of beauty." She uses more passages from this essay, as well as "The Woods in Summer" (September 1911) and "The Woods in Winter" (December 1911) in later chapters of *The Blue Castle*.

"~~Well, I don't see~~ NOTE L1 ~~NOTE F9 NOTE L1~~ what you want to get a book for, anyhow. You waste too much time reading."

"Of what value is my time?" ~~said Miranda~~ asked Valancy bitterly.

"Doss! Don't speak in that tone to <u>me</u>."

"We need some tea," said Cousin Stickles. "She might go and get that if she wants a walk – though this damp weather is bad for colds[.]"

They argued the matter for ten minutes longer and finally Mrs. ~~Stirling~~ Frederick agreed rather grudgingly that ~~Miranda~~ Valancy might go.

NOTE L1: "You are mistaken. It cannot possibly have been more than two weeks. ~~And~~ I dislike contradiction. And I do not see

They argued the matter for ten minutes longer and finally Mrs. Frederick Stirling agreed rather grudgingly that Valancy might go.

"Got your rubbers on?" called Cousin Stickles, as Valancy left the house.

Cousin Stickles had never once forgotten to ask that question where Valancy went out on a damp day.

"Yes."

"Have you got your flannel petticoat on?" asked Mrs. Frederick.

"No."

"Valancy, I really do—Valancy, you are really leaving this minute and feel— No."

"Mother, I don't need a flannel petticoat. My skirt—, no is plenty warm enough."

"Valancy, remember you had bronchitis

IV X[1]

"Got your rubbers on?" called Cousin Stickles, as ~~Miranda~~ Valancy left the house.

Christine Stickles had never once forgotten to ask that question when ~~Miranda~~ Valancy went out on a damp day.

"Yes."

"Have you got your flannel petticoat on?" asked Mrs. ~~Stirling~~ Frederick.

"No."

"~~Doss, you are really trying. Go upstairs this minute and put it on.~~ NOTE M1 ^I really do not understand you^ ~~NOTE U9~~

"Mother, I don't <u>need</u> a flannel petticoat. My ~~gingh~~ sateen one is ~~plenty~~ warm" ^enough."^

"Doss, remember you had bronchitis two years ago. Go and do as you are told."[2]

~~Miranda~~ Valancy went, though nobody will ever know just how near she came to hurling the rubber[-] plant ^on the veranda^ into the street before she went. She hated that gray flannel petticoat ~~mre~~ more than any other garment ^she owned.^ Olive never had to wear flannel petticoats. Olive wore ruffled silk and sheer ~~laun~~ lawn and ~~filmy~~ filmy laced flounces. But Olive's father had "married money" and Olive never had ~~bronchitis~~ bronchitis. So there you were.

~~NOTE J1~~ NOTE N1

~~Meide Miranda~~ ^She^[3] turned at the corner and looked back down the ugly, prim[,] ^respectable^ street where she lived. The Stirling house was the ugliest on it – more like a red brick box than anything else. Too high

1: It is not clear why "X" was pencilled in and circled here.

NOTE M1: "Doss, I really do not understand you. Do you want to catch your death of cold <u>again</u>?" Her voice implied that Valancy had died of a cold several times already. "Go upstairs this minute & put it on."

2: The period after "told" is replaced by an exclamation point in the published version.

NOTE N1: "Are you sure you didn't leave the soap in the water?" demanded Mrs. Frederick. But Valancy was gone.

3: "She" does not begin a new paragraph in the published version but continues after "gone."

4: "Dubbed-off gables" probably refers to "clipped" gables in which the pointed end of a roof gable is flattened into a triangular shape. In the published version, "-off" is omitted.

NOTE O1: ~~a young house.~~ One of those houses you love the minute you see them.[5]

5: In the published version, this sentence does not stand alone but continues as part of the previous one ("a new house, one…").

NOTE P1: Oh, if I could only have a house of my own – ever so poor, so tiny – but my own.[6] But then," she added bitterly, "there is no use in yowling for the moon when you can't even get a tallow candle.["]

6: The period after "my own" is replaced by an exclamation point in the published version.

7: In the published version, "fully" is substituted for "richly."

NOTE Q1: Yet she was to have this delightful house. ~~And~~ And the nicest little Wedgewood teacups – Valancy had seen them; an open fireplace[,] & monogrammed linen; hem-stitched tablecloths & china closets[.]

8: In the published version, a new paragraph begins at "Valancy was once more seething."

NOTE R1: with its insulting shrieks.

9: In the published version, a new paragraph does not begin here.

---

for its breadth, and made still higher by a bulbous glass cupola on top. NOTE Z ~~It was the ugliest house not only in Deerwood but in the no.~~ About it was the desolate, barren peace of an old house whose life is lived.

There was a very pretty little house[,] ^with leaded casements & dubbed~~-off~~ gables,^[4] just around the corner – a new house NOTE A4 NOTE O1 ~~Clayton Markley~~ ^Clayton MARKLEY^ had built it for his bride. He was to be married to Jennie Lloyd in June. The little house, it was said, was furnished from attic to cellar, in complete readiness for its mistress.

"I don't envy Jennie the man," ~~said~~ thought ~~Miranda~~ Valancy sincerely—Clayton Markley was not one of her many ideals—["]but I do envy her the house. ^X P1^ ~~Its~~ It's such a nice young ~~young~~ house. NOTE P1

In dreamland nothing would do ~~Miranda~~ Valancy but a castle of pale sapphire. ~~But~~ In real life she would have been richly[7] satisfied with a little house of her own. She ~~evned~~ ^envied^ Jennie Lloyd more fiercely than ever to-day. Jennie was not so much better looking than she was, and not so very much younger. ~~NOTE J~~ NOTE Q1 Why did everything come to some girls and nothing to others? ~~Mira~~ It wasn't fair. ~~Miranda~~ Valancy was once more seething[8] with ~~rebellon~~ rebellion as she walked along, a prim, dowdy little figure in her ~~raincoat~~ shabby raincoat and three-year-old hat, splashed occasionally by the mud of a passing motor NOTE R1 ~~with its their raucous, insulting shrieks.~~

Motors[9] were still rather ~~a novelly~~ ^a novelty^ in Deerwood, though they were common in ~~Croyden~~ ^Point^ Port Laurence^ and most of the summer residents up at ~~Mistawis~~ ^Muskoka^[10] had them. In ~~Croyden~~ ^Deerwood^ only some of the smart set had them; for even ~~in~~ Deerwood was divided into sets. There was the smart set – the intellectual set – the old-family set—of which the Stirlings were members—the common run, and a few pariahs. Not one of the Stirling clan had as yet condescended to a motor, though Olive was teasing her ~~mother and~~ father to have one. ~~Miranda~~ Valancy had never even been in a motor car. ~~NOTE M1~~ NOTE S1

10: While Montgomery changed the name of Lake Muskoka to Lake Mistawis, she uses the name Muskoka when referring to the general area around the lake.

NOTE S1: But she did not hanker after this. In truth, she felt rather afraid of motor cars, especially at night. They seemed to her too much like big purring beasts that might turn and crush you – or make some terrible ~~shabby~~ savage leap somewhere. On the steep mountain trails around her Blue Castle only gaily caparisoned steeds might proudly pace; in real life Valancy would have been quite contented to drive in a buggy behind a nice horse.[11] She got a buggy drive only when some uncle or cousin remembered to fling her a chance[,] like a bone to a dog.

11: In her journal, Montgomery comments on her feelings about automobiles vs. horse-driven buggies: "Personally I prefer a buggy with a nice lovable horse like dear little 'Queen.' But I realize a car's good points also, as time and distance-savers.... But I think I shall occasionally remember with regret the old days – and moonlit nights – of buggy driving. A moonlit night loses its charm in a car with its glaring lights." (May 7, 1918)

in Deerwood, though they were
common in ~~Roydon~~ Port Lawrence and ~~north~~ ^northward^
the ~~summoned~~ residents of ~~[crossed]~~
had their. In ~~Roydon~~ ^Deerwood^ only some of
the sical-sel- had them; for even ~~in~~
Deerwood was divided into sets.
There was the sical-sel- — the
intellectual set- — the old-family
set- — of which the Stirlings were
members — the common herd, and
a few pariahs. Not one of the Stirling
class had as yet condescended to
a motor, though Olive was leaving
her ~~[crossed]~~ father. There one.
~~Miranda~~ ^Valancy^ had never even been in
a motor car. Pht 81

Of course she must buy the tea
at little Benjamin's grocery store.
~~[crossed]~~ to accept her offer was
unthinkable. Tel- ~~Miranda~~ ^Valancy^ [crossed].
Valancy

V X[1]

Of course she must buy the tea in Uncle Benjamin's grocery[-]store. ~~Any other course was unth~~ ^To buy it anywhere else^ was unthinkable. Yet ~~Miranda~~ Valancy hated to go to Uncle Benjamin's store on her twenty[-]ninth birthday. There was no hope that he would not remember it.

"Why," demanded Uncle Benjamin[,] ~~genially~~ ^leeringly,^ as he tied up her tea, "are young ladies like ~~bad grammarians~~ ^bad grammarians?"^

~~Miranda~~ Valancy, with Uncle Benjamin's will in the background of her mind, said ~~weakly~~ meekly, "I don't know. Why?"

"Because," chuckled Uncle Benjamin, "they can't decline matrimony."

The two clerks, ^Joe Hammond and Claude Bertram,^ chuckled also, ~~They were~~ and ~~Miranda~~ Valancy disliked them a little more than ever. On the first day Claude Bertram had seen her in the store she had heard him whisper ^to^ Joe, "Who is that?" And Joe had said, "~~Miranda~~ Valancy Stirling ~~— an old maid."^—~~ one of the Deerwood old maids."^ "~~Curable~~ ^Curable^ or incurable?" Claude had asked with a snicker, evidently thinking the question very ~~smart.~~ ^clever.^ ~~Miranda~~ Valancy ~~burned~~ ^smarted^ anew with the sting of that old recollection.

"Twenty[-]nine," Uncle Benjamin was saying. "Dear me, Doss, you're dangerously near the second corner.[2] ^And not even thinking of getting married yet?[3]^ Twenty[-]nine. It seems impossible."

4: "Aprons" is changed to "apron" in the published version. Montgomery wrote about having to wear long-sleeved aprons in her journal entry of January 7, 1910: "I remember one winter when I was sent to school wearing a new style of apron. I think still it was very ugly. Then I thought it hideous. It was a long, sack-like garment with sleeves. Those sleeves were the crowning indignity. Nobody in school had ever worn aprons with sleeves before. When I went to school one of the girls sneeringly remarked that they were 'baby aprons.' This capped all! I could not bear to wear them—but wear them I had to, until they were worn out. But the humiliation never grew less. To the end of their existence—and they did wear horribly well, never getting any fortunate rents or tears—those 'baby' aprons marked for me the extreme limit of human endurance."

Then Uncle Benjamin said an original thing. Uncle Benjamin said[,] "How time does fly!"

"I think it crawls," said ~~Miranda~~ Valancy passionately. Passion was so alien to Uncle Benjamin's conception of ~~Miranda~~ Valancy that he ~~stared at her.~~ ^didn't know^ what to make of her. To cover his confusion[,] he asked another conundrum as he tied up her beans—Cousin Stickles had remembered at the last moment that they must have beans. ^Beans were cheap and filling.^

"What two ages are apt to prove illusory?" asked Uncle Benjamin; and not waiting for ~~Miranda~~ Valancy to "give it up[,]" he added "Mir-age and marri-age."

"M-i-r-a-g-e is pronounced mirazh," said ~~Miranda~~ Valancy shortly, ~~for the moment~~ picking up her tea and her beans. For the moment she did not care whether Uncle Benjamin cut her out of his will or not. She walked out of the store while Uncle Benjamin stared after her with his mouth open. Then he shook his head.

"Poor Doss is taking it hard," he said.

~~Miranda~~ Valancy was sorry by the time she reached the ~~corn~~ next crossing. Why had she lost her patience like that? Uncle Benjamin would be annoyed and would likely tell her mother that Doss had been impertinent—to "me!"—and her mother would lecture her for a week.

"I've held my tongue for ~~20~~ ^twenty^ years," thought ~~Miranda~~ Valancy. "Why couldn't I have held it once more?"

Yes, it was just twenty ~~years~~, ~~Miranda~~ Valancy reflected, since she had first been twitted with her loverless condition. She remembered the bitter moment perfectly. She was just nine years old and she was standing alone in the school playground while the other little girls of her class were playing a game in which you must be chosen by a boy ~~before you could~~ as his partner before you could play. Nobody had chosen ~~Miranda~~ Valancy—little, pale, black-haired ~~Miranda~~ Valancy[,] with her prim, ~~aprons and~~ long-sleeved aprons[4] and odd, slanted eyes.

"Oh," said a pretty little girl to her, "I'm so sorry for you. You haven't got a beau."

~~Miranda~~ Valancy had said ~~then~~ ^defiantly,^ as she ~~said~~ continued to say for twenty years, "I don't ~~want~~ a beau." But this afternoon ~~Miranda~~ Valancy once and for all stopped saying that~~, even to herself. ¶ "I'm going to be honest~~ I'm going to be honest with myself anyhow," she thought savagely. "Uncle Benjamin's riddles hurt me because they are true. I ~~do~~ want to be married. I want a house of my own – I want a husband of my own – I want ^sweet, little fat^ ~~babies~~ of my own" – ~~Miranda~~ Valancy stopped suddenly~~,~~ aghast at her own recklessness. She felt sure that ~~the~~ Rev. ~~Mr.~~ Dr. ~~Stalling~~ STALLING[,] who passed her at this moment read her thoughts and disapproved of them thoroughly. ~~Miranda~~ Valancy was afraid of ~~Mr.~~ Dr. Stalling—had been afraid of him ever since the ^~~Sun~~^~~day~~ Sunday twenty[-]three years before, when he had first come to St. Alban's. ~~It was a rainy day and Miranda~~ Valancy had been too late for Sunday School that day and she had gone into the church ^timidly^ and sat in ~~the Stirling~~ their pew. No one else was in the church—nobody except the new rector, ~~Mr.~~ Dr. Stalling. ~~Mr.~~ Dr. Stalling stood up ~~on~~ ^at the top of the^ ~~the pulpit platform,^ ^in front of the choir door, ~~but~~^ beckoned to her, and said sternly, "Little boy, come up here."

~~Miranda~~ Valancy had stared around her. There was no little boy—there was no one in all the huge church but her^self^. This strange man with the blue glasses couldn't mean her. She was not a boy.

"Little boy," repeated ~~Mr.~~ Dr. Stalling ~~sternly~~ ^more sternly still,^ shaking his fore finger[5] fiercely at her, "come up here at once."

~~Miranda~~ Valancy arose as if hypnotized and walked up the aisle. She was too terrified to do anything else. What dreadful thing was going to happen [to] her? What ~~had~~ happened to her? Had she ~~by an~~ actually turned into a boy? She came to a stop in front of ~~Mr.~~ Dr. Stalling. ~~Mr.~~ Dr. Stalling shook his fore finger—such a long, knuckly, fore finger—at ~~him~~ her and said,

"Little boy, take off your hat."

5: "Fore finger" is written as a single word in the published version, here and elsewhere.

~~Miranda~~ Valancy took off her hat. She had a scrawny little pig=tail hanging down her back[,] but ~~Mr.~~ Dr. Stalling was short sighted[6] and did not perceive it.

"Little boy, go back to your seat and <u>always</u> take off your hat in church.~~"~~<u>Remember!</u>[["]

~~Meranda~~ ~~Miranda~~ Valancy went back to her seat, carrying her hat, ^like an automaton.^ ~~She was frozen with terror and shame.~~ Presently her mother came in.

~~"Miranda,"~~ "Doss," said Mrs. Stirling, "what do you mean by taking off your hat? Put it on instantly."

~~Miranda~~ Valancy put it on instantly. She was ~~sick~~ ^cold^ with fear ~~that~~ ^lest^ ~~Mr.~~ Dr. Stalling ~~would~~ ^should^ immediately summon her up front again. She would have to go[,] of course—it never occurred to her that one could disobey the rector—and the church was full of people now. Oh, what would she do if that ~~dreadful forefinger~~ ^horrible, stabbing forefinger^ were shaken at her again before all those people? ^~~Miranda~~ Valancy^ ~~Doss was sick for a week after~~ sat through the whole service in an agony of dread and was sick for a week afterwards. Nobody knew why – Mrs. ~~Stirling~~ Frederick again bemoaned herself of her delicate child. ~~Miranda had~~

~~Mr.~~ Dr. Stalling found out his mistake and laughed over it to ~~Miranda~~ Valancy – who did not laugh. She never got over her dread of ~~Mr.~~ Dr. Stalling. And now to be caught by him on the street corner, thinking such things!

~~Miranda~~ Valancy ~~wandered into the read~~ got her John Foster book – <u>Magic of Wings</u> – "his latest – all about birds," said Miss Clarkson. She had almost decided that she would go home, instead of going to see Dr. Trent. Her courage ^had^ failed her. She was afraid of offending Uncle James – afraid of angering her mother – afraid of facing gruff, shaggy-browed old Dr. ~~Freint~~ Trent[,] who would probably tell her, as he had told Cousin Gladys, that her trouble was entirely imaginary and that she only had it because she liked to have it. No, she would not go; she would get a bottle of ~~Shortreed's~~ ^Redfern's^ Purple Pills instead. ~~Shortreed's~~

^Redfern's^ Purple Pills ~~was~~ ^were^ the standard med-icine of the Stirling clan. ~~It They had~~ ^Had they not^ cured Second Cousin Geraldine when five doctors had given her up? ~~Miranda~~ Valancy always felt very skepti-cal concerning the virtues of the Purple Pills; but there might be something in them; and it was easier to take them than to face Dr. Trent alone. ~~She would go and read~~ She would glance over the magazines in the read-ing[-]room a few minutes and then go home. ~~-- back to the brick house.~~

~~Mirde Miranda~~ Valancy tried to read a story but it made her furious. On every page was a picture of the heroine surrounded by ^adoring^ men. And here was she, ~~Miranda~~ Valancy Stirling, who could not get a soli-tary beau! ~~Miranda~~ Valancy slammed the magazine shut; she opened Magic of Wings. ~~And the first paragraph she saw was a~~ ^Her eyes fell^ on the paragraph that changed her life.

"Fear is the original sin," wrote John Foster. "Almost all the evil in the world has its origin in the fact that some[ ]one is afraid of something ^NOTE B4 NOTE T1^ ~~and it is beyond all things degrading." NOTE B4~~

~~Miran Miranda~~ Valancy shut Magic of Wings and stood up. She would go and see Dr. Trent.

NOTE T1: It is a cold, slimy serpent coiling about you. It is horrible to live with fear; and it is of all things degrading.["]

VI

The ordeal was not so dreadful, after all. Dr. Trent was as gruff and abrupt as usual[,] but he did not tell her her ailment was imaginary. After he had listened to her symptoms and asked a few questions and made a quick examination[,] he sat for a moment looking at her quite ~~seriously~~ ^intently.^ ~~Miranda~~ Valancy thought he looked as if he were sorry for her. She caught her breath for a moment. Was the trouble serious? Oh, it couldn't be[,] surely – it really hadn't bothered her <u>much</u> – only lately it had got a little worse.

Dr. Trent opened his mouth – but before he could speak the telephone[1] at his elbow rang sharply. He picked up the receiver. ~~Miranda~~ Valancy, watching him, saw his face change suddenly as he listened.

"'Lo – yes – yes – <u>what</u>? – yes – yes" – a brief interval – "My God!"

Dr. Trent dropped the receiver, dashed out of the room and upstairs without even a glance at ~~Miranda~~ Valancy. She heard him rushing madly about overhead, barking out a few remarks to somebody[—]presumably his housekeeper. Then he came tearing ~~down stairs~~ ^downstairs^ with a club bag in his hand, snatched his hat and coat from the rack, jerked open the ~~street~~ [street] door and rushed down the street in the direction of the station.

~~Miranda~~ Valancy sat alone in the little office, feeling more absolutely foolish than she had ever felt before in her life. Foolish – and humiliated. So this was all that had come of her heroic determination to live up to John Foster and cast fear aside. ~~NOTE C4~~ NOTE U1 ~~She Not only~~

44

~~was she of no importance as daughter, relative, or friend = she was not even impor had not even importance as a patient.~~ Dr. Trent had forgotten her very ~~existence~~ ^presence^ in his excitement over whatever message had ~~come from~~ come by the telephone. She had gained nothing by ignoring Uncle James and flying in the face of family tradition.

~~She felt foolishly like crying~~

For a moment she was afraid she was going to cry. It <u>was</u> all so – ridiculous. Then she heard Dr. Trent's housekeeper coming down the stairs. ~~Mird Miranda~~ Valancy rose and went to the office door.

"The doctor forgot all about me," she said with a twisted smile. ~~"I = I had consulted him about a little ailment = but the phone rang before~~

"Well, that's too bad," said Mrs. Patterson sympathetically. "But it wasn't much wonder, poor man. That was a telegram they 'phoned over from the ~~Point~~ Port. His son has been terribly injured in an auto accident in Montreal~~, and they don't think he'll live~~. The doctor had just ten minutes to catch the train. I don't know what he'll do if ~~Ned doesn't recover =~~ & anything happens to Ned—he's just bound up in that boy. You'll have to come again, Miss Stirling. I hope it's nothing serious."

"Oh, no, nothing serious," agreed ~~Miranda.~~ Valancy. She felt a little less humiliated. It was no wonder poor Dr. Trent had forgotten her at such a moment. Nevertheless, she felt very flat and discouraged as she went down the street.

~~Miranda~~ Valancy went home by the shortcut of Lover's Lane[2]. She did not often go through Lover's Lane – but it was getting near supper[-]time and it would never do to be late. Lover's Lane wound back of the village, under great elms and maples, and deserved its name. It was hard to go there at any time and not find some canoodling couple – or young girls in pairs, arms intertwined, earnestly talking over their little secrets. ~~Miranda~~ Valancy didn't know which made her feel more self-conscious and ~~envious.~~ ^uncomfortable.^ This evening[3] she encountered both. She met Connie Hale and

2: Montgomery named a wooded path in Cavendish, Prince Edward Island, "Lover's Lane" and walked there frequently. She wrote it into her first novel, *Anne of Green Gables*, as one of Anne's favourite places. It is a feature of the Green Gables property at L. M. Montgomery's Cavendish National Historic Site.

3: In the published version, a new paragraph begins with "This evening."

NOTE V1: Never had she felt so utterly colorless & skinny & insignificant.

4: "Tin Lizzie" was the nickname for the Ford Model T, produced from 1908 to 1927.

5: Montgomery's husband purchased a Gray-Dort automobile in 1921. Gray-Dorts were manufactured in Chatham, Ontario, from 1915 to 1925. It is unclear why Montgomery chose to name the brand of Barney's automobile a "Grey-Slosson." She altered the spelling of "Gray" in Gray-Dort to "Grey-Dort" in her journals. As for "Slosson," it is possible she was inspired to use the name of author and entomologist Annie Turnbull Slosson (1838–1926) as a link to Barney's interest in the natural world. In the published version, "Grey-Slosson" is not hyphenated.

6: In the published version, a new paragraph begins with "It was Barney Snaith's car."

NOTE W1: "up back" in Muskoka.

NOTE X1: – a little, whimsical grin that gave him the look of an amused gnome.

Kate Bayley, in new ^pink^ organdy dresses with flowers stuck coquettishly in their glossy[,] bare hair. ~~Miranda~~ Valancy had ~~nevr~~ never ^had a pink dress or^ worn flowers in her hair. Then she passed a ~~young boy~~ young couple she didn't know, dandering along, oblivious to everything but themselves. The young man's arm was around the girl's waist quite shamelessly. ~~Miranda~~ Valancy had never walked with a man's arm about her. She felt that she ought to be shocked—they might leave that sort of thing for the screening twilight, at least—but she wasn't shocked. In another flash of desperate, stark honesty she owned to herself that she was ^merely^ envious. When she passed them she felt quite sure they were laughing at her – pitying her – "there's that queer little old maid ~~Miranda~~ Valancy Stirling. They say she never had a beau in her whole life" – ~~Miranda~~ Valancy fairly ran to get out of Lover's Lane. ~~NOTE K1~~ NOTE V1

Just where ~~it~~ ^Lover's Lane^ debouched on the street[,] an old ~~disreputable Ford~~ ^car^ was parked. ~~Miranda~~ Valancy knew that ~~Ford~~ ^car^ well ^– by sound, at least^ – [and] everybody in Deerwood knew it. This was before the phrase "tin Lizzie" had come into circulation – in Deerwood at least; but if it had been known, this ^car^ was the tinniest of Lizzies[4] – ^though it was not a Ford but an old Grey-Slosson.^[5] Nothing more battered and disreputable could be imagined. It was Barney Snaith's car[6] and Barney himself was just scrambling up from under it, in overalls plastered with mud. ~~Miranda~~ Valancy gave him a swift, furtive look as she hurried by. This was ~~not the first time she had seen B~~ ^only the second time she had ever seen^ the notorious Barney Snaith, though she had heard enough about him in the ~~four~~ five years that he had been living NOTE W1 ~~up at Mistawis~~ ^back Muskoka^ ^at in Muskoka.^ The first time had been nearly a year ago, ~~up~~ on the ~~Mistawis~~ ^Muskoka^ road. He had been crawling out from under his car then, too, and he had given her a cheerful grin as she went by ~~NOTE N1~~ NOTE X1. ~~She always remembered that Sun= and his over-long tawny hair with a dash of red in it,~~ ^his deep brown eyes,^ ~~his and his ears that stuck~~

~~out just enough to give him an alert look but not enough to be flying jibs.~~ He didn't look bad – she didn't believe he was bad, in spite of the wild yarns that were always being told of ~~him~~ him. Of course he went tearing in that ~~terrible~~ ^terrible^ old ~~Ford~~ ^Grey-Slosson^ through Deerwood at hours when all ~~resp~~ decent people were in bed – often with old "Roaring ~~Sandy~~ Abel," ~~waking~~ ^who made the night^ hideous with his howls – "both of them dead drunk, ~~and mind you.~~ ^my dear!"^ And every[ ]one knew that he was an escaped convict and a ~~runaway~~ ^defaulting^ bank clerk and a murderer in hiding. ~~NOTE F1~~ NOTE Y1 But still ~~Miranda~~ Valancy didn't believe he was bad. Nobody with a smile ~~tha~~ like that could be bad, no matter what he had done. ~~NOTE L1~~ NOTE Z1

~~He~~ ^~~Barney Snaith~~ BARNEY SNAITH^ looked even more disreputable than usual just now. It was very evident that he hadn't shaved for days[,] and his hands and arms, bare to the shoulders, were black with grease. But he was whistling gleefully to himself and he seemed so happy that ~~Miranda~~ Valancy envied him. ~~=she~~ She envied him his light heartedness and his irresponsibility and his mysterious little cabin up on an island NOTE A2 ~~in Mistawis~~ ^Lake Muskoka^ ~~= even his rackety old Ford.~~ ^Grey-Slosson.^ Neither he nor his car had to be respectable and live up to traditions. When he ~~passed~~ ^rattled past^ her a few minutes later, bareheaded, leaning back in his Lizzie at a ~~rak~~ raffish angle, his longish hair blowing in the wind~~,~~[,] ~~NOTE R3~~ NOTE B2 she envied him again. Men had the best of it, no doubt about that. This outlaw was happy, whatever he was or wasn't. She, ~~Miranda~~ Valancy Stirling, respectable, well-behaved to the last degree, was unhappy ^and had always been unhappy.^ And ^So^ there you were.

~~Mian~~ ~~Miranda~~ Valancy was ^just^ in time for supper. The sun had clouded over[,] and a ^dismal,^ drizzling rain was falling again. Cousin Stickles had the neuralgia. ~~Miranda~~ Valancy had to do the family darning and there was no time for "Magic of Wings"[.] NOTE A1 NOTE C2 | 7 ~~She~~ ^Miranda^ darned all the evening and listened to Mrs. ~~Stirling George~~ Frederick and Cousin

NOTE Y1: and an infidel & an illegitimate son of old Roaring Abel Gay & the father of ~~Abel Gay's~~ Roaring Abel's illegitimate grandchild & a counterfeiter & a forger & a few other awful things

NOTE Z1: ⟨It was that night the Prince of the Blue Castle changed from a being of grim jaw & hair with a dash of premature gray to a rakish individual with over-long, tawny hair, dashed with red, dark-brown eyes, & ears that stuck out just enough to give him an alert look but not enough to be called flying jibs. But he still retained something a little grim about the jaw.

NOTE A2: in Lake Mistawis—even his rackety old Grey-Slosson.

NOTE B2: a villainous-looking old black pipe in his mouth,

NOTE C2: "Can't the darning wait till to-morrow," she pleaded.
"To-morrow will bring its own duties," said Mrs. Frederick inexorably.
Valancy

7: In the published version, a new paragraph begins with "Valancy darned."

~~Christine~~ Stickles talking the eternal ^niggling^ gossip of the clan[,] ~~NOTE O1 NOTE~~
~~B1~~ NOTE D2 ~~Ten o'clo~~ ❡ Half past nine o'clock and so, as Mr. Pepys[8] would say, to
bed. ~~NOTE J1~~ NOTE E2 ❡ ~~Miranda's~~ Valancy's day of destiny had come and gone. She
ended it as she had begun it in tears.

NOTE D2: as they knitted drearily at interminable black stockings. They discussed Second Cousin Lilian's approaching wedding in all its bearings. On the whole, they approved. Second Cousin Lilian was doing well for herself.

"Though she hasn't hurried," said Cousin Stickles. "She must be twenty[-]five."

"There have not – fortunately – been many old maids in our connection," said Mrs. Frederick bitterly.

Valancy flinched. She had run the darning needle into her finger.

Third Cousin Aaron Gray had been scratched by a cat & had blood-poisoning in his finger. "Cats are most dangerous animals," said Mrs. Frederick. "I would never have a cat about the house."

She glared significantly at Valancy through her terrible glasses. Once, five years ago, Valancy had asked if she might have a cat. She had never referred to it since[,] but Mrs. Frederick still suspected her of harboring the unlawful desire in her heart of hearts.

Once Valancy sneezed. Now, in the Stirling code[,] it was very bad form to sneeze in public.

"You can always repress a sneeze by pressing your finger on your upper lip," said Mrs. Frederick rebukingly.

8: "Mr. Pepys" refers to Samuel Pepys (1633–1703), an Englishman well-known for his diary in which he recounts events of the period as well as his own observations about daily life. He frequently ended the day's entry with "and so to

bed," a phrase often repeated by others since.

NOTE E2: But first Cousin Stickles' neuralgic back must be rubbed with Redfern's liniment.[9] Valancy did that. Valancy always had to do it. She hated the smell of Redfern's Liniment – she hated the smug, beaming, portly, be-whiskered, be-spectacled picture of Dr. Redfern on the bottle. Her fingers smelled of the horrible stuff after she got into bed, in spite of all the scrubbing she gave them.

9: In the published version, "liniment" is capitalized.

45   54 b

~~Section IV~~

VI

There was a rose bush on the ~~little Stirling lawn,~~ lawn, growing beside the gate. It was called ~~("Rose's"~~ rose bush." Cousin ~~Aussie~~ ~~Georgiana~~ Georgiana had given it to ~~Miranda~~ Valancy five years ago and ~~Miranda~~ Valancy had planted it joyfully. She loved roses. But ~~of course~~ — the rose bush never bloomed. That was her fate. ~~Miranda~~ Valancy did everything she could think of and took the advice of everybody in the clan, but still the rose bush would not bloom. It ~~thrived~~ thrive ~~and~~ grew luxuriantly with great leafy branches untouched of rust or spider; but not even a bud had ever appeared on it. ~~Miranda,~~ Valancy,

VII

There was a rosebush on the ~~Stirlings lawn,~~ ^little Stirling lawn,^ growing beside the gate. It was called "Doss's rosebush." Cousin ~~Georgiana~~ ^~~Gussie~~^ ^Georgiana^ had given it to ~~Miranda~~ Valancy five years ago and ~~Miranda~~ Valancy had planted it joyfully. She loved roses. But – of course – the rosebush never bloomed. That was her ~~fate~~ ^luck^. ~~Miranda~~ Valancy did everything she could think of and took the advice of everybody in the clan, but still the rosebush would not bloom. It ~~thrived~~ ^throve^ and grew luxuriantly with great leafy branches untouched of rust or spider; but not even a bud had ever appeared on it. ~~Miranda~~ Valancy, looking at it ~~on the~~ ^two^ days after her birthday, was filled with a sudden, overwhelming hatred for it. The thing wouldn't bloom: very well, then, she would cut it down. She marched to the ^tool-room in the^ barn for her garden knife and she went at the rosebush viciously. A few minutes later horrified Mrs. ~~Stirling~~ George Frederick came out to the ~~walk~~ ^veranda^ and beheld her daughter slashing ~~inanely~~ ^insanely^ among[1] the rosebush boughs. Half of them were already strewn on the walk. The bush looked sadly dismantled.

"Doss, what on earth are you doing? Have you gone crazy?"

"No," said ~~Miranda~~ Valancy. She meant to say it defiantly[,] but habit was too strong for her. She said it deprecatingly. "I – I just made up my mind to cut this bush down. It is no good. It never blooms – never will bloom."

"That is no reason for destroying it," said Mrs. ~~Stirling~~ George Frederick sternly. "It was a beautiful bush and quite ornamental. You have made a sorry-looking thing of it."

1: This word is difficult to decipher in the manuscript, which is probably why it is circled. It is not corrected in the manuscript, but it looks to be "among," which appears in the published version.

NOTE F2: There's nothing like Redfern's Bitters for building a body up. Cousin James says the Purple Pills are the best[,] but I know better. My poor dear husband took Redfern's Bitters right up to the day he died.

"Roses ^trees^ should <u>bloom</u>," said Miranda a little obstinately.

"Don't argue with <u>me</u>, Doss. ~~And~~ Clear up that mess and leave the bush alone. I don't know what ~~Cousin Georgiana~~ ^~~Gussie~~^ ^Georgiana^ will say when she ~~shees~~ sees how you have ~~mistreated it.~~^hacked it to pieces.^ Really, I'm surprised at you. And to do it without consulting <u>me</u>!['']

"The bush is mine," muttered ~~Miranda~~ Valancy.

"What's that? What did you say, Doss?"

"I ^only^ said the bush was mine," repeated ~~Miranda~~ Valancy humbly.

Mrs. ~~Stirling George~~ Frederick turned without a word and marched back into the house. ~~Miranda~~ The mischief was done now. ~~Miranda~~ Valancy knew she had offended her mother deeply and would not be spoken to or noticed in any way for two or three days. Cousin Stickles would see to ~~Miranda's~~ Valancy's bringing-up but Mrs. ~~Stirling George~~ Frederick would preserve the ^stony^ silence of ~~offended~~ ^outraged^ majesty.

~~Miranda~~ Valancy sighed and put away her garden knife, hanging it precisely on its precise nail in the tool-shop. She cleared ~~up the~~ ^away^ the severed branches and swept up the leaves. Her lips twitched as she looked at the straggling bush. It had an odd resemblance to ^its^ shaken, scrawny ~~little~~ donor, little Cousin ~~Georgiana Gussie~~ Georgiana herself.

"I certainly have made an awful looking thing of it," thought ~~Miranda~~ Valancy. ℂ But she did not feel repentant – only sorry she had offended her mother. Things would be so uncomfortable until she was forgiven. Mrs. ~~Stirling George~~ Frederick was one of those women who can make their anger felt all over a house. Walls and doors ~~were~~ ^are^ no protection from it.

"You'd better go ^up town^ and git the mail," said Cousin Stickles, when ~~Miranda~~ Valancy went in. "<u>I</u> can't go – I feel all sorter peaky and piny this spring. I want you to stop at the drugstore and git me a bottle of ~~Shortreed's~~ ^Redfern's^ Blood Bitters. ~~NOTE R1~~ NOTE F2 Don't let them charge you more'n ~~ninety~~ ^ninety^ cents.

I kin git it for that at the ~~Point~~ Port. And what <u>have</u> you been saying to your poor mother?" ~~NOTE D4~~ NOTE G2

~~Merden Miranda~~ Miranda went up-town. She got Cousin Stickles['] bottle of bitters and then she went to the Post Office[2] and asked for her mail at the General ~~Deel~~ Delivery. Her mother did not have a box. They got too little mail to bother with it. ~~Miranda~~ Valancy didn't expect any mail ^except^ ~~=it was not the day for~~ the <u>Christian Times</u>, which was the only paper they took. ~~And~~ They hardly ever got any letters. But ~~Miranda~~ Valancy rather liked to stand in the office and watch ~~old~~ Mr. Carewe,[3] the gray-bearded, Santa-Clausy old clerk, handing out letters to ^the^ lucky people who did get them. He did it with such a detached, impersonal, Jove-like[4] air[,] as if it did not matter in the least to him what supernal joys or shattering horrors might be in those letters for the people ~~they were addressed to~~ ^to whom they were addressed.^ Letters had a fascination for ~~Miranda.~~ NOTE Q1 NOTE H2 ~~She had never got any~~ ^her only^ letters ~~in her life, save~~ were occasional perfunctory notes from relatives ~~and she did not expect she ever would. There was nobody to write to her.~~ ^or advertising circulars^ ^or an advertising circular.^

Consequently she was immensely surprised when Mr. ~~Cree~~ Carewe NOTE T1 NOTE I2 poked a letter ^out^ at[5] her. Yes, it was addressed to her plainly, in a fierce, black hand "Miss ~~Miranda~~ Valancy Stirling, Elm Street, Deerwood" – and the postmark was Montreal. ~~Miranda~~ Valancy picked it up with a little quickening of her breath. Montreal! It must be from Doctor Trent. He had remembered her[,] after all. ~~NOTE U1~~ NOTE J2

NOTE G2: Do you ever stop to think, Doss, that you kin only have one mother?"
"One is enough for me," thought Valancy undutifully, as she went up town.

2: In the published version, "Post Office" is written as "post-office."

3:"Carewe" is Montgomery's altered spelling of the name of Mr. Crewe, the mail carrier who brought mail to Cavendish and other community post offices along the way from Hunter River. Montgomery referred to him in her journal entry of August 12, 1903: "Old Santa Clausy Mr. Crewe with his bushy gray head and his limp, was fate's incongruous messenger."

Montgomery's grandparents kept the Cavendish post office in their home. The desk with its "pigeonholes" is on display at the Site of Lucy Maud Montgomery's Cavendish Home in Cavendish.

4: Jove/Jovian: comparing to the god Jupiter (also known as Jove) in Roman mythology. He was considered "king of the gods" and the god of sky and thunder.

NOTE H2: Valancy, perhaps because she so seldom got any. In her Blue Castle exciting epistles, bound with silk and sealed with crimson, were always being brought to her by pages in livery of gold and blue, but in real life

NOTE I2: looking even more Jovian than usual,

5: In the published version, "at" is changed to "to."

NOTE J2: Valancy met Uncle Benjamin coming in as she was going out and was glad the letter was safely in her bag.
"What," said Uncle Benjamin, "is the difference between a donkey and a postage stamp?"
"I don't know. What?" answered Valancy dutifully.
"One you lick with a stick & the other you stick with a lick. Ha, ha!"
Uncle Benjamin passed in, tremendously pleased with himself.

6: In the published version, "were at present" is changed to "at present were."

NOTE K2: Valancy had never had anything to hide.

7: An aneurism (or aneurysm) is a weak spot in an artery that can rupture.

Cousin Stickles pounced on the ~~Ch~~ <u>Times</u> when ~~Miranda~~ Valancy got home[,] but it did not occur to her to ask if there were any letters. Mrs. ~~Stirling George~~ Frederick would have asked it[,] but ~~Mere~~ Mrs. ~~Stirling's George~~ Frederick's lips were ^at present^[6] sealed. ~~Miranda~~ Valancy was glad of this. If her mother had asked if there were any letters ~~Miranda~~ Valancy, ~~having a Washingtonian incapability of telling a lie, for words~~ would have had to admit there was. Then she would have had to let her mother and Cousin Stickles read the letter and all would be discovered.

~~Miranda's~~ Her heart acted strangely on ~~her~~ ^the^ way upstairs[,] and she sat down by her window for a few minutes before opening her letter. She felt very guilty and deceitful. She had ~~new~~ ^never^ before kept a letter secret from her mother. Every letter she had ever written or received had been read by Mrs. ~~Stirling.~~ Frederick. That had never mattered. ~~NOTES:~~ NOTE K2 But this <u>did</u> matter. She could not have any[ ]one see this letter. But her fingers trembled with a consciousness of wickedness and unfilial conduct as she opened her ~~letter~~ ^it^—trembled a little too, perhaps, with apprehension. She felt quite sure there was nothing seriously wrong with her heart but – one never knew.

Dr. Trent's letter was like himself—blunt, abrupt, concise, wasting no words. Dr. Trent never beat about the bush. "Dear Miss Sterling" –

~~Montreal~~

~~May 28, 19=~~

~~Dear Miss Sterling ~~

and then a page of black, positive writing. ~~Miranda~~ Valancy seemed to read it at a glance; ~~then~~ she dropped it on her lap, her face ^ghost-^ ~~as~~ white^. ~~as the snow~~ ^the^ cherry blossoms as snow.

Dr. Trent told her that she had a very dangerous and fatal form of heart disease—angina pectoris – evidently complicated with an aneurism – whatever that was –[7] and in the last stages. He said without mincing matters that ~~he could do nother~~ nothing could be done for her. If she took great care of herself she might live a year – ~~possibly two~~ – but she might also die at any moment—Dr. Trent never troubled himself about euphemisms. She must be careful to avoid all excitement and all severe muscular effort[s]. ~~NOTE V1~~ NOTE L2 She was to get the prescription he enclosed filled and ~~take a~~ carry it with her always, taking a dose whenever her attacks came on. And he was hers truly, H. B. Trent.

~~Miranda~~ Valancy sat for a long while by her window. Outside was a world drowned in the light of a spring afternoon ~~that~~—skies entrancingly blue, winds perfumed and free[,] ~~NOTE I9~~ NOTE M2 ~~Across the vacant lot~~ Over at the railway station a group of young girls were[8] waiting for a train; she heard their gay laughter as they chattered and joked. The train roared in and roared out again. But none of these things had any reality. Nothing had any reality except the fact that she had only another year to live.

When she was tired of sitting at her window she went over and lay down on her bed, staring at the ^cracked, discolored^ ceiling. The curious numbness that follows on a staggering blow possessed her. She did not feel anything except a boundless surprise and incredulity – behind which was the conviction that Dr. Trent knew his business and that she, ~~Miranda~~ Valancy Stirling, who had never lived, was about to die.

When the gong rang for supper ~~Miranda~~ Valancy got up and went downstairs ^mechanically, from force of habit.^ She wondered that she had been let alone so long. But of course her mother would not pay any attention to her just now. ~~Miranda~~ Valancy was thankful for this. She thought the quarrel over the rosebush had been really, ^as Mrs. ~~Frank~~ Frederick herself might have said,^ Providential. She could not eat anything[,] but both Mrs. ~~Stirling~~ ~~George~~ Frederick and Cousin Stickles thought this was because she was ~~deservedly~~ deservedly unhappy over her mother's attitude[,] and her lack of appetite was not commented on. ~~Miranda~~ Valancy forced herself to swallow a cup of tea; and then sat and watched the others eat[,] with an odd feeling that years had passed since she had sat with them at the ~~diner~~ dinner[-]table. She found herself smiling inwardly to think

NOTE L2: She must eat & drink moderately, she must never run, she must go upstairs & uphill with great care. Any sudden jolt or shock might be fatal[.]

NOTE M2: ~~NOTE X9~~ lovely, soft, blue hazes at the end of every street.

8: In the published version, "were" is corrected to "was."

9: "Choose" is corrected to "chose" in the published version.

NOTE M2 N2: Valancy could not be allowed to have headaches without interference.

NOTE O2: Here, try a spoonful of vinegar."
"Piffle," said Valancy rudely, getting up from the table. She did not care just then if she was rude. She had had to be so polite all her life. NOTE S3
"You go & get right into bed," ^she^ said Cousin Stickles,[11] thoroughly alarmed,

NOTE S3: If it had been possible for Cousin Stickles to turn pale she would have. As it was not she turned yellower.
"Are you sure you ain't feverish, Doss? You sound like it. (Finish Note O2)[10]

10: "Finish Note O2" seems to be a reminder to Montgomery herself or to the typist to add Cousin Stickles's remark ("You go & get right into bed") after NOTE S3.

11: In the published version, Cousin Stickles's speech continues uninterrupted ("...You sound like it. You go and get right into bed,"), and "said Cousin Stickles" replaces "she said."

12: In the published version, this sentence is not a separate paragraph but continues after "she turned."

13: In the published version, this sentence is not a separate paragraph but continues after "gasped."

14: In the published version, "liniment" is capitalized.

NOTE P2: And it has the vilest smell of any liniment I ever saw.

what a commotion she could make if she choose.[9] Let her just ^merely^ tell them what was in Dr. Trent's letter and there would be as much fuss made as if – Miranda Valancy thought bitterly – she was they really cared two straws about her.

"Dr. Trent's housekeeper got word from him to-day," said Cousin Stickles, so suddenly that Miranda Valancy dro jumped guiltily. Was there anything in thought waves? "Mrs. Judd next door was talking to her up town. They think his son will recover[,] but Dr. Trent wrote that if he did he was going to take him abroad as soon as he was able to travel and wouldn't be back here for a year at least."

"That will not matter much to us," said Mrs. Stirling George Frederick majestically. "He is not our doctor. I would not have"—here she looked ^or seemed to look^ accusingly at Miranda ^right through^ Valancy—"have him to doctor a sick cat."

"No, of course not," agreed Cousin Stickles.

"May I go upstairs and lie down," said Miranda Valancy faintly. "I – I have a headache."

"What has given you a headache?" asked Cousin Stickles, since Mrs. Stirling George Frederick would not. The question had to be asked. NOTE C4 NOTE N2

"You ain't in the habit of having headaches. I hope you're not taking the measles ^mumps.^ NOTE G2 NOTE O2 You go and git into bed "and I'll come up and rub your forehead and the back of your neck with Shortreed's liniment Redfern's Liniment."

Miranda Valancy had reached the door[,] but she turned.

"I won't be rubbed with Shortreed's Redfern's liniment," she said.[12]

Cousin Stickles stared. ^and gasped^[.]

"What – what do you mean?" she gasped.[13]

"I said I wouldn't be rubbed with Shortreed's Redfern's liniment,"[14] repeated Miranda Valancy. "Horrid, sticky smelly stuff[!] NOTE I 19 NOTE P2 It's no good. I want to be left alone, that's all."

~~Miranda~~ Valancy went out, ^leaving^ Cousin Stickles ~~was~~ aghast.

"She's feverish – she <u>must</u> be feverish," ~~gasped~~ ^ejaculated^ Cousin Stickles.

Mrs. ~~Stirling~~ ~~George~~ Frederick went on eating her supper. It did not matter ~~to her~~ whether ~~Miranda~~ Valancy ~~had~~ was or was not feverish. ~~Miranda~~ Valancy had been guilty of impertinence to <u>her</u>.

71

"She's feverish — she must be feverish," ejaculated Cousin Stickles.

Mrs. Stirling went on eating her supper. I did not want to her shelter Valancy had was or was not feverish. Valancy had been quietly impertinent to her.

VII

Amanda did not sleep that night. She lay awake all through the long dark hours — thinking — thinking. She made a discovery that surprised her; she who had been afraid of almost everything in life, was not afraid of death. It did not seem in the least terrible to her. And she need not now be afraid of

VIII

Miranda Valancy did not sleep that night. She lay awake all through the long dark hours – thinking – thinking. She made a discovery that surprised her: she[,] who had been afraid of almost everything in life, was not afraid of death. It did not seem in the least terrible to her. And she need not now be afraid of anything else. Why had she been afraid of things? Because of life. Afraid of Uncle Benjamin because of the menace of poverty in old age. NOTE Q2 ~~But now~~ ^she would never be old = neglected = tolerated.^ ~~there would be no old age.~~ Afraid of being an old maid all her life. But now ~~there would be no life.~~ ^she would not be an old maid very long.^ Afraid of offending her mother and her clan because she had to live with and among them ~~NOTE W1~~ NOTE R2 But now she hadn't. ~~Miranda~~ Valancy felt a curious freedom.

But she was still horribly afraid of one thing – the fuss the whole jamfry[1] of them would make when she told them. ~~Miranda~~ Valancy shuddered at the thought of it. She couldn't endure it. Oh, she knew so well how it would be. First there would be indignation—yes, ~~the indignation would come first.~~[2] Indignation on the part of Uncle James because she had gone to ~~Dr. Trent~~ a doctor ^– any doctor –^ without consulting ~~him~~ HIM. Indignation on the part of her mother for being so sly and deceitful – "to your own mother, Doss." Indignation on the part of the whole clan because she had not gone to Dr. Marsh. ⁋ Then would come the solicitude. She would be taken to Dr. Marsh[,] and when Dr. Marsh confirmed Dr. Trent's diagnosis she

NOTE Q2: But now she would never be old – neglected – tolerated.

NOTE R2: and couldn't live peaceably if she didn't give in to them.

1: jamfry = clan or mob; from the Scottish term "clamjamfry"

2: The phrase "the indignation would come first" is left out of the published version; "yes, indignation on the part of Uncle James" starts after the dash.

would be taken to ~~specil~~ specialists in Toronto and Montreal[.] ~~NOTE X1~~ NOTE S2 And when the specialists could do nothing for her Uncle James would insist on her taking Purple Pills – "I've known them to affect a cure when <u>all</u> the doctors had given up" – and her mother would insist on ~~Shortreed's~~ ^Redfern's^ ^Blood^ Bitters and Cousin Stickles would insist on rubbing her over the heart every night with ~~Shortreed's~~ ^Redfern's^ Liniment on the grounds that it <u>might</u> do good and <u>couldn't</u> do harm; and everybody else would have some pet dope for her to take[.] ~~NOTE X3~~ NOTE T2 And she would be watched and checked like a baby and never let do anything or go anywhere alone. Perhaps she would not ~~be~~ even be allowed to sleep alone lest she die in her sleep. Cousin Stickles or her mother would insist on sharing her room and bed. Yes, undoubtedly they would.

~~I think~~ It was this last ~~com~~ thought that really decided ~~Miranda~~ Valancy. She could not put up with it and she wouldn't. As the clock in the hall below struck twelve ~~Miranda~~ Valancy suddenly and definitely made up her mind that she wouldn't ^not^ tell anybody. She had always been told, ever since she could remember, that she must hide her feelings. "It is not ladylike to have feelings," Cousin Stickles had once told her disapprovingly. Well, she would hide them with a vengeance.

But though she was not afraid of death she was not indifferent to it. She found that she <u>resented</u> it; it was not fair that she should have to die when she had never lived. Rebellion flamed up in her soul as ~~she~~ the dark ~~hours~~ ^hours^ passed by—not because she had no future but because she had no past.

"I'm poor – I'm ugly – I'm a failure – and I'm near death," she thought. She could see her own obituary notice in the Deerwood <u>Weekly Times</u>, copied into the ~~Point~~ ^Port Laurence^ Journal. "A deep gloom was cast over Deerwood etc., etc." – "leaves a large circle of friends to ~~mour~~ mourn" etc.[,] etc., etc. – lies, all lies. ~~NOTE Y1~~ NOTE U2 Nobody would miss her. ~~It~~ ^Her death^ would not matter a straw to anybody. ~~NOTE Z1~~ NOTE V2

~~Miranda~~ Valancy ~~went over~~ ^reviewed^ her whole life ~~as she lay there~~ between midnight and the early spring dawn. It was a very ~~colorless~~ ^drab^ existence, but here and there an incident loomed out with a significance out of all proportion to its real importance. These incidents were all unpleasant in one way or another. Nothing really pleasant had ever happened to ~~Miranda~~ Valancy.

"I've never had one ^wholly^ happy hour in my life—not one," she thought. "I've just been a colorless nonentity. I remember reading somewhere once that there is an hour in which a woman might be happy all her life if she can but find it! I've never found my hour—never, never. And I never will now. If I could only have had that hour ~~I don't~~ I'd be willing to die."

Those significant incidents kept bobbing up in her mind ~~NOTE Z3~~ NOTE W2 without any sequence of time or place. For instance, ~~there was~~ that time when, at ~~seven fifteen~~ ^sixteen,^ she had blued a tubful of clothes too deeply. And the time when, at eight, she had "stolen" some raspberry jam from ~~the~~ ^Aunt Wellington's^ pantry. ~~Miranda~~ Valancy never heard the last of those two misdemeanors. At almost every clan gathering they were raked up ~~and~~ against her as jokes. Uncle Benjamin hardly ever missed re-telling NOTE X2 ~~it~~ – he had been the one to catch her, her face all stained ^and streaked.^ ~~with raspberry jam.~~

"I have ^really^ done so few bad things that they have to keep harping on the old ones," thought Miranda. "Why, I've never even had a quarrel with any[ ]one. I haven't an enemy. What a spineless thing I must be not to have even one enemy."[5]

~~There was~~[6] That incident of the dust pile at school when she was ~~six~~ ^seven^. ~~Miranda~~ Valancy always recalled it when ~~Mr.~~ Dr. Stalling referred to the text, ~~"From~~ "To him that hath shall be given and from him that hath not shall be taken even that which he hath."[7] Other people might puzzle over that text but it never puzzled ~~Miranda~~ Valancy. The whole relationship between herself and Olive, dating from the day of the dust pile, was a commentary on it.

NOTE W2: like unbidden ghosts,

NOTE X2: the raspberry jam incident –

5: In the published version, an exclamation point replaces the period after "enemy."

6: In the published version, the sentence begins with "There was."

7: A quote from Mark 4:25, also used in Chapters XXVII and XLII.

She had been going to school a year[,] but Olive, who was a year younger, had just begun and had about her all the glamor of a "a new girl" and an exceedingly pretty girl at that. It was at recess and all the girls, big and little, were out on the road in front of the school making dust piles. The aim of each girl was to have the biggest pile. ~~Miranda~~ Valancy was good at making dust piles—there was an art in it—and she had secret hopes of leading. But Olive's, working off by herself, was ~~suddenly~~ ^suddenly^ discovered to have a ~~quite tremendous dust pile~~ ^larger dust pile than anybody.^ ~~Miranda~~ Valancy felt no jealousy. Her dust-pile was quite ~~as big as anybody elses~~ ^enough to please her^. Then ~~suddenly~~ one of the older girls had an inspiration.

"Let's put all our dust on Olive's pile and make a tremendous one," she exclaimed.

A frenzy seemed to seize the girls. They swooped down on the dust-piles with pails and shovels and in a few seconds Olive's pile was a veritable pyramid. In vain ~~Miranda~~ Valancy, ^with scrawny, outstretched little arms,^ tried to protect hers. She was ruthlessly swept aside, her dust-pile scooped up and poured on Olive's. ~~Miranda~~ Valancy turned away resolutely and began building another dust-pile. Again a bigger girl pounced on it. ~~Miranda~~ Valancy stood before it, flushed, ~~tearful,~~ indignant, arms ^outspread[.]^

"Don't ~~you touch~~ ^take^ it," she pleaded. "Please don't take it."

"But <u>why?</u>" demanded the older girl. "Why won't you help to build Olive's bigger[?]"

I want my own little dust-pile," said ~~Miranda~~ Valancy piteously.

Her plea went ~~unheard~~ ^unheeded.^ While she argued with one girl another scraped up her dust-pile. ~~Miranda~~ Valancy turned away, her heart swelling, her eyes full of tears.

"Jealous – you're jealous," said the girls mockingly.
~~NOTE A2~~ NOTE Y2

But ~~Miranda~~ Valancy was ~~not jealous.~~ ^neither jealous nor selfish.^ It was only that she wanted a dust-pile of her own—small or big mattered not. A team of horses came down the street – Olive's dust-pile was scattered over the roadway – the bell rang – the girls trooped into school and had forgotten the whole affair ~~in a~~ before they reached their seats. ~~Miranda~~ Valancy never forgot it. To this day she resented it in her secret soul. But was it not symbolical of her life? ~~She had never had her own dust-pile. Everything went to Olive.~~

"I've never been able to have my own dust-pile," thought ~~Miranda~~ Valancy.

~~Then there was~~ NOTE Z2 ~~NOTE Z9~~

The boy who had tried to kiss her at a party when she was fifteen. She had not let him – she had evaded him and run. He was the only boy who had ever tried to kiss her. Now, ~~fif~~ fourteen years later, ~~Miranda~~ Valancy found herself wishing that she had let him.

~~There was~~ The time she had been made to apologize to Olive for something she hadn't done. Olive had said that ~~Miranda~~ Valancy had pushed her into the mud and spoiled her new shoes <u>on purpose</u>. ~~Miranda~~ Valancy knew she hadn't. It had been an accident—and even that wasn't her fault—but nobody would believe her. She had to apologize[8] ^ – and kiss Olive to "make up." ^ ~~And~~ The injustice of it burned in her soul tonight. ~~There was~~ ℂ That summer when Olive had the most beautiful hat, trimmed with creamy yellow tulle, with a wreath of red cherries and little tulle bows under the chin.[9] ~~Miranda~~ Valancy had wanted a hat like that more than she had ever wanted anything. She pleaded ~~for one and~~ ^for one and^ had been laughed at.[10] All summer she had to wear a horrid little brown sailor with ~~lastic~~ elastic that cut behind her ears. None of the girls would go around with her because she was so shabby—nobody but Olive. People had thought Olive so sweet and unselfish.

"I was an excellent foil for her," thought ~~Miranda~~ Valancy. "Even then she knew that."

~~Mirdl Miranda~~ Valancy had tried to win a prize ^for attendance^ in Sunday School once. But Olive won it. There were so many Sundays ~~Miranda~~ Valancy had to stay home because she had colds. She had once tried to

NOTE Z2: ℂ The enormous red moon she had seen rising right at the end of the street one autumn evening of her sixth year. She had been sick & cold with the awful, uncanny horror of it. So near to her. So big. She had run in trembling to her mother & her mother had laughed at her. She had gone to bed & hidden her face under the clothes in terror lest she might look at the window & see that horrible moon glaring in at her through it.

8: In the published version, "apologize" is spelled "apologise."

9: In the published version, the description of the hat changes to "trimmed with creamy yellow net, with a wreath of red roses and little ribbon bows under the chin."

10: In the published version, there is a dash instead of a period after "laughed at," and "All" is not capitalized.

"say a piece" in school one Friday afternoon and had broken down in it. Olive was a good reciter and never got stuck.

NOTE C2 NOTE A3

The time Cousin Betty Stirling was married‡[.] Somehow ~~Miranda~~ Valancy got wind of the fact that Betty was going to ask her to be ^one of^ her bridesmaids. ~~Miranda~~ Valancy was secretly ~~delighted. It~~ uplifted. It would be a delightful thing to be a bridesmaid. And of course she would have to have a new dress for it – a pretty ~~light~~ new dress – a pink dress. Betty wanted her bridesmaids to dress in pink.

But Betty had never asked her after all. ~~Miranda~~ Valancy couldn't guess why but long after her ^secret^ tears of disappointment had been dried Olive told her. Betty, after much consultation and reflection, had decided that ~~Miranda~~ Valancy was "too insignificant" – she would "spoil the effect." That was nine years ago. But tonight ~~Miranda~~ Valancy caught her breath with the old pain and sting of it.

NOTE V3 NOTE B3

The winter she went to dancing school‡[.] Uncle James had decreed she should go and had paid for her lessons. How she had looked forward to it.[!] And how she had hated it! She had never had a voluntary partner. The teacher always had to tell some boy to dance with her[,] and generally he had been sulky about it. Yet ~~Miranda~~ Valancy was a good dancer, as light on her feet as thistledown. Olive, who ~~was~~ never lacked eager partners, was heavy.

NOTE A3: ❡ The night she had spent in Port Laurence with Aunt Isabel when she was ten. Byron Stirling was there. From[11] Montreal, twelve years old, conceited, clever. At family prayers in the morning Byron had reached across and given Valancy's thin arm such a savage pinch that she screamed out with pain. After prayers were over she was summoned to Aunt Isabel's bar of judgment. But when she said Byron had pinched it. He said she cried out because the kitten scratched her. He said she had put the kitten up on her chair and was playing with it when she should have been listening to Uncle David's prayer. He was believed. In the Stirling clan the boys were always believed before the girls. Valancy was sent home in disgrace because of her exceedingly bad behavior during family prayers & she was not asked to Aunt Isabel's again for many moons.

11: In the published version, "From" does not begin a new sentence but continues the previous sentence after a semicolon instead of a period.

NOTE B3: That day in her eleventh year when her mother had badgered her into confessing something she had never done. Valancy had denied it for a long time but eventually for peace' sake she had given in and pleaded guilty. Mrs. Frederick was always making people lie by pushing them into situations where they had to lie. Then her mother had made her kneel down on the parlor floor, between herself and Cousin Stickles, and say, "Oh, God, please forgive me for not speaking the truth." Valancy had said it but as she rose from her knees she muttered, "But oh God, you know I did speak the truth." Valancy had not heard of Galileo[12] but her fate was similar to his. She was punished just as severely as if she ~~hadent~~ hadn't confessed and prayed.

12: Galileo Galilei (1564–1642) was an Italian astronomer convicted of heresy by the Roman Inquisition of 1633 for his support of Copernicus's theory that the earth revolved around the sun. Galileo was required to deny his theory but is said to have added, "And yet it [the earth] moves." He was imprisoned for the remainder of his life.

The night of Margaret Blunt's party. She had made such pathetic efforts to appear be pretty that night. Rob Walker was to be there[;] and two nights before, on the moonlit veranda of Uncle Uncle Heebert's house ^Herbert's cottage at Mistawis MISTAWIS,^ Rob had really seemed attracted by ^to^ her. At Margaret's party Rob never even asked her to dance – did not even notice her at all. She was a wallflower[,] as usual. That, of course, was years ago. People in Deerwood had long since given up inviting Miranda Valancy to dances. But the to Miranda Valancy its humiliation and disappointment were of the other day. Her cheek face burned in the darkness as she recalled herself, sitting there with her pitifully crimped, thin hair, her new cream organdy dress and the cheeks she had pinched for an hour before coming[,] in an effort to make them red. All that came of it was a wild story that Miranda Valancy Stirling was rouged at Margaret Blunt's Blunt's party[.] and In those days in Deerwood that was enough to wreck your character forever. It did not wreck Miranda's ^Valancy's, or even damage it.^ People knew she couldn't be fast if she tried. They only laughed at her.

"I've had nothing but a second-hand existence," decided Miranda Valancy. "All the great emotions of life have passed me by. I've never even had grief. And have I ever really loved anybody? Do I really love mother? No, I don't. I'm going to ^That's the truth,^

NOTE C3: The affair of the button[-]string,[13] when she was ten. All the girls in school had button[-]strings. Olive had a very long one with a great many beautiful buttons. Valancy had one. Most of the buttons on it were very common=place[,] but she had six beauties that had come off Grandmother Stirling's wedding gown— sparkling buttons of gold and glass, much more beautiful than any Olive had. Their possession conferred a certain distinction on Valancy. She knew every little girl in school envied her the exclusive possession of those beautiful buttons. When Olive saw them on the button[-]string she had looked at them narrowly but said nothing—then. The next day Aunt Wellington had come to Elm Street & told Mrs. Frederick that she thought Olive should have some of those buttons— Grandmother Stirling was just as much Wellington[']s mother as Frederick[']s. Mrs. Frederick had agreed amiably. She could not afford to fall out with Aunt Wellington. Moreover, the matter was of no importance whatever. Aunt Wellington carried off four of the buttons, generously leaving two for Valancy. Valancy had torn these from her string and flung them on the floor.[14] She had not yet learned that it was unladylike to have feelings – and had been sent supperless to bed for the exhibition.

13: Putting buttons on a thread was a popular hobby in Victorian times. The thought was that when a girl had one thousand buttons on her button string, she would meet the man she would marry.

14: In the published version, a dash is substituted for the period after "floor," and "She" is not capitalized.

NOTE D3: whether it is disgraceful or not. I don't love her – I've never loved her. What's worse I don't even like her. So

15: Montgomery did not cross this sentence out in the manuscript even though she wrote it into NOTE D3.

NOTE E3: It was three o'clock in the morning – the wisest and most accursed hour of the clock. But sometimes it sets us free.
  "I've been trying to please other people all my life & failed," she said. "After this I shall please myself. I shall never pretend anything again. I've breathed an atmosphere of fibs and pretences and evasions all my life.

16: From *The History of the Saracens*, by Simon Ockley (1678–1720), published in the early 1700s.

NOTE F3: schoolgirl complexion on the old carriage[-]shop.

~~absolutely honest with myself whether it is disgraceful or not. After this~~ I don't love her – I've never loved her[15] | ~~NOTE Y3~~ ~~and so I've never loved anybody.~~ I don't know anything about any kind of love. My life has been empty – empty. Nothing is worse than emptiness. Nothing!" ~~Miranda~~ Valancy ejaculated the last "nothing" aloud passionately. Then she moaned and stopped thinking about anything for awhile. One of her attacks of pain had come on.

When it was over ~~NOTE B2~~ something had happened to ~~Miranda~~ Valancy – perhaps the culmination of the process that had been going on in her mind ever since she had read Dr. Trent's letter. ~~NOTE W3~~ NOTE E3

~~"I've lived in other people's opinions all my life," she said aloud. "After this I'm going to live in my own – as long as I do live. I've breathed an atmosphere of fibs and pretentions all my life. I shall~~ ^never^ ~~pretend no more~~ ^ a thing again^. What a luxury it will be to tell the truth! I may not be able to do much that I want to do but I won't do another thing that I don't want to do. Mother can ~~pout~~ pout for weeks – I shan't worry over it. 'Despair is a free man – hope is a ~~slave."~~ slave."[16]

~~Miranda had voiced her decal declaration of independence. She got~~ ^Valancy got^ up and dressed, with a ^deepening of that^ curious sense of freedom. When she had finished with her hair she opened ~~her~~ the window and hurled the jar of pot-pourri over into the next lot. It smashed gloriously against the NOTE F3 ~~postered wall of the old carriage~~ ^school girl complexion^ ~~shop~~.

"I'm sick of the fragrance of dead things," said Miranda.

IX

Uncle Herbert and Aunt ~~Alberta's~~ Alberta's silver wedding was ~~always~~ ^delicately^ referred to among the Stirlings ^during the following year^[1] as "the ^weeks^ time we first noticed poor ~~Miranda~~ Valancy was – a little – <u>you</u> understand?"

Not for worlds would any of the Stirlings have said out and out ^at first^ that ~~Miranda's mind was deranged~~ ^Valancy^ had gone mildly insane or even that her mind was slightly deranged. Uncle Benjamin was considered to have gone entirely too far when he had ejaculated "She's dippy – I tell you, she's dippy," and was only excused because of the ~~outragerous~~ outrageousness of ~~Miranda's~~ Valancy's conduct at the aforesaid wedding dinner. ~~NOTE~~ ~~H2~~

But Mrs. ~~George Stirling~~ Frederick and Cousin Stickles had noticed a few things that made them uneasy <u>before</u> the dinner. It had begun with the rosebush, of course; and ~~Miranda~~ Valancy ~~was~~ never was really "quite right" again. She did not seem to worry in the least over the fact that her mother was not speaking to her. ~~or y~~ You would never suppose she noticed it at all. ~~NOTE I2~~ NOTE G3 She had announced coolly that she did not intend to answer to the name of "Doss" any longer. ~~If they wanted.~~ She had told Cousin Stickles that she wished she would give up wearing that brooch with Cousin Artemas Stickles['] hair in it. She had moved her bed in ~~the~~ her room to ~~the~~ the opposite corner. She had read <u>Magic of Wings</u> ~~all on~~ Sunday afternoon. When Cousin Stickles had rebuked her ~~Miranda~~ Valancy had said indifferently, "Oh, I forgot it was Sunday"—and <u>had gone on reading it.</u>

1: In the published version, "year" is changed to "weeks."

NOTE G3: She had flatly refused to take either Purple Pills or Redfern's Bitters.

2: From Shakespeare's *King Lear*, Act 1, Scene 4: "How sharper than a serpent's tooth it is To have a thankless child!"

~~She had swept the parlor one day~~ ^and dusted^ ~~but had everything in it but the enormous Family Bible.~~ ❡ Cousin Stickles had seen a terrible thing—she had caught ~~Miranda~~ Valancy sliding down the bannister. ~~Cousin~~ Cousin Stickles did not tell Mrs. ~~Stirling George~~ Frederick this – poor Amelia was worried enough as it was. But it was ~~Miranda's~~ Valancy's announcement on Saturday night that she ~~meant to go~~ was not going to go to the Anglican church any more that broke through Mrs. ~~Stirling's George's~~ Frederick's ~~stubborn~~ ^stony^ silence.

"Not going to church anymore! Doss, have you absolutely taken leave—"

"Oh, I'm going to church," said ~~Miranda~~ Valancy airily. "I'm going to the Presbyterian church. But to the Anglican church I will not go."

This was even worse. Mrs. ~~Stirling George~~ Frederick had recourse to tears, having found outraged majesty had ceased to be effective.

"What have you got against the Anglican church?" she sobbed.

"Nothing – only just that you've always made me go there. If you'd made me go to the Presbyterian church I'd want to go to the Anglican."

"Is that a nice thing to say to your mother? Oh, how true it is that it is sharper than a serpent's tooth to have a thankless child?"[2]

"Is that a nice thing to say to your daughter?" said unrepentant ~~Miranda.~~ Valancy.

~~"I thi really think we ought to take her to a doctor," said Cousin Stickles that night, remembering the bannister.~~

~~"We will wait a few days to see if she will come~~

So ~~the Miranda's~~ Valancy's behavior at the silver wedding was not quite the surprise to Mrs. ~~George~~ Frederick and Christine Stickles that it was to the rest. They were doubtful about ~~the~~ the wisdom of taking her but concluded it would ~~cau~~ "make talk" if they didn't. ~~Perhaps~~ Perhaps she would behave herself[,] and so far ~~nobody~~ ^no outsider^ suspected there was anything queer about her. By a special mercy of Providence it had poured torrents Sunday morning[,] so ~~Miranda~~ Valancy had not carried out her ~~awful~~ ^hideous^ threat of going to the Presbyterian church.

~~Miranda~~ Valancy would not have cared in the least if they had left her at home. ~~These family celebrations~~ ^assemblies^ ~~of sensible, depress~~ These family ~~cle~~ celebrations were all hopelessly dull. ^{NOTE H3} ~~But the Stirlings always celebrated everything. Even Mrs. George gave a dinner party~~ ^It was a custom long-established custom^ on her wedding day[3] and Cousin Stickles had friends in to supper on her birthday. ~~Miranda~~ Valancy hated these entertainments because they had to pinch and save and contrive for weeks afterwards to pay for them. But she ~~rather~~ wanted to go to the silver wedding. It would hurt Uncle ~~Heebert's~~ Herbert's feelings if she stayed away[,] and she rather liked Uncle Herbert. Besides, she wanted to look over all her relatives from her new angle. It would be an excellent place to make public her declaration of independence if occasion offered.

"Put on your brown silk dress," said Mrs. Stirling.

As if there ~~was~~ ^were^ anything else to put on! ~~Miranda~~ Valancy had only the one festive dress—that snuffy-brown silk ~~Uncle~~ Aunt ~~Wellington~~ ^Isabel^ had given her. Aunt ~~Wellington~~ ^Isabel^ had decreed that ~~Miranda~~ Valancy should never wear colors. They did not become her. When she was young they allowed her to wear white but that had been tacitly dropped for some years. ~~Miranda~~ Valancy put on the brown silk. It had a high collar and long sleeves. ~~Miranda~~ She had never had a dress with low ~~sleeves~~ ^neck^ and ~~below~~ ^elbow^ sleeves, although they had been worn, even in Deerwood, for over a year. But she did not do her hair pompadour. She knotted it low on her neck, ^and^ pulled it out over her ears. ~~and~~ She thought it became her – only the little knot was so absurdly small. Mrs. ~~George~~ Frederick resented the hair but decided it was wisest to say nothing on the eve of the party. It was so important that ~~Miranda~~ Valancy should be kept in good humor[,] if possible[,] until it was over. Mrs. ~~George~~ Frederick did

NOTE H3: But the Stirlings always celebrated everything. It was a long-established custom. Even Mrs. Frederick gave a dinner party

3: "Wedding day" is changed to "wedding anniversary" in the published version.

4: The "wee sma's" (an abbreviations of "smalls") are the hours just after midnight.

NOTE 13: "He'll be picked up dead some morning – he'll fall under his horse's hoofs & be trampled to death," said Cousin Stickles reassuringly.

not reflect that this was the first time in her life that she had thought it ~~necessary to defer to Miranda.~~ ^necessary to consider ~~Miranda's humors.~~ Valancy's humors.^ But then ~~Miranda~~ Valancy had never been "queer" before.

On their way to Uncle Herbert's—Mrs. ~~George~~ Frederick and Cousin Stickles walking in front, ~~Miranda~~ Valancy trotting meekly along behind—~~Roaring Abel passed~~ ^Roaring Abel drove past^ them. Drunk as usual but not in the roaring stage. Just drunk enough to be excessively polite. He raised his disreputable old ~~tartaer~~ tartan cap with the air of a monarch saluting his subjects and swept them a grand ~~p~~ bow. Mrs. ~~George~~ Frederick and Cousin Stickles ~~responded with the fante faintest of bows. They~~ dared not cut Roaring Abel altogether. He was the only person in Deerwood who could be got to do odd jobs of carpentering and repairing when they needed to be done[,] so it would not do to offend him. But they responded with only the stiffest, slightest of bows. ~~Roar~~ Roaring Abel must be kept in his place.

~~Miranda~~ Valancy, behind them, did a thing they were fortunately spared seeing. She smiled gaily and waved her hand to Roaring Abel. Why not? She had always liked the old sinner. He was such a jolly, ^picturesque,^ unashamed reprobate and stood out against the drab respectability of Deerwood ~~like a~~ ^and its^ customs like a flame-red flag of revolt and protest. Only a few nights ~~agone~~ ^ago^ Abel had gone through Deerwood ~~at~~ in the wee ~~smas,~~ sma's,[4] ~~yelling and blasp~~ shouting oaths at the top of his stentorian voice which could be heard for miles, and lashing his horses into a furious gallop as he ~~tore through~~ along prim, proper Elm Street.

"Yelling and blaspheming like a fiend," shuddered Cousin Stickles at the breakfast[-]table.

"I cannot understand why the judgment of the Lord has not fallen upon that man long ~~ago~~ ^ere this^," said Mrs. ~~George~~ Frederick ^petulantly,^ as if she thought Providence was very dilatory and ought to have a gentle reminder.

~~NOTE J2~~ NOTE 13

~~Miranda~~ Valancy had said nothing, of course; but she wondered to herself if Roaring Abel's periodical sprees were ^not^ his ^futile^ protest against the poverty and drudgery ^and monotony^ of his existence. NOTE J3 ~~NOTE A4~~ ~~and in a way she sympathized with him.~~ So she waved at him to-day with a sudden fellow feeling and Roaring Abel, not too drunk to be astonished, nearly fell off his seat in his amazement. ~~NOTE L2~~ NOTE K3 .

NOTE J3: <u>She</u> went on dream sprees in her Blue Castle. Roaring Abel, having no imagination, could not do ~~this~~ that. <u>His</u> escapes from reality had to be concrete.

NOTE K3: ⁋By this time they had reached Maple Avenue & Uncle Herbert's house, a large pretentious structure peppered with meaningless bay windows & excrescent[5] porches. A house that always looked like a stupid, prosperous, self-satisfied man with warts on his face.

"A house like that," said Valancy solemnly, "is a blasphemy."

Mrs. Frederick was shaken to her soul. <u>What</u>[6] had Valancy said? Was it profane? Or only just queer? Mrs. Frederick took off her hat in ~~Mrs.~~ Aunt Alberta's spare[-] room with trembling hands. She made one more feeble attempt to avert disaster. She held Valancy back on the landing as Cousin Stickles went down stairs.

"Won't you try to remember you're a lady?" she pleaded.

"Oh, if there were only any hope of being able to forget it," said Miranda wearily.

Mrs. Frederick felt that she had not deserved this from Providence.

5: excrescent = superfluous

6: In the published version, "What" is not italicized.

judgment of the Lord has al-
fallen upon that, we all long ago,"
said Miss George, as if she thought
Providence was very dilatory and
ungul. to have a gentle reminder.
Amanda had one's richness of
errors; but she wondered to herself
of Roaring Abel's periodical sprees
were being a protest against the
poverty and drudgery) his existence.
and in a way she sympathized
with him. So she waved at him
to-day with a sudden fellow feeling
and Roaring Abel, not too drunk to
be astonished, nearly fell off his seat
in his amazement.

"Bless this food to our use
and not al- we are about to
receive make us truly thankful
and consecrate our lives to they

X

"~~For what we are about to receive make us truly thankful~~ ^Bless this food to our use^ and consecrate our lives to Thy service," said Uncle Herbert briskly. ℭ Aunt Wellington frowned. She always considered Herbert's graces entirely too short and "flippant." ~~NOTE B4~~ NOTE L3 As a protest she kept her head bent a ~~second peceptable~~ perceptible time after all the rest had been lifted. When she permitted herself to sit upright she found ~~Miranda~~ Valancy looking at her. Ever afterwards Aunt Wellington averred that she had known from that moment that there was something wrong with ~~Miranda~~ Valancy. In those ~~queer~~ ^odd^ ^queer^ slanted eyes of hers – "we should always have known she was not entirely <u>right</u> with eyes like that" – there was an odd gleam of mockery and amusement – as if ~~Miranda~~ Valancy were laughing at <u>her</u>. Such a thing was unthinkable, of course. Aunt Wellington at once ~~refused~~ ^ceased^ to think ~~of it.~~

~~Miranda~~ Valancy was enjoying herself. ~~=for the first time.~~ She had never enjoyed herself at a "family reunion" before[.] ~~NOTE E5~~ NOTE M3 ~~-- she ha. Her clan had always considered her very shy and backward~~ ^dull^. ~~NOTE R4~~

"She has no social presence whatever," Aunt Wellington had decreed once and for all. Nobody dreamed that ~~Miranda~~ Valancy was dumb in their presence ^merely^ because she was afraid of them. Now she was no longer afraid of them. The shackles had been stricken off her soul. ~~Miranda~~ ^She^ was quite prepared to talk if occasion offered. Meanwhile she was giving herself such freedom of thought as she had never dared to take before. ~~Just at first she was almost afraid to think~~

NOTE L3: A grace, to be a grace in Aunt Wellington's eyes, had to be at least three minutes long & uttered in an unearthly tone between a groan & a chant.

NOTE M3: In social functions as in childish games she had only "filled in." Her clan had always considered her very dull. She had no parlor tricks. And she had been in the habit of taking refuge from the boredom of family parties in her Blue Castle which resulted in an absent-mindedness that increased her reputation for dullness and vacuity.

73

NOTE N3: – "loosening things up a bit" as he would have said.

NOTE O3: examining relentlessly every one in this depressing assembly of sensible people and watching their little squirms with a detached, amused smile.

NOTE P3: herself the cleverest woman in the clan[,]

NOTE Q3: Had not her son Howard been all through teething at eleven months? And could she not tell you the best way to do everything from cooking mushrooms to picking up a snake? What a bore she was! What ugly moles she had ~~R~~ on her face!

~~such thoughts. They were so vivid.~~ She let herself go with a wild, inner exultation[,] as Uncle Herbert carved the turkey. ~~Here~~ Uncle Herbert gave ~~Mid~~ ~~Miranda~~ Valancy a second look that day. Being a man[,] he didn't know what she had done to her hair[,] but he thought surprisedly that Doss was not such a bad-looking girl[,] after all; and he put ~~a~~ ^an extra^ piece of white meat on her plate.

"What ~~herb~~ herb is most injurious to a young lady's beauty?" propounded Uncle Benjamin by way of ~~her~~ starting conversation. ~~NOTE U2~~ NOTE N3

~~Miranda~~ Valancy, whose duty it was to say, "What?" did not say it. Nobody else said it, so Uncle Benjamin ~~felt that = had to say "Thyme" after a p~~ after an expectant pause had to ~~say~~ answer[,] "Thyme[,]" and felt that his riddle had fallen flat. He looked resentfully at ~~Miranda~~ Valancy, who had never failed him before[,] but ~~Miranda~~ Valancy did not seem ~~to~~ even to be aware of him. She was ~~looking~~ gazing around the table[,] ~~NOTE Q2~~ NOTE O3 ~~and there was a little amused, ^detached^ satirical smile on her face as~~ ~~NOTE Q2~~

So these were the people she had always ~~been afraid of~~ ^held in reverence & fear^. She seemed to see them with new eyes. ⟨ Big, capable, patronizing, ^voluble^ Aunt Mildred, who thought ~~NOTE M2~~ NOTE P3 ~~no~~ her husband ~~was like hers~~ a little lower than the angels and her children wonders. ~~NOTE L4~~ NOTE Q3 ~~What a bore she was! Miranda counted her chins and the ^ very ugly^ moles on her face ^What ugly moles she had on her face.^~~ ⟨ Cousin Gladys, who was always praising her son who had died young[,] and always fighting with her living one. She had neuritis – or what she called neuritis. It jumped about from one part of her body to another. It was a convenient thing. If anybody wanted her to go somewhere she didn't want to go she had neuritis in her legs. And always if any mental effort was required she could have neuritis in her head. You can't <u>think</u> with neuritis in your head, my dear.

"What an old humbug you are," thought ~~Miranda~~ Valancy impiously.

Aunt Isabel. ~~NOTE W2~~ NOTE R3 "~~I wonder what would happen to her face if she smiled" speculated Miranda. Aunt Isabel had always criticized her~~ ^was the critic of the clan.^ More members of it than ~~Miranda~~ Valancy were afraid of her. She had, it was conceded, a biting tongue.

"I wonder what would happen to your face if you ^ever^ smiled,["] ~~NOTE P2 NOTE S3~~ speculated ~~Miranda~~ Valancy unblushingly.
~~NOTE M4~~ NOTE T3 | 1

Little Cousin Georgiana. Not such a bad little soul. But dreary – very. Always looking as if she had just been starched and ironed ~~NOTE L6~~ NOTE U3 ~~Uncle~~ ℂ Uncle James, handsome, black, ~~sarcastic~~ ^with his sarcastic trap-like mouth^ ~~NOTE M6 NOTE J5~~ NOTE V3. ℂ Uncle Benjamin, wheezy, ~~pussy-mouthed~~ mouthed. With great pouches under ~~his~~ eyes ^that held nothing in reverence^. ℂ Uncle Wellington. Long, pallid face, thin, pale-yellow hair – "one of the fair Stirlings" – thin, scooping body, abominably high forehead with such ugly wrinkles, and – "Eyes[4] about as intelligent as a fish's," thought ~~Miranda~~ Valancy. "Looks like ^a cartoon of himself."^

Aunt Wellington. Named Mary but called by her husband[']s name to distinguish her from Great-aunt Mary. A massive, dignified, permanent lady. Splendidly arranged, iron-gray hair. Rich, fashionable ~~crepe~~ ^beaded^ dress. Had her moles removed by electrolysis – which Aunt Mildred thought was a wicked evasion of the purposes of God.

NOTE R3: ~~Mira~~ Valancy counted her chins. Aunt Isabel was the critic of the clan. She had always gone about squashing people flat.

NOTE T3: Second Cousin Sarah Taylor, with her great, pale expressionless eyes, who was noted for the variety of her pickle recipes and for nothing else. So afraid of saying something indiscreet that she never said anything worth listening to. So proper that she blushed when she saw the advertisement picture of a corset and had put a dress on her Venus de Milo[2] statuette which made it look "real tasty."

1: S3 was used in Chapter VII.

2: The Venus de Milo statue was found on the Greek island of Milos in 1820 and is now displayed in the Louvre in Paris. The statue is thought to depict Aphrodite, the Greek goddess of love, whose Roman counterpart was Venus. The torso of the figure is unclothed.

NOTE U3: Always afraid to let herself go. The only thing she really enjoyed was a funeral. You knew where you were with a corpse. Nothing more could happen to it. But while there was life there was fear.

NOTE V3: and iron-gray sideburns, whose favorite amusement was to write controversial letters to the Christian Times,[3] attacking modernism. Valancy always wondered if he looked as solemn when he was asleep as he did when awake. No wonder his wife had died young. Valancy remembered her. A pretty, sensitive thing. Uncle James had denied her everything she wanted and showered on her everything she didn't want. He had killed her – quite legally. She had been smothered and starved.

3: Although Montgomery neglected to underline "Christian Times," it is italicized in the published version.

4: "Eyes" is not capitalized in the published version.

Uncle Herbert with his spiky gray hair. Aunt Alberta[,] ~~NOTE N~~ NOTE W3 ~~enormously fat.~~ ^NOTE N2^ Miranda let them off easily in her judgment because she liked them, even if they were ~~stupid.~~ ~~NOTE N5~~ NOTE X3

Then she looked across the table at Olive. ~~NOTE S3~~ NOTE Y3 ~~The slanted brown eyes~~ ^Miranda's elfin^ lost their mocking glitter and became pensive and sorrowful. You could not ignore or disdain Olive. It was quite impossible to deny that she was beautiful and effective ~~NOTE E6~~ NOTE Z3 . Her mouth might be a trifle heavy – she might show her fine, ^white regular^ teeth rather too lavishly when she smiled. But when all was said and done[,] Olive justified Uncle Benjamin's summing up—"a ~~A stunning~~ stunning girl." Yes~~, Miranda~~ Valancy agreed in her heart, Olive was stunning. NOTE A4

~~Rich, golden brown hair = large sparkling blue eyes = neck of snow and face of rose. Tall = queenly. Pale~~ Everything ^that^ Miranda was not. ~~NOTE R2~~

Olive was only a year younger than ~~Miranda~~ Valancy, ~~NOTE O2~~ NOTE B4 But nobody ever dreaded old maidenhood for her. Olive's ~~footsteps~~ had been surrounded by a crowd of eager beaus since her early teens, just as her mirror was always surrounded by a fringe of ^cards,^ photographs, ~~and~~ programmes and invitations. At ~~twenty~~ ^twenty one^ ~~NOTE S2~~ NOTE D4 | 7 Olive had been engaged to Will ~~Desemond~~ Desmond, lawyer in embryo. Will Desmond had died and Olive had mourned for

---

NOTE W3: who twisted her mouth so unpleasantly in talking & had a great reputation for unselfishness because she was always giving up a lot of things she didn't ~~like~~ want.

NOTE X3: in Milton's expressive phrase, "stupidly good."[5] But she wondered for what inscrutable reason Aunt Alberta had seen fit to tie a black velvet ribbon around each of her chubby arms above the elbow.

5: The phrase "stupidly good" is from *Paradise Lost*, Book 9, by English poet John Milton (1608–1674). "That space the Evil One abstracted stood From his own evil, and for the time remained Stupidly good, Of enmity disarmed, Of guile, of hate, of envy, of revenge."

NOTE Y3:= Olive, who had been held up to her as a paragon of beauty, behaviour and success as long as she could remember. "Why can't you hold yourself like Olive, Doss? Why can't you stand correctly like Olive, Doss? Why can't you speak prettily like Olive, Doss? Why can't you make an effort,[6] Doss?" Valancy's elfin eyes

6: "Effort" is not italicized in the published version.

NOTE Z3: —and sometimes she was a little intelligent.

NOTE A4: ¶ Rich, golden-brown hair, elaborately dressed, with a sparkling bandeau holding its glossy puffs in place; large, brilliant blue eyes & thick silken lashes; face of rose & bare neck of snow, rising above her gown; great pearl bubbles in her ears; the blue-white diamond flame on her long-smooth, waxen finger with its rosy, pointed nail. Arms of marble, gleaming through green chiffon & shadow lace. Valancy felt suddenly thankful that her own scrawny arms were decently swathed in brown silk. Then she resumed her tabulation of Olive's charms.

Tall. Queenly. Confident. Everything that Valancy was <u>not</u>. Dimples, too, in cheeks & chin. "A woman with dimples always gets her own way," thought Valancy, in a recurring spasm of bitterness at the fate which had denied her even one dimple.

NOTE B4: though a stranger would have thought that there was at least ten years between them[.]

NOTE D4: At eighteen, when she had graduated from Havergal College,[8]

7: There is no Note C4.

8: Havergal College, established in 1894, is an independent girls' school in Toronto.

him ~~dutifully~~ ^properly^ for two years. When she was twenty[-] ~~three five~~ three ~~she -- she another engagement~~ she had a hectic affair with ~~a~~ Donald Jackson. But ~~Unc~~ Aunt and Uncle Wellington disapproved of that and ~~fi- nall~~ in the end Olive dutifully gave him up. Nobody in the Stirling clan—whatever outsiders might say—~~hent- ed~~ hinted that she did so because Donald himself was cooling off. However that might be, Olive's third venture met with everybody's approval. Cecil Price ~~-- one of the Point Prices --~~ was clever and handsome and "one of the ~~Point~~ ^Port Laurence^ Prices." Olive had been engaged to him for ~~two~~ ^three^ years. ~~He was to be a mining engineer from a School of Mines~~ ^He had just graduated in civil engineering^ and next year they were to be married ^as soon as he landed a contract.^ Olive's hope chest was full to overflowing with exquisite things and Olive had already confided to ~~Miranda~~ Valancy what her wedding[-]dress was to be. ~~NOTE T2~~ NOTE E4 ~~Miranda~~ Valancy knew also—though Olive had not told her— that the bridesmaids were selected and that she was not among them.

~~Miranda~~ Valancy had, after a fashion, always been Olive's confidant ~~NOTE V2~~ NOTE F4 Olive always told ~~Miranda~~ Valancy all the details of her love affairs[,] ~~NOTE Z4~~ NOTE G4 ~~Miranda~~ Valancy could not comfort herself by thinking these affairs ~~imaginary~~ ^mythical.^ Olive really had them. Many men had gone mad over her besides the three fortunate ones.

"I don't know what the poor idiots see in me, ~~to make them~~ ^that drives them to make such double idiots of themselves,"^ Olive was wont to say ~~affectedly.~~ ~~Miranda~~ Valancy would have liked to say[,] "I don't either," but truth and diplomacy both restrained her. She <u>did</u> know, perfectly well. Olive Stirling was one of the girls about whom men do go mad just as indubitably as she, ~~Miranda,~~ Valancy, was one of the girls at whom no man ever looked twice. ⸤ NOTE H4

NOTE E4: Ivory silk draped with lace, white satin court train, lined with pale green georgette, heirloom veil of Brussels lace.

NOTE F4: – perhaps because she was the only girl in the connection who could not bore Olive with return confidences.

NOTE G4: from the days when the little boys in school used to "presecute"[9] her with love letters.

9: In the published version, "presecute" is changed to "persecute."

NOTE H4: "And yet," thought Valancy, summing her up with a new and merciless conclusiveness, "she's like a dewless morning. There's <u>something</u> lacking."

these affairs ~~mythically~~ mystical. Olive
really had them. Many men had
gone mad over her besides the
three fortunate ones.

"I don't know what ~~the~~ poor
idiots see in me, ~~that things those~~
~~to make them~~ think such doubly idiols of themselves,"
Olive was wont to say. ~~affectedly.~~
~~Miranda~~ Valancy would have liked to say
"I don't either" but — truth and diplomacy both restrained her. She did
know, perfectly well. Olive Stirling
was one of the girls about whom men
do go mad just as indubitably as
she, ~~Miranda~~ Valancy was one of the girls
at whom no one ever looked
twice. ~~P H 4.~~ ~~114.~~ ⊕ V

Meanwhile the dinner in its
earlier stages was dragging its
slow length along true to Stirling
form. ~~so 94~~ Uncle Herbert made his
hardy perennial joke when he helped

XI

Meanwhile the dinner in its earlier stages was dragging its slow length along[1] true to Stirling form. ~~NOTE B6~~ NOTE I4 Uncle Herbert made his hardy perennial joke when he helped Aunt Wellington to the cold meat – "Mary, will you have a little lamb?" – Aunt ~~Mildred~~ ^Isabel^ ^Mildred^ told the same old story of once finding a lost ring in a turkey's crop. Uncle ~~Herbert~~ ^Benjamin^ told ~~a~~ ^his favorite^ prosy tale of how he had once chased and punished a now famous man for stealing apples. ~~NOTE T4 NOTE X2~~ NOTE J4

Cousin Gladys,[5] ^likewise^ as usual, had a grievance. Her visiting nephews had nipped all the buds off her house-plants and chivied[6] her brood of fancy chickens—"squeezed some of them actually to death, my dear."

"Boys will be boys," reminded Uncle ~~Her but~~ ^Herbert^ tolerantly.

"But they needn't be ~~rampant~~ ^ramping,^ rampageous animals," retorted Cousin Gladys, looking round the table for appreciation of her wit. Everybody smiled except ~~Miranda~~ Valancy. Cousin Gladys remembered <u>that</u>.[7] A few minutes later, when Ellen Hamilton was being discussed, Cousin Gladys spoke of her

---

1: From "An Essay on Criticism" (Part 2), a poem by Alexander Pope (1688–1744), written in 1711. The line in the poem reads: "That, like a wounded snake, drags its slow length along."

NOTE I4: The room was chilly, in spite of the calendar, & Aunt Alberta had the gas[-]logs lighted. Everybody in the clan envied her those gas[-]logs except Valancy. Glorious open fires blazed in every room of her Blue Castle when autumnal nights were cool but she would have frozen to death in it before she would have committed the sacrilege of a gas[-]log.

NOTE J4: Second Cousin Jane described all her sufferings with an ulcerating tooth. Aunt Wellington admired the pattern of Aunt Alberta's silver teaspoons and lamented the fact that one of her own had been lost.

"It spoiled the set. I could never get it matched. And it was my wedding[-]present from dear old Aunt Matilda. ^(next page)^[2] Aunt Isabel[3] thought the seasons were changing & couldn't imagine what had become of our good, old-fashioned springs. Cousin Georgiana, as ~~Cou~~ usual, discussed the last funeral & wondered audibly, "Which[4] of us will be the next to pass away." Cousin

Georgiana could never say anything as blunt as "die." Valancy thought she could tell her but didn't.

2: This seems to be a reminder that NOTE J4 continues on the next page of the manuscript.

3: In the published version, a new paragraph begins at "Aunt Isabel."

4: In the published version, "Which" is not capitalized.

5: In the published version, "Cousin Gladys" does not begin a new paragraph.

6: chivied = harassed, annoyed

7: In the published version, "that" is not italicized.

8: NOTE Y2 was used in Chapter VIII. No note has been added here.

9: Luisa Tetrazzini (1871–1940) was an Italian opera star.

NOTE K4: Aunt Alberta remarked vaguely that the greatest happiness was to be found in "the poetry of life" & hastily gave some ~~order~~ directions to her maid to prevent any[ ]one asking her what she meant.

NOTE L4: "We are all too ~~pious~~ prone," continued Mrs. Frederick, determined not to lose so good an opportunity, "to live in selfishness, worldliness and sin."

10: From Alexander Pope's poem "An Essay on Criticism," Part 3 (1711). The line in the poem reads: "For fools rush in where angels fear to tread."

---

as "one of those shy, plain girls who can't get husbands," and glanced significantly at ~~Miranda~~ Valancy. ~~Uncle~~ ℂ Uncle James thought the conversation was sagging to a rather low plane of personal gossip. He tried to elevate it by starting an abstract discussion on "the greatest happiness." Everybody was ~~compelled~~ ^asked^ to state his or her idea of "the greatest happiness." ^ NOTE Y2 ^8 ℂ Aunt Mildred thought the greatest happiness—for a woman—was to be "a loving and beloved wife and mother." ~~Mrs. George thought it was to spend your life in service for others and Cousin Stickles agreed with her.~~ Aunt Wellington thought it would be to travel in Europe. Olive thought it would be to be a great ~~musician~~ singer ^like Tetrazzini.^9 Cousin Gladys remarked mournfully that her greatest happiness would be to be free – absolutely free – from ~~nurul~~ neuritis. Cousin Georgiana's greatest ~~husband~~ happiness would be "to have ^her^ dear ^dead brother^ Richard back." ~~NOTE O3~~ NOTE K4 Mrs. ~~George~~ Frederick said the greatest happiness was to spend your life in loving service for others and ~~Aunt Iso~~ ^Cousin^ Stickles and Aunt Isabel agreed with her – Aunt Isabel with a ~~resenffut~~ resentful air, as if she thought Mrs. ~~George~~ Frederick had taken the wind out of her sails by saying it first. ~~NOTE P3~~ NOTE L4

The other women all felt rebuked for their ~~selfish~~ ^low^ ideals[,] and Uncle James ~~felt~~ ^had a conviction^ that ~~he had indeed succeeded in raising the plane of~~ the conversation had been uplifted with a vengeance.

"The greatest happiness," said ~~Miranda~~ Valancy ^suddenly and^ distinctly ~~and defiantly~~ "is to ~~scneeze~~ ^sneeze^ when you want to."

Everybody stared. Nobody felt it safe to say anything. Was ~~Miranda~~ Valancy trying to be funny? It was incredible. Mrs. ~~George~~ Frederick, who had been breathing easier since the dinner had progressed so far ~~with Miranda behaving well,~~ ^without any outbreak on the part of ~~Miranda~~ Valancy,^ began to tremble again. But she ~~diemed~~ ^deemed^ it the part of prudence to say nothing. Uncle Benjamin was not so prudent. He rashly rushed in where Mrs. ~~George~~ Frederick feared to tread.[10]

"Doss," he chuckled, "what is the difference between a young girl and an old maid?"

"One is happy and careless and the other is cappy and hairless," said ~~Miranda~~ Valancy. "You have asked that riddle at least fifty times in my recollection, Uncle Ben. Why don't you hunt up some new riddles if riddle you must?" ~~NOTE C5~~ NOTE M4

Uncle Benjamin's mouth fell open, ^and stayed open^[.][11] Never in his life had he, ~~NOTE Z2 Benjamin's~~ NOTE N4 been spoken to so. And by ~~Miranda~~ Valancy of all people! He looked feebly around the table to see what the others thought of it. Everybody was looking ^rather^ blank. Poor Mrs. ~~George~~ Frederick had shut her eyes. And her lips moved tremblingly – ~~perhaps in prayer~~ ^as if she were praying. Perhaps she was.^ ~~Aunt Alberta was distressed, Uncle Herbert~~ The situation was so unprecedented that nobody knew how to ~~meet~~ meet it. ~~Miranda~~ Valancy went on calmly eating her salad as if nothing out of the usual had occurred.

Aunt Alberta, to save her dinner, plunged into ~~a story of~~ an account of how a dog had bitten her recently. Uncle James, to back her up, asked where the dog had bitten her recently. ⟨ "Just a little below the Catholic Church" said Aunt Alberta. ⟨ At this[12] point ~~Miranda~~ Valancy laughed. Nobody else laughed. What was there to laugh at?

"Is that a vital part?" asked ~~Miranda~~ Valancy.

"What do you mean?" said bewildered Aunt Alberta, and Mrs. ~~George~~ Frederick was almost driven to ~~conclude~~ ^believe^ that she had served God all her years for naught.

Aunt Isabel concluded that it was up to her to suppress ~~Doss Miranda~~ Valancy.

"Doss, you are horribly thin," she said. "^You are <u>all</u> corners.^ Do you <u>ever</u> try to fatten up a little[?]~~;~~"

"No," ~~said Miranda, attacking the salted almonds with new a relish.~~ ^Miranda^ ^Valancy was not asking quarter ~~nor~~ or giving it.^ "But I can tell you where you'll find a beauty parlor in ~~Point~~ Port Laurence – where they can ~~reduce~~ reduce the number of your chins."

NOTE M4: It is such a fatal mistake to try to be funny if you don't succeed.["]

11: In the published version, this sentence was changed to "Uncle Benjamin stared foolishly."

NOTE N4: Benjamin Stirling, of Stirling and Frost,

12: In the published version, "this" is changed to "that."

13: There has been some confusion over how to pronounce "Valancy." Here Montgomery makes it clear that the accent is on the first syllable (not the second as some have suggested); however, in the published version, "Val-an-cy" is entirely in italics.

14: In the published version, the period after "Valancy" is replaced by a comma, and "The" is lower case.

NOTE O4: "Doss," said Uncle Benjamin, thinking it might cow Valancy, "do you remember the time you stole the raspberry jam?"
Valancy flushed scarlet—with suppressed laughter, not shame. She had been sure Uncle Benjamin would drag that jam in somehow.
"Of course I do," she said. "It was good jam. I've always been sorry I hadn't time to eat more of it before you found me. Oh, look at Aunt Isabel's profile on the wall. Did you ever see anything so funny?"
Everybody looked, including Aunt Isabel herself, which of course destroyed it. But Uncle Herbert said kindly,

NOTE P4: It was the first time any[ ]one had been called ~~in~~ "old dear" in Deerwood. The Stirlings thought Valancy had unveiled the phrase & they were afraid of her from that moment. There was something so uncanny about such an expression. But in poor Mrs. Frederick[']s opinion the reference to a satisfying meal was the worst thing Valancy had said yet. Valancy had always been a disappointment to her. Now she was a disgrace.

15: In the published version, "She thought" does not start a new paragraph but continues the previous paragraph, after "disgrace."

~~"Mi-ran-da!"~~ "Val-an-cy!"[13] The protest was wrung from Mrs. ~~George~~ Frederick. She meant her tone to be stately and majestic as usual[,] but it sounded more like an imploring whine. And she did not say "Doss."

"She's feverish," said Cousin Stickles to Uncle Benjamin in an agonized whisper. "We've thought she's seemed feverish for several days."

"She's ~~dipp~~ gone dippy in my opinion," growled Uncle Benjamin. "If not she ought to be spanked. Yes, spanked."

"You can't spank her," Cousin Stickles was much agitated. "She's twenty[-]nine years old."

"So there is that advantage at least in being twenty[-]nine," said ~~Miranda~~ Valancy, whose ears had caught this aside.

"Doss," said Uncle Benjamin, "when I am dead you may say what you please. ~~But~~ As long as I am alive I demand to be treated with respect[.]"

"Oh, but you know we're all dead," said ~~Miranda~~ Valancy.[14] ~~"Some of~~ The whole Stirling clan. Some of us are buried and some aren't—yet. That is the only difference." ~~NOTE 14 NOTE M3 NOTE 13 NOTE M3~~ NOTE O4

"I – I wouldn't eat any more if I were you, ~~Mir~~ Dossie," ~~said Uncle Herbert kindly.~~ "It isn't that I grudge it – but don't you think it would be better for yourself? Your – your stomach seems a little out of order."

"Don't worry, ~~old dear,~~ ^about my stomach, old dear,^ said ~~Miranda~~ Valancy. ~~"My stomach is~~ ^It is^ ^It is^ all right. I'm going to keep right on eating. It is so seldom I get the chance of a satisfying meal." ~~NOTE J4~~ NOTE P4

~~This, in Mrs. George's opinion, was the most awful thing Miranda had said yet.~~ She thought[15] she would have to get up and ~~leave~~ ^go away from^ the table. Yet she dared not leave ~~Miranda~~ Valancy there.

Aunt Alberta's maid came in to remove the ^salad^ plates and bring in the des[s]ert. It was a welcome diversion. Everybody brightened up with a determination to ignore ~~Miranda~~ Valancy and talk as if she wasn't there. ~~It did not occ started talking about~~ ^Uncle Wellington mentioned^ Barney Snaith. Eventually somebody did ~~begin talking~~ ^mention^ Barney Snaith at every Stirling function, ~~Miranda~~ Valancy reflected ~~NOTE A3~~ NOTE Q4 She resigned herself to listen. There was a subtle fascination in the subject for her, though she had not yet faced this fact. ~~NOTE K6~~ NOTE R4 ❦ Of course they abused him. Nobody ever had a good word to say of Barney Snaith. All the old, wild tales were canvassed – the defaulting cashier – counterfeiter – infidel –[16] murder-in-hiding legends were thrashed out. ~~Uncle Weller~~ Uncle Wellington was very indignant that such a creature should be allowed to exist at all in the neighborhood of Deerwood. He didn't know what the police ^at ~~Point~~ Port Laurence^ were thinking of. Everybody would be murdered in their beds some night. It was a shame that he should be allowed to be at large after all that he had done.

"What <u>has</u> he done?" asked ~~Miranda~~ Valancy suddenly.

Uncle Wellington stared at her, forgetting that she was to be ignored.

"Done! Done! He's done <u>everything</u>."

"<u>What</u> has he done?" repeated ~~Miranda~~ Valancy ^inexorably.^ "What do you <u>know</u> that ~~he's~~ ^he has^ done? You're always running him down. And what has ever been proved against him?["] ~~Except perhaps that's he's been seen drunk once or twice."~~

"~~I don't need proof,~~" ^"I don't argue with women,"^ said Uncle Wellington, ^"And I don't need proof.^ When a man hides himself up there on an island in ~~Mistawis~~ ^Muskoka^ year in and year out and nobody can find out where he came from or ~~what~~ how he lives, ~~that's~~ ^or what he does there^ <u>that's</u> proof enough. Find a mystery and you find a crime."
~~NOTE N4~~ NOTE S4

"~~Where there is so much smoke there must be some fire," said Cousin Georgiana~~ ^sagaciously.^ I was afraid he was a criminal when he came there first. I <u>felt</u> he had something to hide[.] ~~NOTE J3~~ NOTE T4

NOTE Q4: Whatever he was[,] he was an ~~created being~~ ^individual^ that could not be ignored.

NOTE R4: She could feel her pulses beating to her fingertips.

16: In the published version, the dashes after "counterfeiter" and "infidel" are changed to hyphens.

NOTE S4: "The very idea of a man named Snaith!" said Second Cousin Sarah. "Why, the name itself is enough to condemn him."
"I wouldn't like to meet him in a dark lane," shivered Cousin Georgiana.
"What do you suppose he would do to you?" asked Valancy.
"Murder me," said Cousin ~~Gerog~~ Georgiana solemnly.
"Just for the fun of it?" suggested Valancy.
"Exactly," said Cousin Georgiana unsuspiciously. "When there is so much smoke there must be <u>some</u> fire.[17]

17: "Some" is not italicized in the published version.

NOTE T4: I am not often mistaken in my intentions."

"Criminal! Of course he's a criminal," said Uncle Wellington. "Nobody doubts it" – glaring at ~~Miranda~~ Valancy NOTE K3 NOTE U4 NOTE U4 "~~Why, the man hasn't a friend except old Roaring Abel.~~ And if Roaring Abel had kept away from him[,] as everybody else did[,] it would have been better ~~for~~ – for some members of his family."

Uncle Wellington's rather lame conclusion was due to a marital glance from Aunt Wellington ^reminding him of what he had^ ~~Uncle Wellington had~~ almost forgotten—that there were ~~unmarried women~~ girls at the table.

"If you mean," said ~~Miranda~~ Valancy passionately, "that Barney Snaith is the father of Cecily Gay's child, he <u>isn't</u>." It's a wicked lie."

In spite of her indignation = ~~an indignation she couldn't understand. What did Barney Snaith's crimes crimes matter to <u>her</u>?~~ = ~~Miranda~~ Valancy was hugely amused at the expression in the faces around that ~~festal board~~ ^festal board.^[19] She had not seen ~~such an expression~~ ^anything like it^ since the day, seventeen years ago, when, at ~~Aunt Mildred's~~ Cousin Gladys' thimble party,[20] they discovered

---

NOTE U4: "Why, they say he served a term in the penitentiary for embezzlement. I don't doubt it. And they say he's in with that gang that are pe[r]petrating all those bank robberies round the country."

"<u>Who</u> say?" asked Valancy.

Uncle Wellington knotted his ugly forehead at her. What had got into this confounded girl[,] anyway? He ignored the question.

"He has the identical look of a jail-bird," snapped Uncle Benjamin. "I noticed it the first time I saw him."

"'A fellow by the hand of nature marked,

Quoted & signed to do a deed of shame['],"[18]

~~declaimed Uncle James.~~ He looked enormously pleased over managing to work that quotation in at last. He had been waiting all his life for the chance.

"One of his eyebrows is an arch & the other is a triangle," said Valancy. "Is <u>that</u> why you think him so villainous?"

Uncle James lifted <u>his</u> eyebrows. Generally when Uncle James lifted his

eyebrows the world came to an end. This time it continued to function.

"How do <u>you</u> know his eyebrows so well, Doss?" asked Olive, a trifle maliciously. Such a remark would have ~~cowed~~ covered Valancy with confusion two weeks ago & Olive knew it.

"Yes, how?" demanded Aunt Wellington.

"I've seen him twice and I looked at him closely," said Valancy composedly. "I thought his face the most interesting one I ever saw."

"There is no doubt there is something fishy in the creature's past life," said Olive, who began to think she was decidedly out of the conversation[,] which had centered so amazingly around Valancy. "But he can hardly be guilty of <u>everything</u> he's accused of, you know."

Valancy felt annoyed with Olive. Why should <u>she</u> speak up in even this qualified defence of Barney Snaith? What had <u>she</u> to do with him? For that matter, what had Valancy? But Valancy did not ask herself this question.

"They say he keeps dozens of cats in that hut up back on Mistawis," said Second Cousin Sarah Taylor, by way of appearing not entirely ignorant of him.

Cats! It sounded quite alluring to Valancy[,] in the plural. She pictured an island in Muskoka haunted by pussies.

"That alone shows there is something wrong with him," decried Aunt Isabel.

"People who don't like cats," said Valancy, attacking her dessert with a relish, "always seem to think that there is some peculiar virtue in not liking them."

"The man hasn't a friend ~~except Roaring Able~~ ^Abel^," said Uncle Wellington;

18: From Shakespeare's play *King John*, Act 4, Scene 2.

19: In the published version, "board" is changed to "table."

20: A "thimble party" was a social occasion to which ladies brought their mending or small sewing projects to work on while they talked together.

that she had got – SOMETHING – in her head at school. <u>Lice</u> in her head! ~~Miranda~~ Valancy was done with euphemisms. Poor[21] Mrs. ~~George~~ Frederick was almost in a state of collapse. She had believed—or pretended to believe—that ~~Miranda~~ Valancy still supposed that children were found in parsley beds. ~~NOTE B5~~ NOTE V4

~~Miranda~~ Valancy didn't exactly understand her own indignation. What did Barney Snaith's ~~crimes~~ imputed crimes and misdemeanors matter to her? And why, out of them all[,] did it seem most intolerable that he should have been poor, pitiful little Cecily Gay's false lover? For it <u>did</u> seem intolerable to her. ~~She could~~ She did not mind when they called him a thief and a counterfeiter and a ~~bigamist~~ ^jail[-]bird^; but she could not endure to think that he had loved and ruined Cecily Gay. She recalled his face on the two occasions of their chance meetings—~~his~~ ~~NOTE F3~~ NOTE W4 ~~smile,~~ his twinkle, ^his thin, sensitive, almost ascetic lips,^ his general air of frank dare=deviltry. A man with that smile ^and lips^ might have murdered or stolen but he could not have betrayed. She suddenly hated every[ ]one who said it or believed it of him.

"When <u>I</u> was a young girl I never thought or spoke about such matters, Doss," said Aunt Wellington[,] crushingly.

"But I'm not a young girl," retorted ~~Miranda~~ Valancy, uncrushed. "Aren't you always rubbing that into me? And you are all evil-minded ^senseless^ gossips. Can't you leave poor Cissy Gay alone? She's dying. Whatever she did, God or the Devil has punished her enough for it. <u>You</u> needn't take a hand, too. As for Barney Snaith, the only crime ~~you can really impute to him~~ he has been guilty of is living to himself and minding his own business. ^He can, it seems, get along without you.^ Which <u>is</u> an unpardonable sin, of course, in your little ~~snobcra=ty.~~ ^snobocracy."^

~~Miranda~~ Valancy[22] coined that concluding word suddenly and felt that it was an inspiration. That was exactly ~~was~~ what they were. And not one of them was fit to mend another.

21: In the published version, a new paragraph begins here.

NOTE V4: "Hush – hush," implored Cousin Stickles.
"I don't mean to hush," said Valancy perversely. "I've hush-hushed all my life. I'll scream if I want to. Don't make me want to. And stop talking nonsense about Barney Snaith.["]

NOTE W4: his twisted, enigmatic, engaging smile,

22: In the published version, "Valancy" does not begin a new paragraph.

"~~Miranda,~~ Valancy, your poor father would turn over in his grave if he could hear you," said Mrs. ~~George.~~ Frederick.

"I ~~daresay~~ dare[ ]say, he would like that for a change," said ~~Miranda~~ Valancy brazenly ~~NOTE P5~~ NOTE X4 ❡ But her excitement had been too much for her. She knew, by certain unmistakable warnings, that one of her attacks of pain was coming on. It must not find ~~her here~~ her there. She rose from her chair.

"I am going home now. I only came for the dinner. It was very good, Aunt Alberta, although ~~a dash of cayenne would improve your salad dressing~~ ^your salad dressing is not salt enough and a dash of cayenne would^ improve it."

~~"She's feverish – I've said right along she was fever~~

None of the flabbergasted silver wedding guests could think of anything to say until the lawn gate clanged behind ~~Miranda~~ Valancy ^in the dusk.^ Then –

"She's feverish – I've said right along she was feverish," moaned Cousin Stickles.

Uncle Benjamin punished his ^pudgy^ left hand fiercely with his ^pudgy^ right.

"She's dippy – I tell you she's gone dippy" ^he snorted angrily.^ "That's all there is about it. ~~Dippy~~ Clean dippy."

"Oh, Benjamin," ~~wailed~~ said Cousin Georgiana, ^soothingly,^ "don't condemn her too rashly. We <u>must</u> remember what dear old Shakespeare says – that charity thinketh no evil."[26]
~~NOTE E3~~ NOTE C5

"Do you suppose that ~~m~~the mumps could work on a person that way?" wailed Cousin Stickles.
~~NOTE Y5~~ NOTE Y4 | NOTE N14

NOTE X4: "Doss," said Uncle James heavily, "the Ten Commandments are fairly up to date still – especially the fifth.[23] Have you 'forgotten that?'

"No," said Valancy, "but I thought you had – especially the ninth.[24] Have you ever thought, Uncle James, how dull life would be without the ten commandments.[25] It is only when things are forbidden that they become fascinating."

23: The fifth of the Ten Commandments is "Honour thy Father and Mother." (Exodus 20:12)

24: The ninth commandment is "Thou shalt not bear false witness against thy neighbour." (Exodus 20:16)

25: In the published version, "ten commandments" is capitalized.

26: This quotation is not from Shakespeare but from the Bible, 1 Corinthians 13:4–5: "Charity…thinketh no evil."

NOTE C5: "Charity! Poppycock!" snorted Uncle Benjamin. "I never heard a young woman talk such stuff in my life as she just did. Talking about things she ought to be ashamed to think of[,] much less mention. Blaspheming! Insulting <u>us</u>! What she wants is a generous dose of spank[-]weed & I'd like to

be the one to administer it. H-uh—h-h-h!["]

"The man hasn't a friend except Roaring Abel," said Uncle Wellington.

Uncle Benjamin gulped down the half of a scalding cup of coffee.

NOTE Y4: "I opened an umbrella in the house yesterday," sniffed Cousin Georgiana. "I <u>knew</u> it betokened some misfortune[.]"

NOTE N14: "Have you tried to find out if she has a temperature?["] asked Cousin Mildred.

"She wouldn't let Amelia put the thermometer under her tongue," whimpered Cousin Stickles.

Mrs. ~~George~~ Frederick was openly in tears. All her defences were down.

"I must tell you," she sobbed, "that ~~Miranda~~ Valancy has been acting very strangely for over two weeks now[.] ~~I have hoped against hope that it~~ ^She hasn't been a bit like herself – Christine could tell you. I have hoped against hope that it was only one of her colds coming on. But it is – it must be something worse." ^ ~~She hasn't been a bit like herself.~~ NOTE G3 NOTE Z4

"Don't cry, Amelia," said Herbert kindly NOTE G3 NOTE B3 NOTE M3 NOTE A5 "You'll have to take her to a doctor." NOTE N6 NOTE B5

"I – I suggested consulting a doctor to her yesterday," moaned Mrs. ~~George~~ Frederick. "And she said she wouldn't go to a doctor." – wouldn't!"27 ^Oh, surely I have had trouble enough[!];"^

"And she won't take ~~Shortreed's~~ ^Redfern's^ Bitters," said Cousin Stickles.

"Or anything," said Mrs. ~~George~~ Frederick.

"And she's determined to go to the Presbyterian church," said Cousin Stickles – repressing, however, NOTE C4 NOTE D5 the story of the bannister.

"That proves she's dippy," growled Uncle Benjamin NOTE C3 NOTE B3 NOTE E5 ~~Come, come, Amelia, stop sniffling. Of course, Doss has made a terrible exhibition of herself today but she's not responsible~~ NOTE D3 ~~and~~ ^well,^ ~~fortunately there are no outsiders here,~~ ^sniffed Uncle B.^ ~~We may keep it in the family yet. I'll take her over to Dr. Marsh tomorrow.~~ XX NOTE H3

~~"Let' cheer up. What's the difference between a bee and a donkey~~ "Why are chorus girls like fine stock raisers?"

"Why?" asked Cousin Stickles, since it had to be asked and ~~Miranda~~ Valancy wasn't there to ask it.

"Like to ~~ex hi~~ exhibit calves," chuckled Uncle Benjamin.

Cousin Stickles thought Uncle Benjamin a little indelicate. Before Olive, too. But then, he was a man. ₵ Uncle Herbert was thinking that things were rather dull now that Doss had gone.

NOTE Z4: "This is bringing on my neuritis again," said Cousin Gladys, putting her hand to her ~~hear~~ head.

NOTE A5: pulling nervously at his spiky gray hair. He hated "family ructions." Very inconsiderate of Doss to start one at his silver wedding. Who would have supposed she had it in her?

NOTE B5: This may be only a – er – a brainstorm. There are such things as brainstorms nowadays, aren't there?"

27: "Wouldn't" is not italicized in the published version.

NOTE D5: to her credit be it said,

NOTE E5: ["]I noticed something strange about her the minute she came in to-day. NOTE I5 There never was anything like that in the Stirlings. It must be from the Barracloughs."

NOTE I5: I noticed it before to-day." (Uncle Benjamin was thinking of "m-i-r-a-zh"). "Everything she said to-day showed an unbalanced mind. That question – 'Was it a vital part'? Was there any sense at all in that remark? None whatever! Poor Mrs. Frederick28 was too crushed to be indignant.
"I never heard ~~heard~~ of anything like that in the Barracloughs," she sobbed.
"Your father was odd enough," said Uncle Benjamin.
(continued on next page)

NOTE I5 *continued*: "Poor pa was – peculiar," admitted Mrs. Frederick tearfully, "but his mind was never affected[.]"

"He talked all his life exactly as Valancy did to-day," retorted Uncle Benjamin. "And he believed he was his own great-great-grandfather born over again. I've heard him say it. Don't tell <u>me</u> that a man who believed a thing like <u>that</u> was ever in his right senses." Come, come, Amelia, stop sniffling. Of course Doss has made a terrible exhibition of herself to-day but she's not responsible. Old maids are apt to fly off at a tangent like that. If she had been married when she should have been she wouldn't have got like this.["]

"Nobody wanted to marry her," said Mrs. Frederick, who felt that, somehow, Uncle Benjamin was blaming her.

"Well, fortunately there's no outsider here," snapped Uncle Benjamin. "We may keep it in the family yet. I'll take her over to see Dr. Marsh to-morrow. I know how to deal with pig-headed people. Won't that be best, James?"

"We must have medical advice certainly," agreed Uncle James.

"Well, that's settled. In the meantime, Amelia, act as if nothing had happened and keep an eye on her. Don't let her be alone. Above all, don't let her sleep alone."

Renewed whimpers from Mrs. Frederick.

"I can't help it. Night before last I suggested she'd better have Christine sleep with her. She positively refused – <u>and locked her door</u>. Oh, you don't know how she's changed." She won't work. At least, she won't sew. She does her usual housework, of course. But she wouldn't sweep the parlor yesterday morning, though we <u>always</u> sweep it on Thursdays. She said she'd wait till it was dirty. 'Would you rather sweep a dirty room than a clean one?' I asked her. She said, 'Of course. I'd see something from my labor then.' Think of it!"

Uncle Benjamin thought of it.
NOTE G5 | 29

"I should never have dreamed it of Doss," said Uncle Herbert. "She has always seemed such a quiet, sensible girl. A bit backward – but sensible."

"The only thing you can be sure of in this world is the multiplication table," said Uncle James, feeling cleverer than ever[.]

"Well, let's cheer up," suggested Uncle Benjamin. ~~"What is the differ~~

28: NOTE E5 continues with this line, following "There never was anything like that in the Stirlings. It must be from the Barracloughs."

NOTE G5: "The jar of pot=pourri"—Cousin Stickles pronounced it as spelled—has disappeared from her room. I found the pieces in the next lot. She won't tell us what happened to it."

29: NOTE F5 is in Chapter XII.

why are chorus girls like fine
stock raisers?"

" Why?" asked Cousin Stickles,
since it had to be asked and
Valancy wasn't there to ask it.

" Like to exhibit calves," chuckled
Uncle Benjamin.

Cousin Stickles thought Uncle
Benjamin a little indelicate. Before
Olive, too. But there, he was a man.

Mrs. Frederick was thinking
that things were rather dull now
that Doss had gone.

XI

Valancy hurried home — hurried
too fast — perhaps. The attack she
had when she thankfully reached
the shelter of her own room was the
worst — yet. It was really very

XII

Miranda Valancy hurried home NOTE S3 NOTE F5 —hurried too fast perhaps. The attack she had when she thankfully reached the shelter of her own room was the worst yet. It was really very bad. NOTE H4 NOTE H5 NOTE H5 | 1 Perhaps – perhaps this was death. Miranda Valancy felt pitifully alone. When she could think at all she wondered what it would be like to have some[ ]one with her who could sympathize – Not some[ ]one who really cared – ^just to hold her hand tight, if nothing else^ – NOTE J4 NOTE H3 NOTE J5| 3 not sues some[ ]one merely fussy ^fussing^ and alarmed. Not her mother or Cousin Stickles. Why did the thought of Barney Snaith come into her mind? Why did she suddenly feel, in the midst of her pain and loneliness ^this hideous loneliness of pain,^ that he would be sympathetic – and sorry for any[ ]one that was suffering[.] = NOTE J10 NOTE K5

She was so bad at first that she could not even get herself a dose of Dr. Trent's prescription. But eventually she managed it[,] and soon after relief came. The pain left her and she lay on her bed, spent, exhausted, wet with ^in^ a cold perspiration. Oh, that had been horrible! She could not endure many more attacks like that. NOTE A6 NOTE L5

Suddenly she found herself laughing. Oh, That dinner had been fun. NOTE D5 NOTE M5 Their faces – oh, their faces! Uncle Benjamin – poor, flabbergasted Uncle Benjamin! Miranda Valancy felt quite sure he would make a new will that very night. Olive would get Miranda's Valancy's share of his fat hoard. Olive had always got Miranda's share of everything. Remember the dust-pile.

NOTE F5: through the faint blue twilight.

NOTE H5: She might die in one of those spells. It would be dreadful to die in such pain.

1: NOTE G5 was used in Chapter XI.

NOTE J5: fussy[2] just to say, "Yes, I know. It's dreadful – be brave – you'll soon be better[;]."

2: In the published version, "some one" is added where Montgomery crossed out "fussy."

3: NOTE I5 was used in the preceding chapter.

NOTE K5: Why did he seem to her like an old, well-known friend? Was it because she had been defending him – standing up to her family for him?

NOTE L5: One[4] didn't mind dying if death could be instant and painless. But to be hurt so in dying!

4: In the published version, "One" does not begin a new paragraph but continues after "like that."

NOTE M5: And it had all been so simple. She had merely <u>said</u> the things she had always <u>thought</u>.

NOTE N5: To laugh at her clan as she had always wanted to laugh was all the satisfaction she could get out of life now. But she thought it was rather pitiful that it should be so. Might she not pity herself a little when nobody else did[?]‡

Valancy got up and went to her window. The moist, beautiful wind blowing across groves of young-leafed wild trees touched her face with the caress of a wise, tender, old friend. The lombardies in Mrs. Tredgold's lawn, off to the left,—Valancy could just see them between the stable & the old carriage[-]shop—were in dark purple silhouette against a clear sky and there was ~~one~~ a milk-white, pulsating star just over one of them, like a living pearl on a silver-green lake. NOTE Q14 ~~A faint, young crescent hung above the dark hills beyond the station.~~ Valancy looked at it over her thin left shoulder.

NOTE Q14: Far beyond the station were the shadowy, purple-hooded woods around Lake Mistawis. A white, filmy mist hung over them & just above it was a faint, young crescent.

~~Miranda~~ NOTE Q5 NOTE N5 ~~got up and went to her window.~~ NOTE H6 NOTE V4 ~~Far over the dark hills ^far^ beyond the station hung a faint silvery crescent. Miranda looked at it over her her ^thin^ left shoulder.~~

"I wish," she said ~~slowly~~ ^whimsically^ ^whimsically,^ ~~and solemnly~~ that I may have <u>one</u> little dust pile before I die."

~~She couldn't see how it could happen.~~

XII

Uncle Benjamin [Pollard?] he had reckoned without his host — when he spoke promised so surely to take Valancy Miranda to a doctor. Mer— Valancy Miranda would eat [it]. laughed in his face

"Why on earth should I go to a Dr. Marsh? There's nothing the matter with my mind. Though you all think I've suddenly gone crazy. Well, I haven't. I've simply grown tired of living in other people's opinions and [I want to] live in my own. What is the matter that?" [She] [3 $\tilde{6}5$]
[15.000]

XIII

Uncle Benjamin found he had reckoned without his host when he ~~spoke~~ promised so airily to take ~~Miranda~~ Valancy to a doctor. ~~Miranda~~ Valancy would not go. ~~Miranda~~ Valancy laughed in his face.

"Why on earth should I go to ~~a~~ Dr. Marsh? There's nothing the matter with my ~~mind~~ mind. Though you all think I've suddenly gone crazy. Well, I haven't. I've simply grown tired of living in other people's opinions and ~~in~~ have ~~mad~~ decided to live in my own.[1] NOTE O14 ~~What is the matter with that? ^So, that's that!^ It~~ NOTE F6 ~~XXX~~

"Doss," said Uncle Benjamin solemnly and helplessly, "you are not like yourself."

"Who am I like then?" asked ~~Miranda~~ Valancy.

Uncle Benjamin was rather posed.

"Your grandfather[2] Barraclough," he answered desperately.

"Thanks." ~~Miranda~~ Valancy looked pleased. "That's a real compliment. I remember Grandfather Barraclough. He was one of the few human beings I _have_ known— almost the only one. Now, it is of no use to scold or entreat or command, Uncle B.[3] – or exchange anguished glances with mother[4] and Cousin Stickles. I am not going to any doctor. ~~NOTE U6~~ NOTE O5 So what are you going to do about it?"

What indeed! ~~Miranda was~~ ^It was not^ seemly— or even possible—to ~~make~~ ^hale^ ~~Miranda~~ Valancy doctor=wards by physical force. And in no other way could it be done, seemingly. Her mother's tears and imploring entreaties availed not. ❡ ~~NOTE P6~~ NOTE P5 Olive, sent by her mother to see if _she_ had any influence over ~~her~~

1: In the published version, this sentence reads "I've simply grown tired of living to please other people and have decided to please myself."

NOTE O14: It will give you something to talk about besides my stealing the raspberry jam. So that's that."

2: In the published version, "grandfather" is capitalized.

3: "Uncle B." is changed to "Uncle Benjamin" in the published version.

4: In the published version, "mother" is capitalized.

NOTE O5: And if you bring any doctor here I won't see him.

NOTE P5: "Don't worry, mother," said Valancy, lightly but quite respectfully. "It isn't likely I'll do anything very terrible. But I mean to have a little fun.["]

"Fun!" Mrs. Frederick uttered the word as if Valancy had said she was going to have a little tuberculosis.

NOTE Q5: "More as if she were talking to herself, than to me. Indeed, mother, all the time I was talking to her she gave me the impression of not really listening. And that wasn't all. When I finally decided that what I was saying had no influence over her I begged her, when Cecil came next week, not to say anything queer before him, at least. Mother, what do you think she said?"

"I'm sure I can't imagine," groaned Aunt Wellington, prepared for anything.

"She said, 'I'd rather like to shock Cecil. His mouth is too red for a man's.' Mother, I can never feel the same to Valancy again."

"Her mind is affected, Olive," said Aunt Wellington solemnly. "You must not hold her responsible for what she says."

When Aunt Wellington told Mrs. Frederick what Valancy had said to Olive ~~Valancy~~ Mrs. Frederick wanted Valancy to apologize.

"You made me apologize to Olive fifteen years ago for something I didn't do," said Valancy. "That old apology will do for now."

NOTE R5: They were all there except Cousin Gladys who ~~was~~ had been suffering such tortures of neuritis in her head "ever since poor Doss went queer" that she couldn't undertake any responsibility.

NOTE S5: "It is" – solemnly – "easier to scramble eggs than unscramble them."

NOTE T5: who put up his hand to conceal a smile several times.

~~Miranda~~ Valancy, came away with flushed cheeks and angry eyes. She told her mother that nothing could be done with ~~Miranda~~ Valancy. After <u>she</u>, Olive, had talked to her just like a sister, tenderly and wisely, all ~~Miranda~~ Valancy had said, ~~laughing~~ narrowing her funny eyes to mere slips[5] was, "<u>I</u> don't show my gums when I laugh." ~~NOTE Q6~~ NOTE Q5

Another solemn family conclave was held. ~~NOTE R6~~ NOTE R5 They decided —that is, they accepted a fact that was thrust in their faces—that the wisest thing was to leave ~~Miranda~~ Valancy alone for awhile – "give her her head" as Uncle Benjamin expressed it – "keep a careful eye on her but let her pretty much alone." The term of "watchful waiting" had not been invented then, but that was practically the policy ~~Miranda's~~ Valancy's distracted relatives decided to follow.

"We must be guided by developments," said Uncle Benjamin ~~NOTE G10~~ NOTE S5 Of ~~couse~~ ^course^ – if she becomes violent –"

Uncle James consulted Dr. Ambrose Marsh. Dr. Ambrose Marsh approved their decision. He pointed out to irate Uncle James – who would have liked to lock ~~Miranda~~ Valancy up somewhere[,] out of hand – that ~~Miranda~~ Valancy had ^not,^ as yet, really done or said anything that could be construed as proof of lunacy – and without proof you cannot lock people up ^in this ~~age~~ degenerate age.^ Nothing that Uncle James had reported seemed very alarming to Dr. Marsh, ~~NOTE V6~~ NOTE T5 But then he himself was not a Stirling. And he knew very little about the old ~~Miranda~~ Valancy. Uncle James ~~stalked out and drove back to Deerwood, thinking that~~ Ambrose Marsh wasn't much of a doctor[,] after all[,] and that Adelaide Stirling might have done better for herself.

XIV

L ife cannot stop because tragedy enters it. Meals must be ~~prepared~~ ^made ready^ though a son dies and porches must be ~~resp~~ repaired even if your only daughter is going out of her mind. Mrs. ~~George,~~ Frederick, in her systematic way, had long ago appointed the second week in June for the repairing of the front porch, the roof ~~was~~ ^~~of w~~ of^ which was sagging dangerously. Roaring Abel had been ~~spoken for~~ ^engaged to do it^ many moons before and Roaring Abel promptly appeared on the morning of the first day of the second week, and fell to work. Of course he was drunk. Roaring Abel was never anything but drunk. But he was only in the first stage, which made him talkative ^and genial^. The odor of whiskey on his breath nearly drove Mrs. ~~George~~ Frederick and Cousin Stickles wild at dinner. Even ~~Miranda~~ Valancy, with all her emancipation, did not like it. But she liked Abel and she liked his vivid, eloquent talk; and after she washed the dinner dishes she went out and sat on the steps and talked to him. Mrs.[1] ~~George~~ Frederick and Cousin Stickles thought it a terrible proceeding but what could they do? ~~Miranda~~ Valancy only smiled mockingly at them when they called her in ~~and sat on.~~ ^and did not go.^ It was so easy to ~~del~~ defy once you got started. The first step was the only one that really counted. They were both afraid to say anything more to her lest she might make a scene before Roaring Abel[,] who would spread it all over the country ~~NOTE W6~~ NOTE U5 It was too cold a day, in spite of the June sunshine, for Mrs. ~~George~~ Frederick to sit at the ^~~porc~~^ dining[-]room window and listen to what was said. She had to shut the window and ~~Miranda~~

1: In the published version, a new paragraph begins here.

NOTE U5: with his own characteristic comments & exaggerations.

NOTE V5: who told her his troubles between intervals of hammering gaily in time to his Scotch songs. Valancy liked to hear him. Every stroke of his hammer fell true to the note[.]

NOTE W5: His years had been a wild, colorful panorama of follies & adventures, gallantries, fortunes & misfortunes.

2: Montgomery changed "Cecily" to "Cecilia" here but continues to call her "Cecily" several more times.

3: In the published version, "Sissy" is spelled "Cissy."

Valancy and Roaring Abel had their talk to themselves. But if Mrs. ~~George~~ Frederick had known what the outcome of that talk was to be she would have prevented it, if the porch was never repaired.

~~Miranda~~ Valancy sat on the steps, defiant of the chill breeze of this cold June which had made ~~Cousin~~ ^Aunt^ Isabel aver the seasons were changing. She did not care whether she caught a cold or not. It was delightful to sit there in that cold, beautiful, fragrant world and feel free. She filled her lungs with the ^clean, lovely^ wind and held out her arms to it and let it ~~make her~~ tear her hair to ~~pie~~ pieces while she listened to Roaring Abel~~.~~[,] ~~NOTE C7~~ NOTE V5

~~Abel~~ Old Abel Gay, in spite of his seventy years, was handsome still[,] in a stately, patriarchal manner. His tremendous beard, falling down over his blue flannel shirt, was still a flaming, untouched red, though his shock of hair was white as snow, and ^his eyes were a fiery, youthful blue.^ His enormous, reddish white eyebrows were more like moustaches than eyebrows ~~and his eyes were a fiery blue~~. Perhaps this was why he always kept his upper lip scrupulously shaved. His cheeks ~~and~~ were red and his nose ought to have been[,] but wasn't. It was a fine, upstanding, aquiline nose, such as the noblest Roman of them all might have rejoiced in. Abel was six feet two in his stockings, broad-shouldered, lean-hipped. In his youth he had been a famous lover, finding all women too charming to bind himself to one. ~~NOTE B7~~ NOTE W5 He had been forty[-]five before he married—a pretty slip of a girl whom his goings[-]on killed in a few years. Abel was piously drunk at her funeral and ~~never~~ insisted on repeating the 55th fifty-fifth chapter of Isaiah ~~whe~~—Abel knew most of the Bible and all the Psalms by heart—while the minister, whom he disliked, prayed or tried to pray. Thereafter his house was run by an ^untidy^ old cousin who cooked his meals and kept things going after a fashion. In this unpromising environment little ~~Cecily~~ ^Cecilia^[2] Gay had grown up.

~~Miranda~~ Valancy had known ~~Cecily~~ "Sissy[3] Gay" fairly well in the democracy of the public school, though Cissy had been ~~four~~ ^three^ years younger than she. After they left school their paths diverged and she had seen nothing of her. Old Abel was a Presbyterian. That is, he got a Presbyterian preacher to marry him, baptize his child and bury his wife; and he knew more about Presbyterian theology than most ministers, ~~But~~ which made him a terror to them in arguments. But Roaring Abel never went to church. Every Presbyterian minister who had been in Deerwood had tried his hand – once – at ~~converting~~ ^reforming^ Roaring Abel. But he had not been pestered of late. ~~years.~~ Rev. Mr. Bentley had been in Deerwood for eight years but he had not sought out Roaring Abel since the first ~~year of~~ ^three months^ [of] his pastorate. He had called on Roaring ~~Able~~ Abel then and found him in the theological stage of drunkenness – which always followed the ~~chatty agre social stage~~ ^sentimental stage^ ~~and preceded the maudlin sentimental weeping the~~ sentimental maudlin one and preceded ~~NOTE Z7~~ NOTE X5 ~~the roaring blasphemous one = which was the last. Abel never went beyond it. He had never been "dead drunk" in his life.~~ He told Mr. Bentley that he was a sound Presbyterian and sure of his election. He had no sins—that he knew of—to repent of.

NOTE X5: the roaring, blasphemous one, in which he realized himself temporarily & intensely as a sinner in the hands of an angry God, was the final one. Abel never went beyond it. He ~~fel~~ generally fell asleep on his knees & awakened sober but he had never been "dead drunk" in his life.

NOTE Y5: ⁋ Abel had seen that Cissy was properly baptized – jovially drunk at the same time himself. He made her go

NOTE Z5: in that delicate, elusive fashion of beauty which fades so quickly if life is not kept in it by love and tenderness.

"Have you never done anything in your life that you are sorry for?" asked Mr. Bentley.

Roaring Abel scratched his bushy white head and pretended to reflect.

"Well, yes," he said finally. "There ~~was a woman~~ ^were some women^ I might have kissed and didn't. I've always been sorry for <u>that</u>."

Mr. Bentley went out and went home.
~~NOTE H19~~ NOTE Y5

~~But Roaring Abel made Cissy~~ ^Cecilia^ go to church and Sunday School regularly. The church people took her up and she was in turn a member of the Mission Band, the Girls Guild and the Young Women's Missionary Society. She was a faithful, unobtrusive, sincere, little worker. Everybody liked Cissy Gay and was sorry for her. She was so ~~pretty and~~ modest and sensitive ^and pretty^ ~~NOTE L10~~ NOTE Z5 But ~~that~~ ^then liking & pity^ did not prevent them

NOTE A6: Nobody ever knew who the father was. Cecily kept her poor pale lips tightly locked on her sorry secret. Nobody dared ask Roaring Abel any questions about it. ~~Rumour~~ Rumor and surmise laid the guilt at Barney Snaith's door because diligent inquiry among the other maids at the hotel revealed the fact that nobody there had ever seen Cissy Gay "with a fellow." She had "kept herself to herself" they said, rather resentfully. "Too good for <u>our</u> dances. And now look!"

NOTE B6: Women would not go to Roaring Abel's house. Mr. Bentley had gone once when he knew Abel was away[,] but the dreadful old creature who was scrubbing the kitchen floor told him Cissy wouldn't see ~~him~~ any[ ]one.

NOTE C6: where[4] a girl was dying of consumption.[5]

4: In the published version, this phrase begins with "a house."

5: Consumption = tuberculosis. A vaccine for tuberculosis became available in about 1920. L. M. Montgomery's mother died of tuberculosis in 1876.

NOTE D6: Abel described Rachel picturesquely. "I ler face' looked as if it had wore out a hundred bodies. And she moped. Talk about temper! Temper's nothing to moping. ~~And~~ She was too slow to catch worms and dirty—d——d dirty.

6: In the published version, a new paragraph begins here.

from tearing her in pieces like hungry cats when the catastrophe came. Four years previously Cissy Gay had gone up to a Muskoka hotel as a summer waitress. And when she had come back in the fall she was a changed creature. She ~~shut herself up~~ ^~~had hidden h~~ hid herself away^ and went nowhere. The reason soon leaked out and scandal raged. That winter Cissy's baby was born ~~NOTE X6~~ NOTE A6 . ⁋ ~~It~~ The baby had lived for a year. After its death Cissy faded away. Two years ago Dr. ~~Trent~~ ^Marsh^ had given her only six months to live – her ~~lugs~~ lungs were hopelessly diseased. But she was still alive. Nobody went to see her. ~~NOTE A7~~ NOTE B6 The old cousin had died and Roaring Abel had had two or three disreputable ~~old~~ housekeepers – the only kind who ~~would~~ could be prevailed on to go to ~~such a house~~ ~~NOTE I 10~~ NOTE C6

But the last one had left and Roaring Abel had now no=[ ]one to wait on Cissy and "do" for him. This was the burden of his plaint to ~~Miranda~~ Valancy and he condemned the "hypocrites" of Deerwood and its surrounding communities with some rich, meaty oaths that happened to reach Cousin Stickles['] ears as she passed through the hall and nearly finished the poor lady. Was ~~Miranda~~ Valancy listening to <u>that</u>?

~~Miranda~~ Valancy hardly noticed the ~~oaths~~ profanity. Her attention was focused on the horrible thought of poor, unhappy, disgraced little Cissy Gay, ~~lying~~ ill and helpless in that forlorn old house ^~~out on on in the out= skirts of Deerwood~~^ out on the Mistawis road, without a soul to help or comfort her ^NOTE Y4^ . And this in a nominally Christian community in the year of grace ~~19~~^nineteen^ and some odd!

"Do you mean to say that Cissy is all alone there now[,] with nobody to do anything for her – <u>nobody</u>?"

"Oh, she can move about a bit and get a bite and sup when she wants it. But she can't work. It's ~~mighty~~ ^d——d^ hard for a man to work hard all day and go home at night tired and hungry and cook his own meals. Sometimes I'm sorry I kicked old ~~Sarah~~ ^Rachel^ Edwards out." ~~Abel described Sarah ^Rachel^ picturesquely~~ ^NOTE M10^ NOTE D6 . ~~But she was ^too d====d^ dirty.~~

I ain't unreasonable—I know a man has to eat his peck before he dies[7]—but she went over the limit. What d'ye sp'ose I saw that lady do? She'd made some ~~pumpkin~~ ^punkin^ jam – had it on the table in glass jars ~~without any tops~~ ^with the tops off.^ The dawg got up on the table and stuck his paw into one of them. What did she do? She jest took holt of the ~~dog and~~ ^dawg and^ wrung the syrup off his paw back into the jar! Then screwed the top on and set it in the pantry. I sets open the door and says to her "Go." ^The dame went[,]^ and I fired the jars of ~~punc punl~~ punkin after her, two at a time. Thought I'd die laughing to see old ~~Sarah~~ ^Rachel^ run – with them punkin jars raining after her. She's told everywhere I'm crazy[,] so nobody'll come for love or money."

"But Cissy <u>must</u> have some[ ]one to look after her," insisted ~~Miranda~~ Valancy whose mind was centred on this aspect of the case. She did not care whether Roaring Abel had any[ ]one to cook for him or not. But her heart was wrung for Cecilia Gay.

"Oh, she gits on. Barney Snaith always drops in when he's passing and does anything she wants done. Brings her oranges ^and flowers^ and things. There's a Christian for you. Yet ~~them~~ that sanctimonious, snivelling parcel of St. Andrew[']s people wouldn't be seen on the same side of the road with him. NOTE E6 ~~Their dogs'll go to heaven before they do.~~ NOTE R10

"There are plenty of good people both in St. Andrew[']s and St. ~~Agath~~ George's, who would be kind to Cissy if <u>you</u> would behave yourself," said Miranda severely. "They're afraid to go near your place[.]"

"Because I'm such a ~~roaring old devil?~~ ^sad old dog?^ But I don't bite—never bit any[ ]one in my life[.] ~~NOTE K10~~ NOTE F6 And I'm not asking people to come. Don't want 'em poking and prying ~~round~~ ^about.^ What I want is a housekeeper. ~~I kin pay decent wages if I could get a decent woman. D'ye' think I like old hags?~~ If I shaved every Sunday & went to church I'd get all the housekeepers I'd want. I'd be respectable then. But ~~I tell you~~ what is the use of going to church when it's all settled by predestination? Tell me that, Miss."

7: The saying "You must eat a peck of dirt before you die" originated in the early 1700s. It refers to the fact that there is bound to be a bit of ash or dirt in food, and over a lifetime, this could amount to a "peck" (about two gallons / eight litres).

NOTE E6: Their dogs'll go to heaven before they do. And their minister – slick as if the cat had licked him!["]

NOTE F6: A few loose words spilled around don't hurt any[ ]one.

8: In the published version, "God" is spelled out.

"Is it?" said ~~Miranda~~ Valancy.

"Yes. Can't git 'round it nohow. Wish I could. I don't want either heaven or hell for steady. Wish a man could have 'em mixed in equal proportions."

"Isn't that the way it is in this world?" said ~~Miranda~~ Valancy thoughtfully – but rather as if her thought was concerned with something else than theology.

"No, no," boomed Abel, striking a tremendous blow on a stubborn nail. "There's too much hell here – entirely too much hell[.]‡ That's why I get drunk so often. It sets you free for a little while – free from yourself – yes, by G-d,[8] free from predestination. Ever try it?"

"~~No, I've another way of getting free, said Miranda absently. "But about Cissy now.~~ ^"No, I've another way of getting free," said Valancy absently. "But about Cissy now.^ She <u>must</u> have some[ ]one to look after her—"

"What ^are^ you harping on ~~Cissy~~ ^Sis^ for? Seems to me you ain't bothered much about her ^up to now.^ You never even come to see her. And she used to like you so well."

"I should have," said ~~Miranda~~ Valancy. "But never mind. You couldn't understand. The point is – you must have a housekeeper."

"Where am I to get one[?]; I can pay decent wages if I could get a decent woman. D'ye think I like old hags?"

"Will I do?" said ~~Miranda~~ Valancy.

XV

"Let us be calm," said Uncle Benjamin. "Let us be perfectly calm."

"Calm!" Mrs. ~~George~~ Frederick wrung her hands. "How can I be calm [–] ~~&~~ how could anybody be calm under such a disgrace as this?"

"Why in the world did you let her go?" asked Uncle James.

"Let her? How could I stop her, James? ^It seems^ she packed the big valise and sent it away with Roaring Abel when he went home after supper, while Christine and I were out in the kitchen. Then Doss herself came down with her little satchel, dressed in her ~~suit~~ green ^serge^ suit. I felt a ~~"wh~~ terrible premonition. NOTE I7 NOTE J7 NOTE G6 ~~I said~~ "Doss, where are you going?" and she said, 'I am going to look for my Blue Castle.'"

"Wouldn't you think that would convince Marsh that her mind is affected?" ~~demanded~~ ^interjected^ Uncle James.

"And I said, '~~Miranda~~ Valancy, what do you mean?' And she said, 'I am going to keep house for Roaring Abel and nurse Cissy. He will pay me ~~twenty-five~~ ^thirty^ dollars a month.' I wonder I didn't drop dead on the ~~spoil~~ spot."

"You shouldn't have let her go – you shouldn't have let her out of the house," said Uncle James.

"~~How could I stop~~ "You should have locked the doors – anything—"[1]

"She was between me and the front door. And you can't realize how determined she was. NOTE E7 NOTE H6 That's the strangest thing of all about her. She used to

NOTE G6: I can't tell you how it was[,] but I seemed to know that Doss was going to do something dreadful."
"It's a pity you couldn't have had your premonition a little sooner," said Uncle Benjamin drily.
"I said[,]

1: In the published version, this line is not a separate paragraph but continues as part of the previous one.

NOTE H6: She was like a rock.

103

2: This phrase is from chapter 7 of *The Light That Failed*, Rudyard Kipling's first novel, published in 1890.

3: In the published version, "everything" is in italics, not "said."

NOTE I6: I said to her solemnly, "Doss, when a woman's reputation is once smirched nothing can ever make it spotless again.

4: In the published version, "she" is not in italics.

NOTE J6: Whatever she's been or done[,] she's a human being."
    "Well, you know, when it comes to that, I suppose she is," said Uncle James with the air of one making a splendid concession.

NOTE K6: "An outrageous thing!" said Uncle Benjamin violently. "An outrageous thing!"
    Which relieved his feelings[,] but didn't help any[ ]one else.

5: In the published version, "mother" is capitalized.

be so good and obedient[,] ^and now she's neither to hold nor bind.^[2] But I <u>said</u> everything[3] I could think of to bring her to her senses. I asked her if she had no regard for her reputation ~~NOTE J7~~ NOTE I6 ~~Her~~ Your character ~~would~~ ^will^ be gone forever if ~~she went~~ ^you go^ to Roaring Abel's to wait on a bad girl like Sis Gay![']' And <u>she</u>[4] said, 'I don't believe Cissy was a bad girl[,] but I don't care if she was.' Those were her very words. 'I don't care if she was.'"

"She has lost all sense of decency," ~~said~~ ^exploded^ Uncle Benjamin.

"'Cissy Gay is dying,' she ~~went on~~ ^said[,]^ 'and it's a shame and disgrace that she is dying in a Christian community with no one to do anything for her.'" ~~NOTE D7~~ NOTE J6

"I asked ~~her~~ ^Doss^ if she had no regard for appearances. She said, 'I've been keeping up appearances all my life. Now I'm going in for realities. Appearances can go hang.' <u>Go</u> hang!'" ~~NOTE P10~~ NOTE K6

Mrs. ~~George~~ Frederick wept. Cousin Stickles took up the refrain between her moans of despair.

"I told her—we <u>both</u> told her—that Roaring Abel had certainly killed his wife in one of his drunken rages and would kill her. She laughed and said, 'I'm not afraid of Roaring Abel. He won't kill <u>me</u>[,] and he's too old for me to be afraid of his gallantries.' What did she mean? What <u>are</u> gallantries?"

~~"I said to her," =~~ Mrs. ~~George~~ Frederick saw that she must stop crying if she wanted to regain control of the ~~convesation.~~ conversation.

"<u>I</u> said to her, ~~Miranda,~~ "Valancy, if you have no regard for your own reputation, and your family's standing have you none for <u>my</u> feelings?" She said, ="[']None.[']= Just like that ="[']<u>None</u>![']""

"~~In a~~ Insane people never <u>do</u> have any regard for other people's feelings," said Uncle Benjamin. "That's one of the symptoms."

"I broke out into tears then[,] and she said, 'Come now, mother,[5] be a good sport. I'm going to do an act of

Christian charity[,] and as for ~~my~~ the damage it will do my reputation, why, you know I haven't any matrimonial chances anyhow, so what does it matter?" And with that she turned and went out."

"The last words I said to her," ~~sobbed~~ said Cousin Stickles; ^pathetically,^ "were 'Who will rub my back at nights now?' ~~NOTE J7~~ NOTE L6 ~~and she never even answered me."~~ ~~NOTE F7~~

"I'll see Ambrose Marsh again about ~~her~~ ^Doss this^,["] said Uncle Benjamin ~~NOTE W10~~ NOTE M6

"I'll see Lawyer Ferguson," said Uncle James.
"Meanwhile," added Uncle Benjamin, "let us be calm."

NOTE L6: And she said – she said – but no, I cannot repeat it."
"Nonsense," said Uncle Benjamin. "Out with it. This is no time to be squeamish."
"She said" – Cousin Stickles' voice was little more than a whisper – "she said – 'Oh, darn'!"
"To think I should have lived to hear my daughter swearing," ~~said~~ ^sobbed^ Mrs. Frederick.
"It – it was only imitation swearing," faltered Cousin Stickles, desirous of smoothing things over now that the worst was out. But she had never told about the bannister.

"It will be only a step from that to real swearing," said Uncle James sternly.
~~"And she didn't even take her flannel petticoat" lamented Cousin Stickles.~~
"The worst of this" – Mrs. Frederick hunted for a dry spot on her handkerchief – "is that every[ ]one will know now that she is deranged. We can't keep it a secret any longer. Oh, I can not bear it."
"You should have been stricter with her when she was young," said Uncle Benjamin.
"I don't see how I could have been," said Mrs. Frederick – truthfully

enough."
"The worst feature of the case is that that Snaith scoundrel is always hanging around Roaring Abel's," said Uncle James. "I shall be thankful if nothing worse comes of this mad freak than a few weeks at Roaring Abel's. Cissy Gay can't live much longer."
~~NOTE M6~~ "And she didn't even take her flannel petticoat," lamented Cousin Stickles.

NOTE M6: – meaning Valancy, not the flannel petticoat.

"let - us be calm."

XV

Valancy

Miranda had walked out—to
Roaring Abel's house on the mistawis
road under a sky of purple
and amber, with a queer exhilaration and expectancy in her heart.
Roaring Abel lived in a another little
place and house, quite a way from
the village. It had once been a
snug place enough in the days
when Abel Gay had been young and
prosperous, and the planning,
arched sign over the gate— "A.
Gay, Carpenter" had been fine
and freshly painted. Now it was
a jaded, dreary, old place with
a patched roof and shutters hanging

XVI

M~~iranda~~ Valancy had walked out to Roaring Abel's house on the ~~Muskoka~~ ^Mistawis^ road under a sky of purple and amber, with a queer exhilaration and expectancy in her heart ~~NOTE Q7 NOTE Q10~~ NOTE N6

~~Roaring Abel lived in a~~ ^rambling,^ ~~big tumble down old house,~~ ~~NOTE R10~~ ~~a mile or so from the village. ^was not very like a Blue Castle.^~~ ❡ It had once been a snug place enough in the days when Abel Gay had been young and prosperous, and the ~~punning,~~ ^punning,^ arched sign over the gate – "A. Gay, Carpenter" had been ~~five~~ ^fine^ and freshly painted. Now it was a faded, dreary old place with a ^leprous,^ patched roof and shutters hanging askew. Abel never seemed to do any carpenter jobs about his own house. ~~A bunch~~ ~~NOTE F10 NOTE M7~~ NOTE O6 The garden, which Cissy used to keep neat and pretty, had run wild. On two sides of the house were fields full of nothing but mulleins. Behind the house was a long stretch of useless barrens, full of ~~pine stumps and scrub~~ ^scrub pines and^ spruces ~~NOTE L7~~ NOTE P6 running back to a belt of timber on the shores of Lake Mistawis[,] ^two miles away.^ A rough, ~~rocky~~ ^boulder-strewn^ lane ran through it to the

---

NOTE N6: Back there, behind her, her mother & Cousin Stickles were crying—over themselves, not over her. But here the wind was in her face, soft, dew-wet, cool, blowing along the grassy roads. Oh, she loved the wind! The robins were whistling sleepily in the big firs along the way & the moist air was fragrant with the tang of balsam. ~~The sides of the road were sprinkled with the phantom-like globes of dandelions. Valancy liked them so much better than the flaunting flowers.~~ Big

cars went purring past in the violet dusk—the stream of summer tourists to Muskoka had already begun—but Valancy did not envy any of their occupants. Muskoka cottages might be charming[,] but beyond, in the sunset skies, among the spires of the firs, her Blue Castle towered. She brushed the old years & habits & inhibitions away from her like dead leaves. She would not be littered with them.

Roaring Abel's rambling, tumble-down old house was situated about ~~two~~ three

miles from the village, on the very edge of "up back," as the sparsely-settled, hilly, wooded country ~~arous~~ around Mistawis was called vernacularly. It did not, it must be confessed, look much like a Blue Castle.

NOTE O6: It had a listless air, as if tired of life. There was a dwindling grove of rag-ged, crone-like old spruces behind it.

NOTE P6: with here & there a blossoming bit of ~~wh~~ wild cherry, ~~ghostly fair in the twilight.~~

107

1: In this case, "pestiferous" probably means "rapidly spreading" instead of the more common meanings of "highly infective," "contagious," or "annoying."

NOTE Q6: "So you've come," he said incredulously. "I never s'posed that ruck of Stirlings would let you. ~~Miranda~~ Valancy showed all her pointed teeth in a grin. "They couldn't stop me." "I didn't think you'd so much spunk," said Roaring Abel admiringly. "And look at the nice ankles of her," he added, as he stepped aside to let her in. If Cousin Stickles had heard this she would have been certain that Miranda's doom, earthly and unearthly, was sealed. But Abel's superannuated gallantry did not worry Valancy. Besides, this was the first complement[2] she had ever received in her life & she found herself liking it. She sometimes suspected she had nice ankles[,] but nobody had ever mentioned it before. In the Stirling clan ankles were among the unmentionables. Roaring Abel

2: In the published version, "complement" is corrected to "compliment."

3: From 2 Corinthians 5:17: "Old things have passed away; behold, all things are become new."

woods – a lane white with pestiferous,[1] beautiful daisies. ~~Beyond it ⟨~~ Roaring Abel met Miranda at the door[.] ~~NOTE N7~~ NOTE Q6 ~~and~~ took her into the ~~dirty~~ kitchen[,] where Cissy Gay was lying on the sofa, breathing quickly, with little scarlet spots on her hollow cheeks. ~~Miranda~~ Valancy had not seen Cecilia Gay for years. Then she had been such a pretty creature ^a slight, blossom-like girl,^ with soft, golden hair, clear-cut, ~~features~~ almost waxen features, and ~~enorm~~ large, beautiful, blue eyes. She was shocked at the change in her. Could this be ^sweet^ Cissy – this pitiful~~ly wasted~~ little thing that looked like a tired, broken flower? She had wept all the beauty out of her eyes; they looked ^too big—^ enormous—in her wasted face. The last time ~~Miranda~~ Valancy had seen Cecilia Gay those faded, piteous eyes had been limpid, shadowy blue pools ~~all astar with dream and~~ ^aglow with^ mirth. The contrast was so terrible that ~~Miranda's~~ Valancy's ~~ey~~ own eyes filled with tears. She knelt down by Cissy and put her arms about her.

"Cissy dear, I've come to look after you. I'll stay with you till – till – as long as you want~~ed~~ me."

"Oh!" Cissy put her thin arms about ~~Miranda's~~ Valancy's neck. "Oh – will you? It's been so – lonely. I can wait on myself – but it's been so lonely." It would just be like – heaven – to have some[ ]one here – like you." You were always – so sweet to me – long ago."

~~Miranda~~ Valancy held Cissy close. She was suddenly happy. Here was some[ ]one who needed her – some[ ]one she could help. She was no longer a ~~super=~~ ~~fluous woman~~ superfluity. Old things had passed away; everything had become new.[3]
~~NOTE VI~~

~~"Look at the nice ankles of her," said Roaring Abel complacently, smoking his pipe in the corner.~~
~~Miranda had received her first complement.~~
~~NOTE VI~~

"Most things are predestinated but some are just darn sheer luck," said Roaring Abel, complacently smoking his pipe in the corner.

she cone O deep. she was no longer
a ~~superfluous woman~~ superfluity.
Old things ~~XI~~ had passed away;
everything had become new.

"Look at ~~that~~. the nice cubbles
of her", said Roaring Owl com-
~~placently~~, smoking his pipe in
the ~~corner~~.

Granddad had received her
just emolument.

"Most things are predestinated
but - some are just down sheer
luck; ~~said~~ ~~Roaring~~ Owl, complacently ~~smoking~~ his pipe in
the corner. ~~XV~~

When ~~Valerie~~ had cried
for a ~~week~~ at - Roaring Owl she
feel - as if years had separated

XVII

When ~~Miranda~~ Valancy had lived for a week at Roaring Abel's she felt as if years had separated her from her old life and all the people she had known in it. They were ^beginning to seem^ remote – dream-like – far[-]away [–]; ~~They had ceased to matter~~ and as the days went on they seemed still more so[,] until they ceased to matter altogether.

She was happy[.] ~~NOTE Z10~~ ~~NOTE S7~~ NOTE R6 ~~and busy – very busy. The house had to be cleaned.~~ If ~~Miranda~~ ^she^ found NOTE G7 satisfaction in cleaning dirty rooms she got her fill of it there. Roaring Abel thought she was foolish to bother doing so much more than she was ~~paid~~ ^asked^ to do[,] but he did not ~~unt~~ interfere with her. ~~NOTE Y7~~ NOTE S6 ~~During the day he~~ Abel was ~~always~~ ^generally^ away from home—if not working[,] then shooting or fishing with Barney Snaith.

NOTE R6: Nobody ever bothered her with conundrums or insisted on giving her Purple Pills. Nobody called her Doss or worried her about catching cold. There were no quilts to piece, no abominable rubber[-]plant to water, no ice-cold maternal tantrums to endure. She could be alone whenever she liked, go to bed when she liked, sneeze when she liked. In the long, wondrous, northern twilights, when Cissy was asleep & Roaring Abel away[,] she could sit for hours on the shaky back veranda steps, looking out over the barrens to the hills beyond, covered with their fine, purple bloom, listening to the friendly wind singing wild sweet melodies in the little spruces[,] & drinking in the aroma of the sunned grasses, until darkness flowed over the landscape like a cool welcome wave.
Sometimes of an afternoon,

when Cissy was strong enough, the two girls went into the barrens & looked at the wood-flowers. But they did not pick any. Valancy had read to Cissy the gospel thereof according to John Foster: –
"It is a pity to gather wood-flowers.[1] They lose half their witchery away from the green & the flicker. The way to enjoy wood-flowers is to track them down to their remote haunts – gloat over them – and then leave them with backward glances, taking with us only the beguiling memory of their grace & fragrance."[2]
~~She was in~~ Valancy was in the midst of realities after a lifetime of unrealities. And busy—very busy. The house had to be cleaned. Not for nothing had ~~Miranda~~ Valancy been brought up in the Stirling habits of neatness & cleanliness.

1: In the published version, there is no new paragraph here.

2: This passage was taken from Montgomery's essay, "The Woods in Summer."

NOTE S6: He was very well satisfied with his bargain. Valancy was a good cook. Abel said she got a flavor into things. The only fault he found with her was that she did not sing at her work. "Folks should always sing at their work," he ~~uns~~ insisted. "Sounds cheerful-like." ~~"Everyb"~~ "Not always," retorted Valancy. "Fancy a butcher singing at his work. Or an undertaker." Abel burst into his great broad laugh. "There's no getting the better of you. You've got an answer every time. I should think the Stirlings would be glad to be rid of you. They don't like being sassed back." During the day

111

He generally came home at nights – always very late & ~~almost always~~ ^often^ very drunk. The first night they heard him come howling into the yard[,] Cissy had told ~~Miranda~~ Valancy not to be afraid.

"Father never does anything—he just makes a noise."

~~Miranda~~ Valancy, lying on the sofa in Cissy's room[,] where she had elected to sleep, lest Cissy should ~~want~~ ^need^ attention in the night—Cissy would never have <u>called</u>[3] her—was not at all afraid[,] and said so. By the time Abel had got his horses put away[,] the roaring stage had passed and he was in his room at the end of the hall crying and praying. ~~Miranda~~ Valancy could still hear his dismal moans when she went ^calmly^ to sleep. ~~She smiled as she thought of the horror all the Stirlings would~~ For the most part Abel was ^a^ good-natured creature[,] ^but occasionally he had a temper^. Once ~~when he was angry,~~ ~~Miranda~~ Valancy asked him coolly,

"What is the use of getting in a rage?"

"It's such a d——ed relief," said Abel.

They both burst out laughing together.

"You're a great little sport," said Abel admiringly. "Don't mind my bad French. I don't mean a thing by it. Jest habit. Say, I like a woman that isn't[4] afraid to speak up to me. Sis there was always too meek—too meek. That's why she got adrift. I like you."

"All the same," said Miranda determinedly.[5] "~~NOTE V7~~ NOTE T6 ~~I'm not~~ going to have you tracking mud all over a floor I've just scrubbed. You <u>must</u> use the scraper~~,~~ ^whether you consign it to perdition or not."^

Cissy loved the cleanness and neatness. She had kept it so, too, until her strength failed. She was very sweet ~~and~~ pitifully happy because she had ~~Miranda~~ Valancy with her. It had been so terrible—the long, lonely days and nights with no companionship save those dreadful old women who came to work. Cissy had hated and feared them. She clung to ~~Miranda~~ Valancy like a child.

There was no doubt that Cissy was dying. Yet at no time did she seem alarmingly ill. She did not even cough a great deal. Most days she was able to get up and dress – sometimes even to walk[6] about in the garden ^or the barrens barrens^ for an hour or two. For a few weeks after ~~Miranda's~~ Valancy's coming she seemed so much better that ~~Miranda~~ Valancy began to hope she might get well. But Cissy shook her head.

NOTE U6: I'm so tired, Valancy. Only dying can rest me.

"No. I can't get well. My lungs are almost gone. And I – don't want to. ~~NOTE X10~~ NOTE U6 But it's lovely to have you here—you'll never know how much it means to me. But ~~Miranda~~ Valancy – you work too hard. You don't need to – Father only wants his meals cooked. I don't think you are strong yourself. You turn so pale sometimes. And those drops you take. <u>Are</u> you well, dear?"

"I'm all right," said ~~Miranda~~ Valancy lightly. She would not have Cissy worried. "And I'm not working hard. I'm glad to have some work to do – something that really wants to be done."

"Then" – Cissy slipped her hand wistfully into ~~Miranda's~~ Valancy's – "don't let's talk any more about my being sick. Let's just forget it. Let's pretend I'm a little girl again – and you have come here to play with me. I used to wish that long ago – wish that you could come. I knew you couldn't[,] of course. But how I did wish it! You always seemed so different from the other girls – so kind and sweet – and as if you had something in yourself nobody knew about – some dear, pretty secret. <u>Had</u> you, ~~Miranda?~~ Valancy?"

"I had my Blue Castle," said ~~Miranda~~ Valancy, laughing a little. She was pleased that Cissy had thought of her like this. She had never suspected that anybody liked or admired or wondered about her. ~~She~~ She told Cissy all about her Blue Castle. She had never told any[ ]one about it before.

"Every[ ]one has a Blue Castle, I think," said Cissy softly. "Only ~~the~~ every[ ]one has a different name for it. <u>I</u> had mine – once."

She put her two thin, little hands over her face. ~~Miranda listened~~ waited with a beating heart. ~~Who had destroyed Cissy's Blue Castle? Would Cissy tell her? But Cissy said nothing more – then.~~ She did not tell ~~Miranda~~ Valancy – then – who had destroyed her Blue Castle. But ~~Miranda~~ Valancy ~~had~~ knew that, whoever it was, it was not Barney Snaith.

XVIII

NOTE V6: thumping over the rocks in that crazy lane.

1: In the published version, "Their" does not begin a new paragraph but continues after "looked into his face."

2: In the published version, a new paragraph begins with "His eyes."

NOTE W6: – she wished she could sew the buttons on his coat – and make him cut his hair – and shave every day. There was something in his face – one hardly knew what it was. Tiredness? Sadness? Disillusionment? He had

~~Miranda~~ Valancy was acquainted with Barney by now—well acquainted[,] it seemed, though she had spoken to him only a few times. But then she had felt just as well acquainted with him the first time they had met. She had been in the garden at twilight, hunting for a few ~~flowers~~ ^stalks of white narcissus^ for Cissy's room ~~She had~~ ^when she^ heard that terrible old Grey-Slosson coming down through the woods from Mistawis—one could hear it miles away. ~~Miranda~~ Valancy did not look up as it drew near[,] ~~NOTE P7~~ NOTE V6 She had never looked up, though Barney had gone racketting past every evening since she had been at Roaring Abel's. This time he did not racket past. The old Grey-Slosson stopped with ^even^ more terrible noises ~~even~~ than it made going. ~~Miranda~~ Valancy was conscious that Barney had sprung from it and was leaning over the ramshackle gate. She suddenly straightened up and looked into his face.

~~Their eyes met = ^Their eyes met =^ For just a second their eyes met & locked~~ ^Their[1] eyes met—^ ~~Miranda~~ Valancy was suddenly conscious of a delicious ~~weakness = . w~~Was one of her heart attacks coming on? – ~~b~~But this was a new symptom! ~~=~~. His eyes,[2] which she had always thought brown, now seen close, were deep violet—translucent and intense. ~~= n~~Neither of his eyebrows looked like the other ~~=~~. ~~h~~He was thin—too thin—she wished she could feed him up a bit ~~NOTE P7~~ NOTE W6 ~~= he had~~ dimples in his thin cheeks when he smiled. ~~= a~~All these ~~thing~~ thoughts flashed through ~~Miranda's~~ Valancy's mind in that one moment while his eyes looked into hers.

"Good-evening, Miss Stirling."

~~"Good-evening, Mr. Snaith."~~

Nothing could be more commonplace and conventional. ~~NOTE EH~~ NOTE X6 ~~Miranda~~ couldn't imagine why she was trembling from head to foot—it must be her heart. If only he didn't notice it!

"I'm going over to ^the^ Port ,"[3] ~~as~~ Barney was saying. "~~Is there anything I can do or get~~ ^Can I acquire merit by getting or doing anything ^there^ for you or Cissy^?" ^~~there?~~^

"Will you get some salt codfish for us?" said ~~Miranda.~~ Valancy. It was the only thing she could think of. Roaring Abel had expressed a desire that day for a dinner of ~~biled~~ boiled salt codfish. When her knights came riding to the Blue Castle[,] ~~Miranda~~ Valancy had sent them on many a quest[,] but she had never asked ~~him~~ any of them to get her salt codfish.

"Certainly. You're sure there's nothing else? Lots of room in Lady Jane Grey-Slosson. And she always gets back some time, does Lady Jane."[4]

"I don't think there's anything more," said ~~Miranda~~ Valancy. She knew he would bring oranges for Cissy anyhow—he always did.

Barney did not turn away at once. He was silent for a little. Then he said, slowly & whimsically[:]~~;~~

"Miss Stirling, you're a brick[!]~~;~~ You're a whole cart load of bricks. To come here and look after Cissy – under the circumstances."

"There's nothing so bricky about that," said ~~Miranda~~ Valancy. "I'd nothing else to do. And – I like it here. I don't feel as if I'd done anything specially meritorious. ~~Ro~~ Mr. Gay is paying me fair wages. I never earned any money before – and I like it!" It seemed so easy to talk to Barney Snaith[,] someway—this ~~terrible~~ terrible Barney Snaith of the lurid tales and mysterious past—as easy and natural as ~~if sh~~ talking to herself.

"All the money in the world couldn't ~~pay you for what y~~ ^buy^ what you're doing for Cissy Gay," said Barney. "It's splendid and ~~dear~~ ^fine^ of you. And if there's anything I can do to help you in ~~anyway~~ any

NOTE X6: Any[ ]one might have said it. But Barney Snaith had a way of saying things that gave them poignancy. When he said good-evening you felt that it was a good evening & that it was partly his doing that it was. Also, you felt that some of the credit was yours. Valancy felt all this vaguely[,] but she

3: Montgomery left a space here for entering her name for "the Port" later. She had used "Port Laurence" for the first time in Chapter I but did not write the name here.

4: The Macdonalds nicknamed their new car, a Gray-Dort, "Lady Jane Grey" for the short-lived Queen of England who, although proclaimed queen after Edward VI died in 1553, was then accused of treason so that her cousin Mary could take the throne. After seven months' imprisonment in the Tower of London, she was executed in February 1554. Lady Jane Grey (c. 1537–1554) was called "the Nine Days' Queen" because of her brief reign, July 10 to July 19, 1553.

NOTE U6. "Well, I'm sure he'll be decent to you, apart from his inebriated yowls," said Barney. "And I've told him he's got to stop damning things when you're around[.]"

"Why?" asked Valancy slyly, with one of her odd, slanted glances & a sudden flake of pink on each cheek born of the thought that Barney Snaith had actually done so much for her. "I often feel like damning things myself."

For a moment Barney stared. Was this elfin girl the little, old-maidish creature who had stood there two minutes ago? Surely there was magic & devilry going on in that shabby, weedy old garden.

Then he laughed.

"It will be a relief to have some[ ]one to do it for you[,] then. So you don't want anything but salt codfish?"

"Not to-night. But I

5: Montgomery misnumbers the next four notes, repeating "NOTE U6, NOTE V6, NOTE W6, and NOTE X6" after the first NOTE X6.

NOTE V6: walking down through the barrens, whistling. How that whistle of his echoed through the spruces on those June twilights! Valancy caught herself listening for it every evening – rebuked herself – then let herself go. Why shouldn't she listen for it?

He always brought Cissy fruit & flowers. Once he brought Valancy a box of candy—the first box of candy she had ever been given. It seemed sacrilege to eat it[.]

---

way[,] you have only to let me know. If Roaring Abel ever tries to annoy you—"

"He doesn't. He's lovely to me. I like Roaring Abel," said ~~Miranda~~ Valancy frankly.

"So do I. But there's one stage of his drunkenness – perhaps you haven't encountered it yet – when he sings ribald songs—."

"Oh yes. He came home last night like that. Cissy and I just went to our room and shut ourselves in where we couldn't hear him. ^He apologized this morning.^ I'm not afraid of any of Roaring Abel's stages." ~~NOTE CH~~

NOTE U6 | 5 ." ~~But But I~~ daresay I'll have some errands for you very often when you go to Port__. I can't trust Mr. Gay to remember to bring ^all the^ things I want." ~~NOTE CH~~

Barney had gone away[,] then[,] in his Lady Jane[,] ~~Grey~~ and ~~Miranda~~ Valancy stood in the garden for a long time.

Since then he had called several times NOTE U7 NOTE Q7 NOTE V6 ~~And every time he had stayed and chatted a while.~~ ^C^ ~~Miranda~~ ^She^ found herself thinking of him in season and out of season. She wanted to know if he ever thought about her when she wasn't before ~~him~~ his eyes[,] and if so[,] what. She wanted to see that mysterious house of his back on the Mistawis island. Cissy had never seen it. Cissy, though she talked freely of Barney ^and had known him for five years[,]^ really knew little more of him than ~~Miranda~~ Valancy herself.

"But he isn't bad," said Cissy. "Nobody need ever tell me he is. He ~~h~~ can't have done a thing to be ashamed of?"

"Then why does he live as he does?" asked ~~Miranda~~ Valancy – to hear somebody defend him.

"I don't know. He's a mystery. And of course there's something behind it – but I know it isn't disgrace. Barney Snaith simply couldn't do anything disgraceful, ~~Miranda~~ Valancy."

~~Miranda felt very happy.~~ ^Valancy was not so sure.^ Barney must have done something – some time. ~~he wouldn't bury himself in Mistawis if he hadn't.~~ He was a man of education and intelligence. She had soon discovered that[,] in listening to his conversations and wrangles with Roaring Abel – who was surprisingly well read and could discuss any subject under the sun when sober. Such a man wouldn't bury himself for five years in ~~Mistawis~~ ^Muskoka^ and live and look like a tramp if there were not too good – or bad – a reason for it ^NOTE W6^ ^~~But it didn't~~^ ~~But~~ she was sure now that he had never been Cissy Gay's lover. There was nothing like <u>that</u> between them. Though he ~~love~~ was very fond of Cissy and she of him, as any[ ]one could see. But it was a fondness that didn't worry ~~Miranda.~~ Valancy.

"You don't know what Barney has been to me these past two years," Cissy ~~had~~ ^had^ said simply. "<u>Everything</u> would have been unbearable without him."

"Cissy Gay ~~was~~^= is =^ the sweetest girl I ever knew—and there's a man somewhere I'd like to shoot if I could find him," Barney had said savagely.

Barney was an interesting talker[,] with a knack of telling a great deal about his adventures and nothing at all about himself. ~~One evening~~ ^on the shaky old back verandah^ ^NOTE X6^ ~~he held them all entranced with his weird tales of~~ his adventures with "shacks" on trains while hoboing it across the continent. ~~Miranda~~ Valancy thought she ought to think his stealing rides quite dreadful[,] but didn't. ~~NOTE X8~~ NOTE Y6 ~~and his yarns of the Yukon enthralled her = he had spent two years there.~~

"Found no gold," he said. "Came away poorer than when I went. But such a place to live! Those silences at the back of the north wind <u>got</u> ~~me~~ ^me.^ I've never belonged to myself since."

Yet he was not a great talker. He told a great deal in a few well-chosen words—how well-chosen ~~Miranda~~ Valancy did not realize. ~~And he often relapsed into long moody silences.~~ And he had a knack of saying things without opening his ~~lips~~ ^mouth^ at all.

"I like a man whose eyes say more than his lips," thought ~~Miranda~~ Valancy.

^But then^ She[6] liked everything about him—his tawny hair – his whimsical ^~~enigmatical~~^ smiles – the little glints of fun in his eyes – his loyal affection for

NOTE W6: But it didn't matter. All that mattered was that

NOTE X6: There was one glorious rainy day when Barney & Abel swapped yarns all the afternoon while Valancy mended tablecloths & listened. Barney told weird tales of

NOTE Y6: The story of his working his way to England on a cattle[-]ship sounded more legitimate. And his yarns of the ~~Yub~~ Yukon enthralled her—especially the one of the night he was lost on the divide between Gold Run & Sulphur Valley. He had spent two years out there. Where in all this was there room for the penitentiary & the other things?
 If he were telling the truth. But ~~Miranda~~ Valancy knew he was.

6: In the published version, "She" is lower case.

that ~~awful~~ ^unspeakable^ Lady Jane – his habit of sitting with his hands in his pockets, his chin ~~sunck~~ sunk on his breast, looking up from under his mismated eyebrows. ~~NOTE W7 NOTE X7~~ NOTE P14

"I've been watching a woodpecker all day," he said one evening ^on the shaky old back verandah.^ His account of the woodpecker's doings was satisfying. He had often some gay or ~~cuin cun~~ cunning little anecdote of the wood folk to tell them. And sometimes he and Roaring Abel smoked fiercely the whole evening and never said a word[,] while Cissy lay in the hammock swung between the verandah posts and Miranda sat idly on the steps[,] her NOTE Z7 hands clasped over her knees[,] NOTE Z3 and ~~Miranda sitting there,~~ wondered dreamily if she were really ~~Miranda~~ Valancy Stirling and if it were only three weeks since she had left the ugly old house on Elm ~~Ave~~ Street ~~NOTE Z7~~ NOTE Z6

NOTE P14: She liked his nice voice which sounded as if it might become caressing or wooing with very little provocation. ~~She wondered what tone the he would say "I love you" in, and if he ever had said it to any woman~~ She was at times almost afraid to let herself think these thoughts. They were so vivid that she felt as if the others **must** know what she was thinking.

NOTE Z6: The barrens lay before her in a white moon-splendor, where dozens of little rabbits frisked. Barney, when he liked, could sit down on the edge of the barrens & lure those rabbits right to him by some mysterious sorcery he possessed. Valancy had once ~~seen a squirrel leap from a~~ scrub pine to his shoulder &

sit there chattering to him. It reminded her of John Foster.

It was one of the delights of Valancy's new life that she could read John Foster's books as often and as long as she liked. She could read them in bed if she wanted to. She read them all to Cissy[,] who loved them. She also tried to read them to Abel & Barney[,] who did not love them. Abel was bored & Barney politely refused to listen at all. "Piffle," said Barney. ~~"How can you?" said Valancy. "Listen to this paragraph. It is beautiful —~~ ~~"'She is a rare artist, this old Mother Nature who works for the joy of the working,'[7] & not in any spirit of vain show. This November day the fir woods~~

~~are a symphony of greens & grays, so subtle that you cannot tell where one shade begins to be the other. Gray trunk, green bough, gray-green moss above the white floor. Yet the old gypsy doesn't like unrelieved monotone. She must have a dash of color. See it — a broken, dead fir-bough of a beautiful red-brown swinging among the beards of moss.'[8]~~ ~~"Isn't that beu beautiful?"~~ ~~"Punk," said Barney.~~

7: "For the joy of the working" is from the poem "When Earth's Last Picture is Painted" by Rudyard Kipling (1865–1936).

8: This passage (from Montgomery's essay "The Woods in Winter") is used in later, in Chapter XXXI.

Miranda, ~~slut~~ ~~Valancy~~ wondered drearily if she were
really ~~Miranda~~ Valancy Stirling and if it
were only three weeks since she
had left the ugly old house on
Elm ~~Rose~~ Street. ~~XVI~~ 36

~~XVI~~ XVII

Of ~~course~~ the Stirlings had not ~~left~~
the poor maniac ~~Miranda~~ alone all this time
— a refrained from heroic efforts to
rescue her perishing soul and
reputation. Uncle James came one
day and, finding ~~Miranda~~ Valancy
alone in the kitchen, as he supposed, gave her a terrible talking-
to — told her she was breaking
her mother's heart and disgracing
her family. B7
"But ~~why~~?" said ~~Miranda~~ Valancy. "I'm
doing honest work for honest pay.

XIX

Of course[,] the Stirlings had not left ~~Miranda~~ ^the poor maniac^ alone all this time or refrained from heroic efforts to rescue her perishing soul and reputation. Uncle James[,] ~~NOTE B8~~ NOTE A7 came one day and, finding ~~Miranda~~ Valancy alone in the kitchen, as he supposed, gave her a terrible talking-to—told her she was breaking her mother's heart and disgracing her family.

"But _why_?" said ~~Miranda~~ Valancy ~~NOTE C8~~ NOTE B7. "I'm doing honest work for honest pay. What is there in that that is disgraceful?"

"Don't quibble, ~~Miranda~~ Valancy," said Uncle James solemnly. "This is no fit place for you to be, and you know it ~~NOTE D8~~ NOTE C7 ~~That~~ drunken, blasphemous old scoundrel[—]" =

"Were you by any chance referring to _me_, Mister Stirling[?]," demanded Roaring Abel, suddenly appearing in the ~~back veranda~~ doorway. ~~He had been smoking a peaceful pipe out there.~~ of the back veranda where he had been smoking a peaceful pipe and listening to "old Jim Stirling['] s" ~~tirades~~ tirade with huge enjoyment. His ~~read~~ red beard fairly ~~bristled~~ bristled with indignation and his huge eyebrows quivered. But cowardice was not among James Stirling['] s shortcomings.

"I was. And[,] furthermore[,] I want to tell you that you have acted an iniquitous part in luring this ^weak and^ unfortunate girl away from her home ^and friends^ and I will have you punished yet for it—"

James Stirling got no further. Roaring Abel crossed the kitchen at a bound, caught him by his collar and his trousers[,] and hurled him through the

2: paling = picket fence

NOTE D7: "The next time you come back here," he bellowed, "I'll ~~through~~ throw you through the window—& all the better if the window is shut[!]; Coming here, thinking yourself God to put the world to rights!"

NOTE E7: She had once been afraid of this man's judgment. Now she saw clearly that he was nothing but a rather stupid, little, village tin-god.
Roaring Abel turned with his great broad laugh.
"He'll think of that for years when he wakes up in the night. The Almighty made a ~~mista~~ mistake in making so many Stirlings. But since they are made[,] we've got to reckon with them. Too many to kill out. NOTE R14 NOTE X14
~~But if they come here bothering you I'll shoo 'em off before a cat could lick its ear!~~

NOTE X14: But if they come here bothering you I'll ~~shoo him~~ shoo 'em off before a cat could lick its ear.

3: Montgomery used this little scene in her story "Our Neighbors at the Tansy Patch" (*Canadian Home Magazine*, April 1918). The story was published in *After Many Years: Twenty-one "Long-Lost" Stories by L. M. Montgomery* (Nimbus, 2017).

NOTE F7: She had to own to herself that she was

4: Montgomery did not strike out "She" or "was" in the manuscript even though she wrote them into NOTE F7.

doorway, ^and^ over the garden paling[2] ~~into~~ with as little apparent effort as he might have employed in whisking a troublesome kitten out of the way NOTE L11 NOTE D7. ❡ ~~Miranda~~ Valancy candidly and unashamedly owned to herself that she had seen few more satisfying sights than Uncle James' coat-tails flying out into the asparagus bed. NOTE I11 NOTE L11 NOTE M11 NOTE E7

The next time they sent ~~Mr.~~ ^Dr.^ Stalling. Surely Roaring Abel would not throw him into asparagus beds. ~~M~~Dr. Stalling was not so sure of this & had no great liking for the task. He did not believe ~~Miranda~~ Valancy Stirling was out of her mind. She had always been queer. He, ~~M~~Dr. Stalling, had never been able to understand her. Therefore, beyond doubt, she was queer. She was only just a little queerer than usual now. And ~~M~~Dr. Stalling had his own reasons for disliking Roaring Abel. When ~~M~~Dr. Stalling had first come to Deerwood he had had a liking for long hikes around Mistawis and Muskoka. On one of those occasions he had got lost and after much wandering ~~fell~~ ^had fallen^ in with Roaring Abel with his gun over his shoulder.

~~M~~Dr. Stalling had ~~continued~~ ^contrived^ to ask his question in about the most ~~idiotic~~ ^idiotic^ manner possible. He said, "Can you tell me where I'm going?"

"How the devil should I know where you're going, ^gosling?"^[3] retorted Abel contemptuously. ❡ ~~M~~Dr. Stalling was so enraged that he could not speak for a moment or two and in that moment Abel had disappeared into the woods. ~~M~~Dr. Stalling had eventually found his way home[,] but he had never hankered to encounter Abel Gay again.

Nevertheless he came now to do his duty. ~~Miranda~~ Valancy greeted him with a sinking heart. NOTE F7 She ^~~had to own to herself that she~~^ was[4] terribly afraid of ~~Mr.~~ ^Dr.^ Stalling still. She had a miserable conviction that if he shook his long, bony finger at her and told her to go home[,] she ~~would have to obey.~~ ^dared not disobey.^

"Mr. Gay," said ~~M~~Dr. Stalling politely ^& condescend-
ingly.^[5] "May I see Miss Stirling alone for a few minutes?"

Roaring Abel was a little drunk – just drunk enough
to be excessively polite and very cunning. He had been
on the point of going away when ~~M~~Dr. Stalling arrived[,]
but now he sat down in a corner of the ~~sitting~~ parlor and
folded his arms.

"No, no, m~~in~~ister," he said solemnly. "That wouldn't do
– wouldn't do at all. I've got the reputation of my household to keep up. I've got to ~~tap~~ chaperone this young lady.
Can't have any sparkin' going on here behind my back."

Outraged ~~M~~Dr. Stalling looked so terrible that
~~Miranda~~ Valancy wondered how Abel could endure his
aspect. But Abel was not worried at all.

"D'ye know anything about it, anyway?" he asked
genially.

"About what?"

"Sparking," said Abel coolly.

Poor ~~M~~Dr. Stalling, who had never married because he believed in a celebate[6] clergy, would not notice
this ribald remark. He turned his back on Abel and addressed himself to ~~Miranda~~ Valancy.

"Miss Stirling, I am here in ~~accor~~ response to your
mother's wishes. She begged me to come. I am charged
with some messages from her. Will you –" he ~~lifted~~
^wagged^ his forefinger – "will you hear them?"

"Yes," said ~~Miranda~~ Valancy faintly, eying the forefinger. It had a hypnotic effect on her.

"The first is this. If you will leave this – this –"

"House." Interjected Roaring Abel.[7] ^"H-o-u-s-e.^
"Troubled with an impediment in your speech, ain't you,
Mister?"

"This[8] place and return to your home[,] Mr. James
Stirling will himself pay for a good nurse to come here
and wait on Miss Gay."

Back of her terror ~~Miranda~~ Valancy smiled in secret.
Uncle James must indeed regard the matter as desperate
when he ~~loosened~~ ^would loosen^ his purse[-]strings
like that. At any rate, her clan no longer despised her or
ignored her. She had become important to them.

5: In the published version,
the period after "conde-
scendingly" is replaced
by a comma, and "May"
is lower case.

6: In the published version,
"celebate" is corrected to
"celibate.

7: In the published version,
the period after "House"
is replaced by a comma,
and "Interjected" is
lower case.

8: In the published version,
there is a dash before
"this," which is in lower
case, as Dr. Stalling continues his sentence.

NOTE G7: I made a fair bargain with her[,] & she's free to conclude it when she likes. She gives me meals that stick to my ribs. She don't forget to put salt in the porridge. She never slams doors and when she has nothing to say she don't talk. That's uncanny in a woman, you know, Mister. I'm satisfied. If she isn't she's free to go[.]

NOTE W14: "If any[ ]one does" – Abel's voice was uncannily bland & polite – "I'll spatter the road with her brains."

9: In the published version, "complements" is corrected to "compliments."

10: In the published version, "not" is not in italics.

NOTE H7: When he could not understand a thing he straightway condemned it. Simplicity itself!

NOTE I7: "That's a pretty th little thought," remarked Abel meditatively, as he ground some tobacco up in his hand.
Dr. Stalling ignored him.

NOTE J7: Before that pitiless finger she drooped & wilted visibly.
"She's giving in," thought Roaring Abel. "She'll go with him. Beats all, the power these preacher fellows have over women."
Valancy was on the point of obeying Dr. Stalling

11: Montgomery did not strike out this sentence even though she added it into NOTE J7.

"That's my business, Mister," said Old Abel quietly. "Miss Stirling can go if she pleases[,] or stay if she pleases[.] NOTE F8 NOTE G7 NOTE G7 But no woman comes here in Jim Stirling[']s pay. NOTE W14 If I want a nurse I'll Tell him that with Abel Gay's complements[9]."

"MDr. Stalling, a nurse is not what Cissy needs," said Miranda Valancy earnestly. "She isn't so ill as that, ^yet.^ What she wants is companionship—somebody she knows and likes just to live with her. You can understand that, I'm sure."

"But you are

"I understand that your motive is quite – ahem – commendable." Mr. ^Dr.^ Stalling felt that he was very broad-minded indeed – especially as in his secret soul he did not believe Miranda's Valancy's motive was commendable. He hadn't the least idea what her motive could be ^she was up to^ but he was sure it was not ^her motive^ ^her motive was not^[10] commendable NOTE K11 NOTE H7 "But your first duty is to your mother. She needs you. She implores you to come home – she will forgive everything if you will only come home. NOTE H8 NOTE I7 ❲

"She entreats but I, Miss Stirling["] –" MDr. Stalling remembered that he was an ambassador of Jehovah – "I, command. As your pastor and spiritual guide[,] I command you to come home with me – this very day. ^Get your hat and coat and come now."^

MDr. Stalling shook his finger at Miranda Valancy. NOTE I8 NOTE J7 She Miranda Valancy was on the point of obeying him MDr. Stalling.[11] She must go home with him – and give up. She would lapse back to Doss Stirling again and for the her few remaining days or weeks be the cowed, futite ^futile^ creature she had always been. It was her fate – typified by that relentless, uplifted forefinger. She could no more escape from it than Roaring Abel from his predestination. She eyed it as the fascinated bird eyes the snake. Another moment –

"Fear is the original sin," suddenly said a still, small voice away back – back – back of Miranda's Valancy's consciousness. "Almost all the evil in the world has its origin in the fact that some[ ]one is afraid of something."

~~Miranda had forgotten where she had read the w~~

~~Miranda~~ Valancy stood up. She was still in the clutches of fear[,] but her soul was her own again. She would not be false to that inner voice.

"~~M~~Dr. Stalling," she said slowly. "I do not at present owe <u>any</u> duty to my mother. She is quite well; she has all the assistance ^& companionship^ she requires; she does not need me at all. I <u>am</u> needed here. I am going to stay here."

"There's spunk for you," said Roaring Abel admiringly.

~~M~~Dr. Stalling dropped his forefinger. One could not keep on shaking a finger forever.

"~~Miss Stirling,~~ ~~NOTE J8~~ NOTE K7 ~~do you realize what people will say = what they are~~ saying?"

"I can imagine it," said ~~Miranda~~ Valancy, with a shrug of her shoulders. She was suddenly free of fear again. "I haven't listened to the gossip of Deerwood tea-parties and sewing circles twenty years for nothing. But, ~~M~~Dr. Stalling, it doesn't matter in the least to me what they say—not in the least."

~~M~~Dr. Stalling went away then. A girl who cared nothing for public opinion! ~~With a~~ Over whom sacred family ties had no restraining influence! Who hated her childhood memories!

~~IX~~

Then Cousin Georgina came – on her own initiative, for nobody would have thought it worth while to send her. She found ~~Miranda~~ Valancy alone, weeding the ^little^ vegetable garden she had planted, and she made all the platitudinous pleas she could think of. ~~Miranda~~ Valancy heard her patiently. Cousin Georgiana wasn't such a bad old soul. Then she said,

"And now that you have got all that out of your system, Cousin G.[12] can you tell me how to make creamed codfish so that it will not be as thick as porridge and as salt as the Dead Sea?"

———   ———   ———[13]

"We'll just have to <u>wait</u>," said Uncle Benjamin. "After all, Cissy Gay can't live long. Dr. Marsh tells me she may drop off any day." ~~NOTE F9~~ NOTE L7

NOTE K7: "Miss Stirling, is there <u>nothing</u> that can influence you? Do you remember your childhood days—["]
"Perfectly. And hate them."
"Do you realize what people will say? What they <u>are</u>

12: In the published version, G. is spelled out: Georgiana.

13: Montgomery draws three short lines across the page here; in the published version, asterisks are used to indicate a change of scene.

NOTE L7: Mrs. Frederick wept. It would really have been so much easier to bear if Valancy had died. She could have worn mourning then.

Where she say, paid Valoured
her first week's wages — which he
did promptly; ile bills reducing with
the odors of tobacco and whisky —
Valoured promptly went held there —
work and spent every cent of it. M[?]
She got a pretty beaded, smoke grey crepe dress,
at a bargain sale, a pair of silk
stockings, to match a little twisted
gray hat — with a crimson rose on it.
The passed the house or the street
since — Valoured never ever thought
about. it as "home" — but — over ce-
one. no doubt. her mother was
sitting in the parlour room the
lonely June evening playing solitaire
and cheating. Valoured knew
that Mrs Frederick always cheated. the

XX

When Abel Gay paid ~~Miranda~~ Valancy her first month's wages—which he did promptly, in bills reeking with the odors of tobacco and whisky—~~Miranda~~ Valancy ~~promptly~~ went into Deerwood and spent every cent of it. She got a pretty ~~green~~ ^beaded, smoke gray^ ^green^ crepe[1] dress ~~NOTE Q11~~ NOTE M7 at a bargain sale, a pair of silk stockings, to match, ~~satin slippers with green~~ ^& a little twisted ~~green~~ gray^ hat[3] with a ~~scarlet~~ crimson rose on[4] it. NOTE N7 ❦ She passed the house on Elm Street twice—~~Miranda~~ Valancy never even thought about it as "home"—but saw no one. No doubt her mother was sitting in the ~~parlor~~ room this lovely June evening playing solitaire—and cheating. ~~Miranda~~ Valancy knew that Mrs. ~~George~~ Frederick always cheated. She never lost a game. Most of the people ~~Miranda~~ Valancy met looked at her curiously and passed her with a cool nod. Nobody stopped to speak to her.

~~Miranda~~ Valancy put on her ~~green~~ ^smoke gray^ ^green^ dress when she got home. Then she took it off again. She felt so miserably undressed in its low neck and short sleeves. And that low ^~~crimson shimmering crimson~~^ ~~girdle~~ ^crimson girdle^ around the hips seemed positively indecent. She hung it up in the closet, feeling flatly that she had wasted her money. She would never have the courage to wear that dress. John Foster's ~~arraignment~~ ^arraignment^ of fear had no power to stiffen her against this. In this one thing habit and custom were still all powerful. Yet she sighed as she went down to meet Barney Snaith in her ~~her~~ old snuff brown silk. That ~~green~~ ^smoky^[5] thing had been very becoming—

1: In the published version, "crepe" is given the French spelling, "crêpe," here and throughout.

NOTE M7: with a girdle[2] of crimson beads,

2: girdle = a low, wide sash or belt

3: In the published version, this is changed to "crinkled green hat."

4: In the published version, "on" is changed to "in."

NOTE N7: She even bought a foolish, little, beribboned & belaced nightgown.

5: In the published version, "smoky" is changed back to "green."

127

NOTE O7: in a valley on the edge of "up back"—a spireless, little gray building among the pines, with a few sunken graves & mossy gravestones in the small, paling-encircled, grass-grown square beside it. She liked the minister who preached there. He was so simple & sincere. An old man, who lived in Port Laurence & came out by the lake in a little disappearing propeller boat[6] to give a free service to the people of the small, stony farms back of the hills, who would otherwise never have heard any gospel message.

6: "Disappearing propeller" boats were very popular on Lake Muskoka. They were well-made, relatively inexpensive, and the propeller was designed to be moved up into the boat if it hit a rock or other obstacle in the water, thus saving damage to the propeller. The first ones were built in Port Carling on Lake Muskoka in 1916; they continued to be produced by several different companies until the mid-1950s and are considered highly desirable today by collectors.

7: "Oddly enough" begins a new paragraph in the published version.

she had seen ~~that~~ ^so much^ in her one ashamed glance. Above it her eyes had looked like odd brown jewels and the girdle had ~~made~~ ^given^ her flat figure ~~seem girlish and~~ ^an entirely different appearance.^ She wished she could have left it on. But there were some things John Foster did not know.

~~Next Sunday evening in the little Mennonite ch Free Methodist church over the hill~~

Every Sunday evening Miranda went to the little Free Methodist church NOTE A9 NOTE O7 ~~up on the hill. She liked the old minister who preached there. He was so simple and sincere.~~ ^NOTE K8^ ~~She had liked him when he came to see Cissy.~~ She liked the simple service and the ^fervent^ singing = ~~which was~~ ^surprisingly^ ~~good.~~ ^fervent singing.^ She liked to sit by the open window and look out into the ~~fir~~ pine woods. The congregation was always small. The Free Methodists were few in number, ~~and as they came from stony little farms back of the hill they were~~ poor and generally illiterate. But ~~Miranda~~ Valancy loved those Sunday evenings. For the first time in her life she liked going to church. The rumor reached Deerwood that she had ~~been~~ "turned Free Methodist" and sent Mrs. ~~George~~ Frederick to bed for a day. But ~~Miranda~~ Valancy had not turned anything. She ~~was not interested in creeds. What did they matter to~~ went to the church because she liked it and because in some inexplicable way it did her good. Old Mr. Towers believed exactly what he preached and somehow it made a tremendous difference. Oddly enough,[7] Roaring Abel; ~~who~~ disapproved of her going to the hill church as strongly as Mrs. ~~George~~ Frederick herself could have done. He had "no use for Free Methodists. He was a Presbyterian." But ~~Miranda~~ Valancy went in spite of him.

"We'll hear something worse than that about her soon," Uncle Benjamin predicted gloomily. ~~They did.~~

They did.

~~Miranda~~ Valancy ~~never~~ could ^not^ quite explain[,] even to herself[,] just why she ~~went~~ ^wanted to go^ to that party. It was a dance ["]^up^ back" at Chidley Corners; ~~in the heart of the Muskoka country;~~ and dances at Chidley Corners were not, as a rule, the sort of assemblies ~~which~~ ^where^ well-brought-up young ladies were found. ~~Miranda~~ Valancy knew it was coming off, for Roaring Abel had been engaged as one of the fiddlers. ~~The Chidley Corners knew knew that he would fiddle beautifully until he got too drunk. There would be plenty of liquor there.~~ But the idea of going[8] had never occurred to her until Roaring Abel himself broached it at supper.

"You come with me to the dance," he ordered. "It'll do you good—put some color in your face. You look peaked – you want something to liven you up."

~~Meranda Miranda~~ Valancy found herself suddenly wanting to go. She knew nothing at all of what dances at Chidley Corners were apt to be like. Her idea of dances had been fashioned on the correct affairs that went by that name in Deerwood and Port ____ [9] ^Laurence^. Of course she knew the Corners['] dance wouldn't be ^just^ like them. Much more informal, of course. But so much the more interesting. Why shouldn't she go? Cissy was in a week of apparent health and improvement. She wouldn't mind staying alone in the least. She entreated ~~Miranda~~ Valancy to go if she wanted to. And ~~Miranda~~ Valancy did want to go.

She went to her room to dress. A rage against the snuff-brown silk seized her. Wear that to a party[!]~~?~~ Never. She pulled her ~~green~~ ^green^ crepe from its hanger and put it on feverishly. It was nonsense to feel so – so – naked – just because ~~it had~~ ^her^ neck and arms were bare. That was just her old maidishness. She would not be ridden by it. On went the dress – the slippers. ~~NOTE T11~~ NOTE P7 ❧ If she only had a necklace or something. She wouldn't feel so bare then. She ran down to the garden. There were ~~pansies~~ ^clovers^ there – great ~~purple~~ ^crimson^ things growing in the long grass. ~~Miranda~~ Valancy gathered handfuls of them and strung them on a cord. Fastened about her neck they gave her ^the^ ~~a~~ comfortable sensation of a collar and were oddly becoming. ~~As~~ Another circlet of them went round her hair[,]; ~~NOTE Z11~~ NOTE Q7 ~~Excitement brought NOTE S11 color to her face.~~ She flung on her coat & pulled the little, twisty hat over her hair.

8: In the published version, a new paragraph begins here.

9: Montgomery drew a blank line here to fill in later with her name for the Port.

NOTE P7: It was the first time she had worn a pretty dress since the organdies of her early teens. And they had never made her look like this.[10]

10: In the published version, NOTE P7 is a new paragraph.

NOTE Q7: dressed in the low puffs that became her. Excitement brought those faint pink stains to her face[.]

NOTE R11^7^: "Like a ^green^ moonbeam with a gleam of red in it, if there could be such a thing."

11: "Father" is capitalized in the published version.

NOTE S7: but full of the austere charm of northern woods.

NOTE T7: fringed by aspens that were always quivering with some supernal joy.

12: In the published version, a new paragraph begins here.

"You look so nice and – and – different, dear," said Cissy. "~~Lika a moonbeam R~~" NOTE R7

~~Miranda~~ Valancy stooped to kiss her.

"I don't feel right about leaving you alone, Cissy."

"~~Nonsense.~~ ^Oh,^ I'll be all right. I feel better tonight than I have for a long while. ~~I'd be worried if you didn't go. You never get out~~ = I've been feeling badly to see you ~~sticking~~ ^sticking^ here so closely on my account. I hope you'll have a nice time. I never was at a party at the Corners[,] but I used to go sometimes, long ago, to ~~those~~ dances up back. We always ~~heal~~ had good times. And you needn't be afraid of father[11] being drunk tonight. He never drinks when he engages to play for a party. But – there may be – liquor. What will you do if it gets rough?"

"Nobody would molest me."

^"Not seriously, I suppose.^ ~~"Oh, no.~~ Father would see to that. But it <u>might</u> be noisy and – and unpleasant."

"I won't mind. I'm only going as a looker-on. I don't expect to dance. I just want to <u>see</u> what a party up back is like. I've never seen anything except decorous Deerwood."

Cissy smiled rather dubiously. She knew much better than ~~Miranda~~ Valancy what a party "up back" might be like if there ~~was~~ should be liquor. But again there mightn't be. ~~And in any case Cissy knew Roaring Abel would see that Miranda wasn't annoyed.~~

"I hope you'll enjoy it, dear," ^Ce^ she repeated.

~~Miranda~~ Valancy enjoyed the drive there. They went early, for it was ~~twelve miles to Chidley Corners, and they had to go in~~ Abel's old, ragged top-buggy ~~behind his~~. The road was rough and rocky, ~~as~~ ^like^ most ~~Mistawis~~ ^Muskoka^ roads[,] ~~were but~~ NOTE V11 NOTE S7 It ~~would~~ ^wound^ through beautiful, ~~pine woods~~ ^growths of pine^ ^purring pines^ that were ~~places~~ ^ranks^ ^ranks^ of enchantment in the June sunset, and over the curious jade-green rivers of ~~Mistawis~~ ^Muskoka^ NOTE ~~X11~~ NOTE T7. Roaring Abel[12] was excellent company, too. He knew all the stories and legends of the wild, beautiful "up back," and he told them to ~~Miranda~~ Valancy as they drove along. ~~Miranda~~ Valancy had several ^fits of^ inward ~~fits~~ laughter over what Uncle Ben^jamin^ and Aunt Wellington[,] et al.[,] would feel & think & say if they saw her driving with Roaring Abel in that terrible buggy to a dance at Chidley Corners.

At first the dance was quiet enough[,] and ~~Miranda~~ Valancy was amused and entertained. She even danced twice herself[,] with a couple of ^nice^ "up back" boys who danced beautifully and told her she did, too. ~~NOTE A12~~ NOTE U7 ⊄ The big room was decorated with pine and fir boughs, & lighted by Chinese lanterns. The floor was waxed[,] and Roaring Abel's NOTE V7 ~~music was worked magic.~~ The ["]up back["] girls were pretty and prettily dressed. ~~Miranda~~ Valancy thought it the nicest party she had ever attended. ⊄ By eleven o'clock she had changed her mind. A new crowd had arrived—a crowd unmistakably drunk. Whisky began to circulate freely. Very soon almost all the men were partly drunk. ~~NOTE U11~~ NOTE W7 The room grew noisy and reeking. Quarrels started up here and there. Bad language and obscene songs were heard. The girls, swung rudely in the dances, became dishevelled and tawdry. ~~Miranda,~~ Valancy, ~~standing~~ alone in her corner, was feeling disgusted and repentant. Why had she ever come to such a place? Freedom and independence ~~was~~ ^were^ all very well[,] but one should not be a little fool. She might have known what it would be like – she might have taken warning ~~by~~ ^from^ Cissy's guarded sentences. Her head was aching – she was sick of the whole thing. But what could she do? She must stay to the end. Abel could not leave till then. And that would probably be not till three or four in the morning.

The ~~arrival of the~~ new influx of boys had left the girls far in the minority & partners were scarce. ~~Miranda~~ Valancy was pestered with invitations to dance. She refused them all shortly[,] and some of her refusals were not well taken. There were muttered oaths and sullen looks. Across the room she saw a group of the strangers talking together and glancing ~~across~~ ^meaningly^ at her. ~~She became nervous~~ What were they plotting?

NOTE U7: ⊄Another complement[13] came her way—not a very subtle one, perhaps, but Valancy had had too few complements in her life to be over-nice on that point. She overheard two of the "up back" young men talking about her in the dark "lean-to" behind her.

"Know who that girl in green is?"

"Nope. Guess she's from out front. The Port, maybe. Got a stylish look to her."

"No beaut but cute-looking, I'll say. ['] Jever see such eyes?"

13: In the published version, "complement" and "complements" are corrected to "compliment" and "compliments."

NOTE V7: fiddle, purring under his skilled touch, worked magic.

NOTE W7: Those in the porch and outside around the door began howling "come-all-ye's" & continued to howl them.[14]

14: "Come, all ye" was a way of saying "gather around" or "come on in." Many street songs and ballads began with the phrase "Come, all ye [young men, sailors, etc.]." The raucous crowd may have been singing (or "howling") some of those ballads.

15: In the published version, "of" is changed to "for."

16: In the published version, "The next moment" does not begin a new paragraph but continues the previous one.

It was at this moment that she saw, looking Barney Snaith looking in over the ^heads of the^ crowd at the doorway. Miranda Valancy had two distan distinct convictions—one was that she was quite safe now; the other was that this was why she had wanted to come to the dance. She had not looked her motive in the face ^It had been such an absurd hope that she had not recognized it^ before[,] but now she knew she had come because of the possibility that Barney might be there, too. Perhaps She thought that perhaps she ought to be ashamed of[15] this[,] but she wasn't. After her feeling of relief her next feeling was one of anger ^annoyance^ with Barney for coming there unshaved. Surely he might have enough self-respect to groom himself up decently when he went to a party. There he was, bareheaded, stu bristly[-] chinned ^chinned,^ in his old trousers and his blue homespun shirt. Not even a coat. Miranda Valancy could have shaken him in her fury. ^anger.^ No wonder people believed everything bad of him.

But she was not afraid any longer. One of the whispering group left his comrades and came across the room to her, through the whirling couples that now filled it uncomfortably. He was a tall, broad-shouldered fellow, not ill dressed or ill-looking but unmistakeably half drunk. He asked Miranda Valancy to dance. Miranda Valancy declined coolly ^civilly.^ His face turned livid. He caught threw his arm about her and pulled her to him. His hot, whisky whiskied breath burned her face.

"We won't have fine-lady airs here, my girl. If you ain't too good to come here you ain't too good to dance with me ^us^. Me and my pals have been watching you. You've got to give us each a turn, and a kiss to boot."

Miranda Valancy tried desperately ^& vainly^ to free herself. She was being dragged out among ^into^ the maze of shouting, stamping, yelling dancers.

The next moment[16] the man who held her went staggering across the room from a neatly planted blow on the jaw, knocking down whirling couples as he went. Miranda Valancy felt her arm grasped.

"This way – quick," said Barney Snaith. He swung her out through the ^open^ window behind them, ~~from which the whole~~ vaulted lightly over the sill and caught her hand.

"Quick – we must run for it—they'll be after us."

~~Miranda~~ Valancy ran as she had never run before, clinging tight to Barney's hand, wondering why she did not drop dead in such a mad scamper. Suppose she did! What a scandal it would make for her poor people. For the first time ~~Miranda~~ Valancy felt a little sorry for them. Also[,] she felt glad that she had escaped from that horrible row. Also, glad that she was holding tight to Barney's hand. Her feelings were badly mixed and she had never had so many in such a brief time in her life.

They finally reached a quiet corner ~~and~~ in the pine woods. The ~~pursut~~ pursuit had taken a different direction and the whoops and yells behind them were growing faint. ~~Miranda~~ Valancy, out of breath, with a crazily beating heart, collapsed on the trunk of a fallen pine.

"Thanks," she gasped.

"What a goose you were to come to such a place[!];" said Barney.

"I – didn't – know – it – would – be – like this," protested ~~Miranda~~ Valancy.

"You should have known. Chidley Corners!"

"It – was – just – a name – to me."

~~Miranda~~ Valancy knew Barney could not realize how ignorant she was of the regions ["]up back.["] She had lived in Deerwood all her life and of course he supposed she knew. He didn't know how she had been brought up. There was no use trying to explain.

"When I dropped[17] in at Abel's this evening and Cissy told me you'd come here I was amazed. And downright scared. Cissy told me she was worried about you but hadn't liked to say anything to dissuade you for fear you'd think she was thinking selfishly about herself. So I came on up here instead of going to Deerwood."

~~Miranda~~ Valancy felt a sudden delightful glow irradiating soul and body under the dark pines. So he had actually come up to look after her.

17: In the published version, "dropped" is changed to "drifted."

NOTE X7: ❨And yet she was enjoying herself – was full of a strange exultation – ~~but~~ bumping over that rough road beside Barney Snaith. The big trees shot by them. The tall mulleins stood up along the road in stiff, orderly ranks like companies of soldiers. The thistles looked like drunken fairies or tipsy elves as their car-lights flashed[18] over them. This was the first time she had ever been in a car. After all, she liked it. She was not in the least afraid[,] with Barney at the wheel. Her spirits rose rapidly as they tore along. She ceased to feel ashamed. She ceased to feel anything except that she was part of a comet rushing gloriously through the night of space[.]

18: In the published version, "flashed" is changed to "passed."

"As soon as they stop ~~looking~~ ^hunting^ for us we'll sneak around to the ~~Mistawis~~ ^Muskoka^ road. I left Lady Jane down there. I'll take you home. I suppose you've had enough of your party."

"Quite," said ~~Miranda~~ Valancy meekly. The first half of the way home neither of them said anything. It would not have been much use. Lady Jane made so much noise they could not have heard each other. Anyway, ~~Miranda~~ Valancy did not feel conversationally inclined. She was ashamed of the whole affair – ashamed of her folly in going – ashamed of being found in such a place by Barney Snaith. By Barney Snaith, reputed jail-breaker, infidel, forger and defaulter. ~~Miranda's~~ Valancy's lips twitched in the darkness as she thought of it. But she <u>was</u> ashamed.

~~NOTE L8~~ NOTE X7

All at once, just where the pine woods frayed out to the scrub barrens, Lady Jane became quiet—too quiet. Lady Jane slowed down quietly – and stopped.

Barney uttered an aghast exclamation. Got out. Investigated. Came apologetically back.

"I'm a doddering idiot. Out of gas." ~~he said.~~ I knew I was short when I left home but I meant to fill up in Deerwood. Then I forgot all about it in my hurry to get to the Corners."

"What can we do?" ~~said Miranda~~ ^asked Valancy^ coolly.

"I don't know. There's no gas nearer than Deerwood, nine miles away. And I don't dare leave you here alone. There's are always tramps on this road – and some of those crazy fools back at the Corners may come straggling along ~~presently~~ ^presently^. There were boys there from the Port. As far as I can see[,] the best thing to do is for us just to sit patiently here until some car comes along and lends us enough gas to get to Roaring Abel's with."

"Well, what's the matter with that[?]," said ~~Miranda.~~ Valancy.

"We may have to sit here all night," said Barney.

"I don't mind," said ~~Miranda~~ Valancy.

Barney gave a short laugh.

"If you don't[,]¹⁹ I needn't. I haven't any reputation to lose."

"Nor I," said ~~Miranda~~ Valancy comfortably.

"If you don't I will duck. I haven't
any reputation to lose."
"Nor I." ~~~~~ Miranda comfortable.

XIX

"We'll just set here," said Barney,
"and if we think of anything
worth while saying we will say
it. Otherwise, not. Don't imagine
you're bound to talk to me."

~~They sat in silence for a long while.~~
Miranda was perfectly happy. She
knew now quite well that she
~~loved Barney.~~ She must always have
loved him ever since he had
~~insulted~~ ~~at~~ her from under his car
in the mountains road a year ago.
~~It don't matter~~ what he was or
what he had done. She loved him.
~~He was all the world to her.~~ She need

XXI

"We'll just sit here," said Barney, "and if we think of anything worth while saying ~~it~~ we'll say it. Otherwise, not. Don't imagine you're bound to talk to me." ~~NOTE K12~~ NOTE Y7

~~They sat in silence for a long while.~~ ^XX XX^ ~~Miranda was perfectly happy. She knew now quite well that she loved Barney.~~ NOTE F12 ~~must always have loved him ever since he had twinkled at her from under his car on the Mistawis road a year ago. It didn't matter~~ what it was or what he had done. She loved him. NOTE G17?

NOTE Y7: "John Foster says," quoted ~~Miranda~~ Valancy, ="'If you can sit in silence with a person for half an hour & yet be entirely comfortable, you & that person can be friends. If you cannot, friends you'll never be & you need not waste time in trying.'"

"Evidently John Foster says a sensible thing once in a while," conceded Barney.

They sat in silence for a long while. Little rabbits hopped across the road. Once or twice an owl laughed out delightfully. The road beyond them was fringed with the woven shadow lace of trees. Away off to the southwest the sky was full of silvery little cirrus clouds above the spot where Barney's island must be.

Valancy was perfectly happy. Some things dawn on you slowly. Some things come by lightning flashes. Valancy had had a lightning flash.

She knew quite well now that she loved Barney. Yesterday she had been all her own. Now she was this man's. Yet he had done nothing – said nothing. He had not even looked at her as a woman. But that didn't matter. Nor did it matter what he was or what he had done. She loved him without any reservations. Everything in her went out wholly to him. She had no wish to stifle or disown her love. She seemed to be his so absolutely that thought apart from him – thought in which he did not predominate [–] was an ~~impossiblity~~ impossibility. ~~She surrendered herself utterly to the charm of the moment.~~

She had realized, ~~that she love~~ quite simply and fully, that she loved him, in the moment when he was leaning on the car door, explaining that Lady Jane had no ~~glas~~ gas. She had looked deep into his eyes in the moonlight and had known. In just that infinitesimal space of time everything was changed. Old things passed away & all things became new.[1]

She was no longer unimportant, little, old-maid Valancy Stirling. She was a woman, full of love & therefore rich & significant‚—justified to herself. Life was no longer empty and futile and death could cheat her of nothing. Love had cast out her last fear.

Love! What a searing, torturing, intolerably sweet thing it was – this possession of body, soul & mind! With something at its core as fine & remote & purely & ~~purely~~ spiritual as the tiny blue spark in the heart of the unbreakable diamond. No dream had ever been like this. She was no longer solitary. She was one of a vast sisterhood—all the women who had ever loved in the world.

Barney need

1: From 2 Corinthians 5:17: "Old things have passed away, behold all things have become new."

137

~~He was all the world to her.~~ ~~He need~~
^Barney need^ never know it – though she would not
^in the least^ have minded his knowing. ~~it in the least.~~
But <u>she</u> knew it and it made a tremendous difference to
her. Just to love! – ~~s~~She did not ask to be loved. It was
rapture enough just to sit there beside him in silence,
alone in the summer night ~~with the wind~~ in the white
splendor of moonshine, with the wind blowing down
on them out of the pine woods. ~~NOTE Q8~~ NOTE Z7 What a
<mark>tang</mark>, what a zip it had! ~~What a message from vast, inter-
minable spaces of freedom!~~ What a magic of adventure!
~~Miranda~~ Valancy felt as if she had exchanged her shop[-]
worn soul for a fresh one[,] fire-new from the ~~workshop~~
workshop of the gods. As far back as she could look[,]
life had been dull – colorless – savorless. Now she had
come to a little patch of violets, purple & fragrant – hers
for the plucking. ~~NOTE U8~~ NOTE A8

"Ever dream of ballooning?" said Barney suddenly.

"No," said ~~Miranda.~~ Valancy.

"I do – often. Dream of sailing through the clouds
– seeing the glories of sunset – spending hours in the
midst of a terrific storm with lightning playing above and
below you – skimming above a silver cloud floor under a
full moon—wonderful!"

"It does sound so," said ~~Miranda~~ Valancy. "I've stayed
on earth in my dreams."

She told him about her Blue Castle. It was so easy to
tell Barney things. One felt he understood everything—
even the things you didn't tell him. And then she told
him a little of her existence before she came to Roaring
Abel's. She wanted him to see why she had gone to the
~~Corners' up back~~ dance ["]up back.["]

"You see – I've never had any real life," she said. "I've
just – breathed~~.~~ ^Every door has always been shut to
me[.]"^

"But you're ^still^ young," ~~yet,~~ said Barney.

"Oh, I know. Yes, I'm ~~young~~ 'still young' – but that's
so different from <u>young</u>," said ~~Miranda~~ Valancy bitterly.
For a moment she was tempted to tell Barney why her
years had nothing to do with her future, but she did not.

2: NOTES M12 and M8 do not belong here; they may have been older nota-tions, written before Montgomery reworked her Notes section. Montgomery did not cross the references out although the rest of the paragraph was crossed out. The circled phrase—"what it was or what he had done. She loved him."—was included in NOTE Y7 but was not crossed out here.

~~NOTE F12: The soft radiance &splendor of the white moon-world outside,~~

NOTE Z7: She had always envied the wind. So free. Blowing where it listed. Through the hills. Over the lakes.

NOTE A8: No matter who or what had been in Barney's past—no mat-ter who or what might be in his future—no one else could ever have this perfect hour. She surrendered herself utterly to the charm of the moment.

She was not going to think of death to-night.

"Though I never was really young," she went on – "until tonight" she added in her heart. "I never had a life like other girls. You couldn't understand. ~~NOTE B4~~ NOTE B8 ~~I = I got tired of being a mere vegetable.~~ That's why I came to ~~Mr.~~ keep house for Mr. Gay" and look after Cissy."

"And I suppose your people thought ~~ch~~ you'd gone mad."

"They did – and do – literally," said ~~Miranda~~ Valancy. "But it's a comfort to them. They'd rather believe me mad than bad~~, you know~~. There's no other alternative. But I've been <u>living</u> since I came to Mr. Gay's. It's been a delightful experience. I suppose I'll pay for it when I ^have to^ go back – but I'll have <u>had</u> it."

"That's true," said Barney. "If you ~~busy~~ buy your experience it's your own. So it's no matter how much you pay for it. Somebody else's experience can never be yours. Well, it's a funny old world."

"Do you think it really is old?" asked ~~Miranda~~ Valancy ^dreamily.^ I never ~~can~~ believe <u>that</u> in ~~spring,~~ June. It seems so young tonight – somehow. In that quivering moonlight – like a young, white girl – waiting."

"Moonlight here on the verge of up back is different from moonlight anywhere else," ~~said~~ ^agreed^ Barney. "It always makes me feel so clean, somehow—body and soul. And of course the age of gold always comes back in spring."[3]

It was two o'clock now.[4] A dragon of black cloud ate up the moon. The spring air grew chill—~~Miranda~~ Valancy shivered. Barney reached back into the innards of Lady Jane and clawed up an old, tobacco-scented overcoat.

"Put that on," he ordered.

"Don't you want it yourself?" protested ~~Miranda.~~ Valancy.

"No. I'm not going to have you catching cold on my hands."

~~NOTE R8~~ NOTE C8

❡ "You've sneezed three times. No use winding up your 'experience' up back with grippe or pneumonia."

NOTE B8: Why[,]"—she had a desperate desire that Barney should know the worst about her—
"I didn't even love my mother. Isn't it awful that I don't love my mother?"
"Rather awful—for her," said Barney drily.
"Oh, she didn't know it. She took my love for granted. And I wasn't any use or comfort to her or anybody. I was just a – a – vegetable. And I got tired of it."

3: This appears to be an allusion to a line from "The Hymn," a poem by John Milton (1608–1674): "Time will run back, and fetch the age of gold."

4: In the published version, this was written as "ten o'clock," which has led to some confusion about the passage of time. Barney and Valancy left the dance sometime after eleven o'clock.

NOTE C8: "Oh, I won't catch cold. I haven't had a cold since I came to Mr. Gay's – though I've done the foolishest things. It's funny, too—I used to have them all the time. I feel so selfish taking your coat.["]

5: The line drawn under "Herbert" is not for emphasis but indicates a blank that Montgomery filled in later.

NOTE D8: The pompous, bewhiskered old humbug!

6: Again, this was written as "ten o'clock" in the published version.

NOTE E8: I never satisfy curiosity.["]

He pulled it up tight about her throat and buttoned it on her. ~~Miranda~~ Valancy submitted with secret delight. How nice it was to have some[ ]one look after you so! She snuggled down into the tobaccoey folds and wished the night could last forever.

Ten minutes later a car swooped down on them from ["]up back.["] Barney sprang from Lady Jane and waved his hand. The car came to a stop beside ~~Lady Jane~~ ^them^. ~~The moon~~ ~~Miranda~~ Valancy saw Uncle Wellington and Olive gazing at her in horror from it.

So Uncle Wellington had got a car[!]. And he must have been spending the evening up at Mistawis with Cousin <u>Herbert</u>.[5] ~~Miranda~~ Valancy almost laughed aloud at the expressions on ~~their~~ ^his^ face~~s~~ as ~~they~~ ^he^ recognized her. ~~NOTE J12~~ NOTE D8

"Can you let me have enough gas to take me to Deerwood?" Barney was asking ^politely.^ But Uncle Wellington was not attending to him.

"~~Miranda~~ Valancy, how came you <u>here</u>?" – ~~with~~ he said sternly.

"By chance or God's grace," said ~~Miranda.~~ Valancy.

~~She had once been afraid of this man's judgment.~~ ~~Now she saw ^clearly^ that he was only a stupid little~~ ^old^ ~~village tin god.~~

"With this jail[-]bird – at two o'clock at night," said Uncle Wellington.[6]

~~Miranda~~ Valancy turned to Barney. The moon had ~~bues~~ escaped from its dragon and in its light her eyes were full of deviltry,

"<u>Are</u> you a jail[-]bird?"

"Does it matter?" said Barney, ^gleams of fun in <u>his</u> eyes.^

"Not to me. I only asked out of curiosity," countered ~~Miranda~~ Valancy.

"Then I won't tell you. ~~NOTE G12~~ NOTE E8 He turned to Uncle Wellington and his voice changed subtly.

"Mr. Stirling, I asked you if you could let me have some gas. If you can, well and good. If not[,] we are only delaying you unnecessarily."

Uncle Wellington was in a horrible dilemma. To give gas to this shameless pair! But not to give it to them! To go away and leave them there in the Mistawis woods— until daylight, likely. It was better to give it to them and let them get out of sight before any[ ]one else saw them.

"Got anything to get gas in?" he grunted sulkily.

Barney produced a two[-]gallon measure from Lady Jane. The two men went to the rear of the Stirling car and began manipulating the tap. ~~Miranda~~ Valancy stole sly glances at Olive over the collar of ~~her~~ Barney's coat. Olive was sitting, ~~grimly~~ grimly staring straight ahead with an outraged expression ~~NOTE O8~~ NOTE F8 ❡ ~~Miranda~~ Valancy could not resist temptation. She leaned forward.

"Olive, does it hurt?"

Olive ~~bit. = coldly, stiffly.~~ ^bit – stiffly.^

"Does _what_ hurt?"

"Looking like that."

For a moment Olive resolved she would take no ^further^ notice of ~~Miranda~~ Valancy. Then duty came uppermost. She must not miss the opportunity.

"~~Miranda~~ ^Doss^," she implored, leaning forward also, "won't you come home – come home tonight?"

^~~Miranda~~ Valancy yawned.^

"You sound like a ~~revival meeting~~ revival meeting," ~~said Miranda~~ ^she said^. "You really do."

"If you will come back—"

"All will be forgiven?"

"Yes," said Olive eagerly. Wouldn't it be splendid if _she_ could induce the prodigal daughter to return? "We'll never cast it up to you ~~NOTE N13~~ NOTE G8 ~~Miranda,~~ ^Doss^ ^Doss^ ~~I can't believe you're a bad = I've always said "You couldn't be bad =~~"

"I don't believe I can be," said ~~Miranda~~ Valancy. "I'm afraid I'm hopelessly proper. I've been sitting here for three hours with Barney Snaith and he hasn't even tried to kiss me. I wouldn't have minded if he had, Olive."

~~Miranda~~ Valancy was still leaning forward. Her little hat with its crimson rose was tilted down over one eye. Olive stared. In the moonlight ~~Miranda's~~ Valancy's eyes – ~~Miranda's~~ Valancy's smile – what had happened

NOTE F8: She did not mean to take any notice of Valancy. Olive had her own secret reasons for feeling outraged. Cecil had been in Deerwood lately & of course had heard all about Valancy. He agreed that her mind was deranged & was exceedingly anxious to find out from whence the derangement had been inherited. It was a serious thing to have in the family – a very serious thing. One had to think of one's – descendants.

"She got it from the Barracloughs" said Olive positively. "There's nothing like that in the Stirlings – nothing!"

"I hope not – I certainly hope not," Cecil had responded dubiously. "But then – to go out as a servant – for that is what it practically amounts to. Your cousin!"

Poor Olive felt the implication. The Port Laurence Prices were not accustomed to ally themselves with families whose members "worked out."

NOTE G8: Doss, there are nights when I cannot sleep for thinking of you."

"And me having the time of my life," said Valancy, laughing.

"Doss, I can't believe you're bad. I've always said you couldn't be bad[-]" =

NOTE H8: – but ~~alluring,~~ provocative, fascinat-ing—yes, abominably so.

7: Seventy cents in 1925 would be about $12.04 today.

NOTE I8: He wanted to give Snaith a piece of his mind[,] but dared not. Who knew what the creature might do if provoked! No doubt he carried firearms. Uncle Wellington looked indecisively at Valancy.

NOTE J8: "The little hussy! The shameless little hussy!" said Uncle Wellington.

to ~~Miranda~~ Valancy! She looked – not pretty – Doss couldn't be pretty ^{~~NOTE H12~~ NOTE H8} – ~~but, fascinating – yes, horribly so.~~ Olive drew back. It was beneath her dignity to say more. After all, ~~Miranda~~ Valancy must be both mad <u>and</u> bad.

"Thanks – that's enough," said Barney behind the car. "Much obliged, Mr. Stirling. Two gallons. ~~Heres – no, I've only got fifty cents. Miss Stirling, have can you by~~ – seventy cents.[7] Thank you."

Uncle Wellington climbed foolishly and feebly into his car[.] ^{~~NOTE N8~~ NOTE I8} ~~He looked full~~ ^indecisively^ at ~~Miranda Valancy,.~~ bBut ~~Miranda~~ Valancy had turned her back on him and was watching Barney pour the gas into Lady Jane's maw.

"Drive on," said Olive decisively. "There's no use in waiting here. Let me tell you what she said to me." ^{~~NOTE J12~~ NOTE J8}

-148-

"Come on", said Alexie decisively.
"There's no use in waiting here.
Let us tell for what she said it
was" just j t

XX

The next thing the Sterling
heard was that Miranda Valancy
had been seen with Barney
finally at a movie theatre
Port —   and   movie in
Port — and   after it al—
supper in a Chinese restaurant
there. This was quite true — and
no one was more surprised al—
it than Miranda Valancy herself. Barney
had come along in   Lady Jane
one   sunlight and told Miranda Valancy
unceremoniously a drive to top in.
if she wanted

"I'm going to the Port". Will you

XXII

The next thing the Stirlings heard was that ~~Miranda~~ Valancy had been seen with Barney Snaith ~~at a noon movie~~ ^in a movie theatre^ in Port ___ [1] ^Laurence^ and ~~later on~~ ^after it^ at supper in a Chinese restaurant there. This was quite true—and no one was more surprised at it than ~~Miranda~~ Valancy herself. Barney had come along in Lady Jane ~~one~~ ^one dim^ at twilight and told ~~Miranda~~ Valancy ^unceremoniously^ if she wanted a drive to hop in.

"I'm going to the Port. Will you go there with me?" ❡His eyes were teasing and there was a bit of defiance in his ~~wo~~ voice. ~~Miranda~~ Valancy, who did not conceal from herself that she would have gone anywhere with him to any place, ~~stepped into Lady Jane~~ ^"hopped in"^ without more ado.

They tore[2] into and through Deerwood. Mrs. ~~George~~ Frederick and Cousin ~~Amelia~~ Stickles, taking a little air on the veranda, saw them whirl by in a cloud of dust and ~~mul~~ mutely sought comfort in each other's eyes. NOTE K8 ~~Miranda~~ NOTE J19 ~~was hatless and her hair was flowing~~ ^wildly^ ~~round her face.~~ NOTE S8 She wore a low-necked dress and her arms were bare. That Snaith creature was in his shirt sleeves, smoking a pipe. They were going at the rate of ~~40~~ ^forty^ miles an hour ^—sixty ~~= 60~~, Cousin Stickles averred.^ Lady Jane could hit the pike when she wanted to. ~~Miranda~~ Valancy waved her hand gaily to her relatives. ~~as she~~ ^they^ ~~passed~~ NOTE O12 NOTE L8

"Was it for this," ~~demanded Mrs. George~~ ^she demanded^ in hollow tones, "that I suffered the pangs of motherhood?"

1: Again, Montgomery drew a blank line here to fill in later with her name for "the Port."

2: In the published version, "They tore" does not start a new paragraph but continues the previous one.

NOTE K8: Valancy, who in some dim; pre-existence, had been afraid of a car[,] was hatless & her hair was blowing wildly round her face. She would certainly come down with bronchitis – and die at Roaring Abel's.

NOTE L8: As for Mrs. Frederick she was wishing she knew how to go into hysterics.

"I will <u>not</u> believe," said Cousin Stickles solemnly, "that our prayers will not yet be answered." ~~NOTE R12~~
~~NOTE R12~~ NOTE M8

Lady Jane flew over the fifteen miles between Deerwood and the Port – through the Port. The way Barney went past traffic policeman[3] was not holy. NOTE N8 ~~Miranda~~ Valancy was crazy with the delight of speeding. Was it possible she had ever been afraid of a car? ~~NOTE P8~~ NOTE O8

They went to the movie—~~Miranda~~ Valancy had never been to a movie. And then, ~~NOTE P12~~ NOTE P8 they went and had fried chicken ^—unbelievably delicious—^ in the Chinese restaurant. After which they rattled home again, leaving a ~~most terrible tale~~ ^devastating trail^ of scandal behind them. Mrs. ~~George~~ Frederick gave up going to church ~~at all.~~ ^altogether.^ She could not endure her friends' pitying glances and questions. But Cousin Stickles went every Sunday. She said they had been given a cross to bear.

NOTE M8: "Who – <u>who</u> will protect that unfortunate girl when I am gone?" moaned Mrs. Frederick.
   As for Valancy, she was wondering if it could really be only a few weeks since she had sat there with them on that verandah. Hating the rubber[-]plant. Pestered with teasing questions like black flies. Always thinking of appearances. Cowed because of Aunt Wellington's teaspoons & Uncle Benjamin's money. Poverty stricken. Afraid of everybody. Envying Olive. A slave to moth-eaten traditions, nothing to hope for ~~or expect.~~
   And now every day was a gay adventure.

3: "Policeman" is changed to "policemen" in the published version.

NOTE N8: The lights were beginning to twinkle out like stars in the clear, lemon-hued twilight air. This was the only time Valancy ever really liked ~~Port Law~~ the town. And she

NOTE O8: She was perfectly happy, riding beside Barney. Not that she deluded herself into thinking ~~she~~ it had any significance. She knew quite well that Barney had asked her to go on the impulse of the moment—an impulse ~~bourn~~ born of a feeling of pity for her & her starved little dreams. She was looking tired after a wakeful night with a heart attack, followed by a busy day. She had so little fun. He'd give her an outing for once. Besides, Abel was in the kitchen, at the point of ~~dunk~~ drunkenness where he was declaring he did not believe in God & beginning to sing ribald songs. It was just as well she should be out of the way for awhile. Barney knew Roaring Abel's repertoire.

NOTE P8: finding a nice hunger upon them,

XXIII

On one of Cissy's wakeful nights, she told ~~Mira Miranda~~ Valancy her poor little story. They were sitting by the open window. Cissy could not get her breath lying down that night. An inglorious gibbous moon was hanging over the wooded hills and in its spectral light Cissy looked frail and lovely and incredibly young. A child. It did not seem possible that she could have lived through all the passion and pain and shame of her story.

"He was stopping at the hotel across the lake. He used to come ~~come~~ over in his canoe at night—we met in the pines down the shore. He was a young college student – his father was a rich man in Toronto. Oh, ~~Miranda~~ Valancy, I didn't mean to be bad – I didn't, indeed. But I loved him so – I love him yet – I'll always love him. And I – didn't know – some things. I didn't – understand. Then his father came and took him away. And – after a little – I found out – oh, ~~Miranda~~ Valancy – I was so frightened. I didn't know what to do." I wrote him – and he came. He – he said he would marry me, ~~Miranda.~~" Valancy."

"And why – and why?" –

"Oh, ~~Miranda,~~ Valancy, he didn't love me any more. I saw that at a glance. He – he was just offering to marry me because he thought he ought to – because he was sorry for me. He wasn't bad – but he was so young – and what was I that he should keep on loving me?"

"Never mind making excuses for him," said ~~Miranda~~ Valancy, a bit shortly. "So you wouldn't marry him?"

"I couldn't – not when he didn't love me anymore. Somehow—I can't explain—it seemed a worse thing to do than – the other. He – he argued a little – but he went away. Do you think I did right, ~~Miranda?~~ Valancy?"

"Yes, I do~~, said Miranda.~~ ^You^ did right. But he—"

"Don't blame him, dear. Please don't. Let's not talk about him at all. There's no need. I wanted to tell you how it was – I didn't want you to think me bad –"

"I never did~~, anyhow,~~" ^think so."^ ~~said Miranda.~~

"Yes, I felt that – whenever you came. Oh, ~~Miranda~~ Valancy, what you've been to me! I can never tell you – but God will bless you for it. I know He will – ~~"~~['] with what measure ye mete.[']"[1]

Cissy sobbed for a few minutes in ~~Miranda's~~ Valancy's arms. Then she wiped her eyes.

"Well, that's almost all. I came home. I wasn't really so very unhappy. I suppose I should have been – but I wasn't. Father wasn't hard on me. And my baby was so sweet while he lived. I was even happy—I loved him so much, the dear little thing. He was so sweet, ~~Miranda~~ Valancy – with such lovely ~~gray~~ ^blue^ eyes – ~~like his father~~ – and little rings of pale gold hair like silk floss – and tiny dimpled hands[.]" – ~~NOTE D9~~ NOTE Q8

"I know," said ~~Miranda,~~ Valancy, ~~winacing~~ ^wincing.^ "I know – a woman ~~always~~ ~~dreams~~" = knows – and dreams[—]" =

"And he was all mine. Nobody else had any claim on him. When he died, oh, ~~Miranda,~~ Valancy. I thought I must die too – I didn't see how anybody could endure such anguish and live. To see his dear little eyes ~~NOTE W12~~ NOTE R8 ~~shut forever = to miss his warm little body lying~~ ^nestled^ ~~against mine at night.~~ ~~NOTE V12~~ It was so awful for the first year – after that ^it was a little easier[,]^ one didn't keep thinking 'this day last year' – but I was so glad when I found out I was dying."

"'Who could endure life if it were not for the hope of death?'" ~~mumerd Miranda~~ ^murmured Valancy^ softly— it was ^of course^ a quotation from some book of John Foster's.

"I'm glad I've told you all about it," sighed Cissy. "I wanted you to know."

Side notes (left margin):

1: From Mark 4:24 and Matthew 7:2: "With what measure ye mete, it shall be measured to you."

NOTE Q8: I used to bite its satin-smooth little face all over – softly, so as not to hurt it, you know –"

NOTE R8: and know he would never open them again – to miss his warm little body nestled against mine at night & think of him sleeping alone & cold, his wee face under the hard frozen earth.

Cissy died ~~three~~ ^a few^ nights after that. Roaring Abel was away. When ~~Miranda~~ Valancy saw the change that had come over Cissy's face she wanted to telephone for the doctor. But Cissy wouldn't let her.

"~~Miranda,~~ Valancy, why should you? He ~~could~~ ^can^ do nothing for me. I've known for several days that – this – was near. Let me die, in peace, dear – just holding your hand. Oh, I'm so glad you're here. Tell father good-bye for me. He's always been as good to me as he knew how – and Barney. Somehow, I think that Barney—"

But a spasm of coughing interrupted and exhausted her. She fell asleep when it was over, still ~~hanging~~ holding to ~~Miranda's~~ Valancy's hand. ~~Miranda~~ Valancy sat there in the silence. She was not frightened – or even sorry. At ~~sunrive~~ ^sunrise^ Cissy died. She opened her eyes and looked ~~at~~ past ~~Miranda~~ Valancy at something—something that made her smile suddenly and happily. And, smiling, she died.

~~Miranda~~ Valancy crossed Cissy's ~~cold~~ hands on her breast and went to the open window. In the eastern sky, amid the fires of sunrise, an old moon was hanging—as slender and lovely as a new moon. ~~Miranda~~ Valancy had never seen an old, old moon before. She watched it pale and fade until it paled and faded out of sight in the living rose of day ^{NOTE W8} NOTE S8 ~~She wasn't in the least sorry Cecilia was dead. She was only sorry for all her suffering in life. She~~ had always thought death dreadful. But Cissy had died so quietly – so pleasantly. And at the very last – something – had made up to her for everything. She was lying there now, in her white sleep, looking like a child. Beautiful! All the lines of shame and pain gone.

Roaring Abel drove in, justifying his name. ~~Miranda~~ Valancy went down and told him. The shock sobered him at once. He slumped down on the seat of his buggy, his great head hanging.

"Cissy dead – Cissy dead," he said vacantly. "I didn't think it would a' come so soon. Dead. ~~NOTE U12~~ NOTE T8 ~~Little~~ Cissy ~~was~~ ^used to be^ a pretty ~~a~~ little girl. And a good little girl."

"She has always been a good little girl," said ~~Miranda~~ Valancy.

NOTE S8: A little pool in the barrens shone in the sunrise like a great golden lily. ~~Birds were singing. The world is always young again for just a few minutes at the dawn.~~[2]

But it[3] suddenly seemed a colder place to Valancy. Again nobody needed her. She was not in the least sorry Cecilia was dead. She was only sorry for all her suffering in life. But nobody could ever hurt her again. Valancy

2: The last two sentences in NOTE S8 were omitted from the published version.

3: In the published version, "it" is changed to "the world."

NOTE T8: She used to run down the lane to meet me with a little white rose stuck in her hair.

XXVII

Valancy herself made Cissy ready for burial, so that no other hands should touch that pitiful, wasted, little body. The old house was spotless on the day of the funeral. Barney Snaith was not at the funeral. He had done all he could to help Valancy before it, and then had gone back to his island. But everybody else was there. Old Sherwood and his folks came. They forgave Cissy splendidly at last. Mr. Bradley gave a very decent funeral address. Valancy had wanted Dr. Mellody, but no. Roaring Abel was obdurate. He was a Pres-

XXIV

M~~iranda~~ Valancy herself made Cissy ready for burial. No hands but hers should touch that pitiful,
wasted, little body. The old house was spotless on the
day of the funeral. Barney Snaith was not ~~at the funeral.~~ ^there. ^ He had done all he could to help ~~Miranda~~
Valancy before it ~~NOTE Y8~~ NOTE U8 and then had gone ^back
to his island.^ ~~away. ^Lady Jane^~~ But everybody else was
there. All Deerwood and ["]up back["] came. They forgave Cissy splendidly at last. Mr. Bradl~~e~~y[1] ~~gave a~~ gave
a very beautiful funeral address. ~~Miranda~~ Valancy had
wanted her old ~~Mennonite~~ ^Free Methodist^ man[,]
but Roaring Abel was obdurate. He was a Presbyterian
and no one but a Presbyterian minister should bury <u>his</u>
daughter. Mr. Bradl~~e~~y was very tactful. He avoided all
dubious points and it was plain to be seen he hoped for
the best. Six reputable citizens of Deerwood bore ~~Cissy's
Cissy~~ ^Cecilia Gay^ to her grave ^in decorous Deerwood
cemetery.^ Among them was Uncle Wellington.

The Stirlings all came to the funeral, men and wom-
en. They had had a family conclave over it. Surely now
that ~~Cecilia~~ ^Cissy^ Gay was dead ~~Miranda~~ Valancy
would come home. She simply could not stay there with
Roaring Abel. That being the case[,] the wisest course
– decreed Uncle James – was to attend the funeral –
legitimize[2] the whole thing, so to speak – show Deerwood
that ~~Miranda~~ Valancy had really done a most creditable
~~thing~~ ^deed^ in going to nurse poor Cecilia Gay and that
her family backed her up in it. ^A^ ~~Death, had made
such~~ ^ ~~had the miracle worker,~~ ^ ^Death, the miracle
worker,^ suddenly made the thing quite respectable.

NOTE U8: – he had
shrouded the pale
Cecilia in white roses
from the garden –

1: Montgomery had given
the minister the name
"Bentley" in previous
chapters, but here she
calls him "Bradley,"
which is spelled "Bradly"
in the published version.

2: "Legitimize" is spelled
"legitimise" in the pub-
lished version.

If ~~Miranda~~ Valancy would return to ^home and^ decency while public opinion was under its influence all might yet be well. ~~NOTE A13~~ NOTE V8 It was the psychological moment – said Uncle James.

So the Stirlings went to the funeral. ~~NOTE X12~~ NOTE W8

℃ And Uncle ~~James~~ ^Wellington^ was a pall bearer.
~~NOTE G9~~ NOTE X8

When the funeral procession had left the house[,] Mrs. ~~George~~ Frederick sought out ~~Miranda~~ Valancy in the kitchen.

"My child," she said tremulously, "you'll come home <u>now?</u>"

"Home," said ~~Miranda~~ Valancy absently. ~~She was~~ ^She was getting on an apron and^ calculating how much tea she ~~should~~ ^must^ put to ~~steep~~ ^steep^ for supper. There would be several guests from ["]up back["]—distant relatives of the Gays' who had ~~never~~ ^not^ remembered them for years. ~~NOTE Y12~~ NOTE Y8

NOTE V8: Society was suddenly forgetting all Cecilia's wicked doings & remembering what a pretty, modest little thing she had been – "and motherless, you know – motherless[!]"‡

NOTE W8: Even Cousin Gladys' neuritis allowed her to come. Cousin Stickles was there, her bonnet dripping all over her face, crying as woefully as if Cissy had been her nearest & dearest. Funerals always brought Cousin Stickles' "own sad bereavement" back.

NOTE X8: Valancy, pale, subdued-looking, her slanted eyes smudged with purple, in her snuff-brown dress, moving quietly about, finding seats for people, consulting in undertones with minister and undertaker, marshalling the "moun "mourners" into the parlor, was so decorous & proper & Stirlingish that her family took heart of grace. This was not—could not be—the girl who had sat all night in the woods with Barney Snaith [– who had] & gone tearing bareheaded through Deerwood & Port Laurence. This was the

~~Miranda~~ Valancy they knew. Really, surprisingly capable & efficient. Perhaps she had always been kept down a bit too much—Amelia really was rather strict—hadn't had a chance to show what was in her. So thought the Stirlings. And Edward Beck from the Port road, a widower with a large family who was beginning to take notice, took notice of Valancy & thought she might make a mighty fine second wife. No beauty – but a fifty-year-old widower, Mr. Beck told himself very reasonably, couldn't expect <u>everything</u>.[3] Altogether, it seemed that Valancy's matrimonial chances were never so bright as they were at Cecilia Gay's funeral.

What the Stirlings & Edward Beck would have thought had they known the back of Valancy's mind must be left to the imagination. Valancy was hating the funeral – hating the people who came to stare with curiosity at Cecilia's marble-white face – hating the smugness – hating the dragging, melancholy singing – hating Mr. Bradley's cautious platitudes. If she

could have had her absurd way[,] there would have been no funeral at all. She would have covered Cissy over with flowers, shut her away from prying eyes, and buried her beside her nameless little baby in the grassy burying[-]ground under the pines of the ["]up-back["] church, with a bit of a kindly prayer from the old Free Methodist minister. She remembered Cissy saying once, "I wish I could be buried deep in the heart of the woods where nobody would ever come to say[,] 'Cissy Gay is buried here' & tell over my miserable story."

But this! However, it would soon be over. Valancy knew if the Stirlings & Edward Beck didn't, exactly what she intended to do then. She had laid[4] awake all the preceding night thinking about it & finally deciding on it.

3: In the published version, "everything" is not italicized.

4: "Laid" is corrected to "lain" in the published version.

NOTE Y8: And she was so tired she wished she could borrow a pair of legs from the cat.

"Yes, home," said Mrs. ~~George~~ Frederick, with a touch of asperity. "I suppose you won't dream of staying here <u>now</u> – alone with Roaring Abel."

"Oh, no. I'm not going to stay <u>here</u>," said ~~Miranda~~ Valancy. "Of course[,] I'll have to stay for a day or two to put the house in order generally. But that will be all. Excuse me, mother,[5] ^won't you?^ I've a frightful lot to ~~do~~ ^do—^ all those [']up back['] people will be here to supper.["]

Mrs. ~~George~~ Frederick retreated in considerable relief[,] and the Stirlings went home with lighter hearts.

"We will just treat her as if nothing had happened when she comes back," decreed Uncle Benjamin. "That will be the best plan.⸗ Just as if nothing had happened.["]

[6]

—————— —————— ——————

5: "Mother" is capitalized in the published version.

6: Montgomery drew three long lines across the bottom of the manuscript page. They are not included in the published version.

XXV

NOTE Z8: I'm going to wet my whistle. Lord, but I'm dry.

On the evening of the day of the funeral Roaring Abel went off for a spree. He had been sober for five ^four^ whole days and could endure it no longer. Before he went[,] ~~Miranda~~ Valancy told him she would be going away the next day. Roaring Abel was sorry[,] and said so. A distant cousin from ["]up back["] was coming to keep house for him—quite willing to do so now since there was no sick girl to wait on—but Abel was not under any delusions concerning her.

"She won't be like you, my girl. Well, I'm obliged to you. You helped me out of a bad hole and I won't forget it. And I won't forget what you did for Cissy. I'm your friend[,] and if you ever want any of the Stirlings ~~polish~~ spanked and sot in a corner, send for me. NOTE Z8 ^I'm ~~going to get a drink wet my whistle~~^ Don't reckon I'll be back afore tomorrow night so if you're going home tomorrow[,] good bye now.["]

"I <u>may</u> go home tomorrow," said ~~Miranda~~ Valancy, "but I'm not going back to Deerwood." ~~You'll~~

"Not going—"

"You'll find the key on the woodshed nail," interrupted ~~Miranda,~~ Valancy, ~~firm,~~ politely and unmistakeably. "The dog will be in the barn and the cat in the cellar. Don't forget to feed her till your cousin comes. The pantry is full and I made bread & pies to-day. Good-bye, Mr. Gay. You have been very kind to me and I appreciate it."

"We've had a d——d decent time of it together, ^and that's a fact,"^ said Roaring Abel. "You're the best ~~little~~ small sport in the world and your little finger is worth the whole Stirling clan tied together. Good-bye and good-luck."

~~Miranda~~ Valancy went ~~upstairs and dre dressed herself in her green crepe and green hat~~ ^out to the garden.^ Her ~~fingers~~ ^legs^ trembled a little ~~as she bus~~ but otherwise she felt ^and looked^ composed. She ~~took something out of a box and slipped~~ held it ^something tightly^ in her hand. ~~as she went down and out to~~ The garden ^was^ lying in the magic of ~~of~~ the warm[,] ^odorous^ July twilight. A few stars were out and the robins were calling ~~NOTE T14~~ NOTE A9. ~~Miranda~~ Valancy stood by the gate expectantly. Would he come? If he did not[—] =

He was coming. ~~Miranda~~ Valancy heard Lady Jane Grey far back in the woods. Her breath came a little more quickly. Nearer – and nearer – she could see Lady Jane now – bumping down the lane – nearer – nearer – he was there ~~and~~ ^–^ he had sprung from the car and was leaning over the gate, looking at her.

"Going home, Miss Stirling[?]."

"I don't know – yet," said ~~Miranda~~ Valancy slowly. Her mind was made up ~~and she did~~ with no shadow of turning, but the moment was very tremendous. ~~NOTE C12~~

"I thought I'd run down and ask if there was anything I could do for you," said Barney.

~~"Yes. There is something you can do for me," said Miranda distinct=~~

~~Miranda~~ Valancy took it with a canter.

"Yes, there is something you can do for me," she said, evenly and distinctly. "Will you marry me?"

For a moment Barney was silent. There was no particular expression on his face. Then he gave an odd laugh.

"Come now! I knew luck was just waiting around the corner for me. All the signs have been pointing that way to-day."

"Wait." ~~Miranda~~ Valancy lifted her hand. "I'm in earnest – but I want to get my breath after that question. ~~You~~ ~~NOTE N14~~ NOTE B9 see = ~~I'm not in the habit of toing about asking men to marry me."~~

~~"No = if~~ "But why= – _why_?" –

"For two reasons." ~~Miranda~~ Valancy was still a little breathless[,] but she looked Barney straight in the eyes,

NOTE A9: through the velvety silences of the barrens

NOTE B9: Of course, with my bringing=up[,] I realize perfectly well that this is one of the things [']a lady should not do[.']‡"

NOTE C9: while all the dead Stirlings revolved rapidly in their graves & the living ones did nothing because they did not know that Valancy was at that moment proposing lawful marriage to the notorious Barney Snaith. "The first reason is, I – I"—Valancy tried to say "I love you" but could not. She had to take refuge in a pretended flippancy. "I'm crazy about you.

1: In the published version, this phrase reads "safe, sane thing to do."

NOTE D9: -- she managed it this time –

2: In the published version, there is no period after "been" and the sentence continues with "just to hear."

NOTE C9 ~~while all the dead Stirlings turned over ^and over^ ^revolved rapidly in their graves and^ in their graves and the living ones did nothing because they didn't know Miranda was proposing ^at that moment lawful marriage^ to the notorious Barney Snaith. "The first reason is – I'm crazy about you.~~ The second is this."

She handed him Dr. Trent's letter.

Barney opened it with the air of a man thankful to find some sane, ^~~harmless~~ safe^ thing to do.[1] As he read it his face changed. He understood—more, perhaps, than ~~even Miranda~~ Valancy wanted him to.

"Are you sure nothing can be done for you?"

~~Miranda~~ Valancy did not misunderstand the question.

"Yes. You know Dr. Trent's ~~is~~ reputation in regard to heart disease. I haven't long to live—perhaps only a few months – a few ~~years~~ ^weeks^. I want to <u>live</u> them. I can't go back to Deerwood—you know what my life was like there. And" NOTE D9 – "I love you. I want to spend the rest of my life with you. That's all."

Barney folded his arms on the gate and looked ~~solemn~~ gravely enough at a ^white,^ saucy star that was winking at him ^~~from the crystal sky~~^ just over Roaring Abel's kitchen chimney.

"You don't know anything about me. I may be a – murderer."

"No, I don't. You <u>may</u> be something dreadful. Everything they say of you may be true. But it doesn't matter to me."

"You care that much for ~~me?"~~ ^me, ~~Miranda?~~ Valancy?"^ said Barney incredulously, looking away from the star and into her eyes – her strange, mysterious eyes.

~~A sudden crimson~~

"I care – that much," said ~~Miranda~~ Valancy in a low voice. She was trembling. He had called her by her name for the first time. It was sweeter than another man's caress could have been.[2] Just to hear him say her name, like that.

"If we are going to get married," said Barney, speaking suddenly in a casual, matter-of-fact voice, "some things must be understood."

"Everything must be understood," said ~~Miranda.~~ Valancy.

"I have things I want to hide," said Barney coolly. "You ~~mus~~ are not to ask me about them."

"I won't," ~~pro~~ said Miranda.

NOTE E9

NOTE E9: "You must never ask to see my mail." "Never."

NOTE F9: You see, I'm not in the habit of going about asking men to marry me.

"And we are never to pretend anything to each other."

"We won't." said ~~Miranda~~ Valancy. "You won't even have to pretend you like me. If you marry me I know you're only doing it out of pity."

"And we'll never tell a lie to each other about anything—a big lie or a petty lie."

"Especially a petty lie," agreed ~~Miranda~~ Valancy."

"And you'll have to live back on my island. I won't live anywhere else."

"That's partly why I want to marry you," said ~~Miranda~~ Valancy.

Barney peered at her.

"I believe you mean it. ~~It's out of the world, you know."~~ ~~"So~~ Well – let's get married, then."

"Thank you," said ~~Miranda~~ Valancy, with a sudden return of primness. She would have been much less embarrassed if he had refused her.

"I suppose I haven't any right to make conditions. But I'm going to make one. You are never to refer to my heart or my liability to sudden death. You are never to urge me to be careful. You are to forget—absolutely forget—that I'm not perfectly healthy. I have written a letter to my mother – here it is – you are to keep it. ^I have explained everything in it.^ If I drop dead suddenly – as I likely will do—["]

"It will exonerate me in the eyes of your kindred from the suspicion of having ~~murdered~~ ^poisoned ~~are~~ you~~;~~[,]"^ said Barney with a grin.

"Exactly." ~~Miranda~~ Valancy laughed gaily. "Dear me, I'm glad this is over. It has been – a bit of an ordeal. ~~NOTE W14~~ NOTE F9 It is so nice of you not to refuse me~~ⁿ~~—or offer to be a brother!" ^ ~~"Or offer to be a brother^~~

"I'll go to the Port tomorrow and get a license. We can be married to-morrow evening. Dr. Stalling, I suppose?"

NOTE G9: Besides, he wouldn't do it. He'd shake his forefinger at me and I'd jilt you at the altar. No,

NOTE H9: A passing car, full of tourists, honked loudly – it seemed derisively.

"Heavens, no." ~~Miranda~~ Valancy shuddered. ~~NOTE B10~~ NOTE G9

~~"~~I want my old Mr. ~~Towers~~ Towers to marry me."

"Will you marry me as I stand?" demanded Barney. ~~NOTE B13 NOTE C13~~ NOTE H9

~~Miranda~~ Valancy looked at him. Blue homespun shirt, ~~mo~~ nondescript hat, muddy overalls. ~~But he was shaved! Unshaved!~~ Unshaved!

"Yes," she said.

Barney put his hands over the gate and took her little, cold ones ^gently^ in his. ~~gently.~~

"~~Miranda,~~ Valancy," he said, trying to speak lightly, ~~"you do you know~~ ^I've always thought you were^ ~~you are a bit of a dear?"~~ "Of course I'm not in love with you – never thought of such a thing as being in love ~~with you.~~ But, do you know[,] I've always thought you were a bit of a dear."

XXVI

The next day passed for ~~Miranda~~ Valancy like a dream. She could not make herself or anything she did seem real. She saw nothing of Barney[,] though she expected he must go rattling past on his way to the Port for a license. ℭ Perhaps he had changed his mind.

But at dusk the lights of Lady Jane suddenly swooped over the crest of the wooded hill beyond the lane. ~~Miranda~~ Valancy was waiting at the gate for ~~him.~~ ^her bridegroom.^ She wore her green dress and her green hat because she had nothing else to wear. She did not ^look or^ feel at all bride-like ~~NOTE G13~~ NOTE I9 But that did not matter. Nothing at all mattered except that Barney was coming for her.

"Ready?" said Barney, stopping Lady Jane with some ~~new~~ ^new,^ horrible noises.

"Yes." ~~Miranda~~ Valancy stepped in and sat down. Barney ~~wore~~ was in his blue shirt and overalls. But they were clean overalls. He was smoking a ~~vile~~ villainous[-] looking pipe and he was bareheaded. NOTE J9 But[2] he was ~~cl~~ shaved. They clattered ~~through Deer~~ NOTE J19 into Deerwood and through Deerwood and hit the long, wooded road to the Port. ~~It was quite dark now — a warm scented dark~~

"Haven't changed your mind?" said Barney.

"No. Have you?"

"No."

That was ~~all their~~ ^their whole^ conversation on the fifteen miles. Everything was more dream[-]like than ever. ~~Miranda~~ Valancy didn't know whether she felt happy. Or terrified. Or just plain fool.

NOTE I9: —she really looked like a wild elf strayed out of the greenwood.

NOTE J9: And[1] he had a pair of oddly smart boots on under his shabby overalls.

1: In the published version, "And" is changed to "But."

2: In the published version "But" is changed to "And."

NOTE K9: when such a thing had not seemed impossible[.]

3: "Barney" is not in italics in the published version.

NOTE L9: No veil – no flowers – no guests – no presents – no wedding[-]cake – but just Barney. For all the rest of her life there would be Barney.

Then the lights of Port Laurence were about them. ~~Miranda~~ Valancy felt as if she were surrounded by the gleaming, hungry eyes of hundreds of great, ~~stealthy~~ stealthy panthers. Barney briefly asked where Mr. Towers lived[,] and ~~Miranda~~ Valancy as briefly told him. They stopped before the shabby little house in an unfashionable street. ~~They stood up together~~ They went in to the small ~~shr~~ shabby parlor. Barney produced his license. So he <u>had</u> got it. ^Also a ring.^ This thing was real. She, ~~Miranda~~ Valancy Stirling, was actually on the point of being married.

They were standing up together before Mr. Towers. ~~Miranda~~ Valancy heard Mr. Towers and Barney saying things. She heard some other person saying things. She herself was thinking of the way she had once planned to be married – away back in her early teens. ~~NOTE H13~~ NOTE K9 White ~~satin~~ silk and tulle veil and orange blossoms; ^~~and bouquet of roses.~~^ no bridesmaid~~;~~. ~~b~~But one flower girl, in a frock of cream shadow lace over pale pink, with a wreath of flowers in her hair, carrying a basket of roses and lilies-of-the-valley. And the groom, a noble-looking creature, irreproachably clad in whatever the fashion of the day decreed. ~~Miranda~~ Valancy lifted her eyes and saw herself and Barney in the little, slanting, ^distorting^ mirror over the mantel=piece. She in her odd, unbridal green hat and dress; Barney in shirt and overalls. But it was <u>Barney</u>.[3] That was all that mattered. ~~NOTE H13~~ NOTE L9

"Mrs. Snaith, I hope you will be very, very happy," Mr. Towers was saying. ¶ He had not seemed surprised at their appearance – not even at Barney's overalls. He had seen plenty of queer weddings ["]up back.["] He did not know ~~Miranda~~ Valancy was one of the Deerwood Stirlings—he did not even know there <u>were</u> Deerwood Stirlings. He did not know Barney Snaith was a fugitive from justice. ^Really,^ he was an incredibly ignorant old man. Therefore he married them and gave them his blessing very gently and solemnly and prayed for them that night after they had gone away. His conscience did not trouble him at all.

"What a nice way to get married," Barney was saying as he put Lady Jane in gear. "No fuss and ~~folly~~ ^flubdub^. I never supposed it was half so easy."

"For heaven's sake," said ~~Miranda~~ Valancy suddenly, "let's forget we <u>are</u> married and talk as if we weren't. I can't stand another drive like the one we had coming in."

Barney howled and threw Lady Jane ^into high^ with an infernal noise ~~into high~~.

"And I thought I was making it easy for you," he said. "You didn't seem to want to talk."

"I didn't. But I ~~do now. At least, I want you to talk.~~ ^wanted you to talk[.]^ I don't want you to make love to me[,] but I want you to act like an ordinary human being. Tell me about this island of yours. What sort of a place is it?"

"The jolliest place in the world. You're going to love it. The first time I saw it I loved it. Old Tom MacMurray owned it then. He built the little shack on it, ^lived there in winter^ and rented it to ~~folks~~ ^Toronto people^ in summer. I bought it from him – became by that one simple transaction a landed proprietor owning a house & an island. There is something so satisfying in owning a whole Island NOTE M19 NOTE M9 ~~I'd wanted to ever since I read Robinson Crusoe. It seemed too good to be true~~ NOTE N19 NOTE M19. You won't find my shack very tidy. I suppose you'll want to make it tidy."

"Yes," said ~~Miranda~~ Valancy, honestly. "I <u>have</u> to be tidy. I don't really <u>want</u> to be. But untidiness hurts me. Yes, I'll have to ~~td~~ tidy up your shack." NOTE D15 NOTE K19 NOTE D15 NOTE N9

NOTE M9: And isn't an uninhabited island a charming idea? I'd wanted to own one ever since I'd read Robinson Crusoe. It seemed too good to be true. And beauty! Most of the scenery belongs to the Government[4] but they don't tax you for looking at it[,] & the moon belongs to everybody.

4: "Government" is not capitalized in the published version.

NOTE N9: "I was prepared for that," said Barney, with a hollow groan.

"But," continued Valancy relentingly, "I won't insist on your wiping your feet when you come in.["]

"No, you'll only sweep up after me with the air of a martyr," said Barney. "Well, anyway, you can't tidy the lean-to. You can't ever enter it. The door will be locked & I shall keep the key."

"Bluebeard's chamber,"[5] said Valancy. "I shan't even think of it. I don't ~~kn~~ care how many wives you have hanging up in it. So long as they're really dead."

¶ "Dead as door-nails. You can do as you like in the rest of the house. There's not much of

it—just one big living[-]room & one small bedroom. Well built, though. Old Tom loved his job! The beams of our house are cedar & the rafters fir. Our living[-]room windows face west & east. It's wonderful to have a room where you can see both sunrise & sunset. I have two cats there. Jigglesqueak[6] and Good Luck.[7] Adorable animiles. Jigglesqueak is a big, enchanting, gray devil cat. Striped[,] of course. I don't care a hang for any cat that hasn't stripes. I never knew a cat who could swear as genteelly & effectively as Jiggles. His only fault is that he snores terribly when he is asleep. Luck is a dainty little cat. Always looking wistfully at you as if he wanted to tell you something. Maybe he will pull it off sometime. Once in a thousand years, you know, one cat is allowed to speak. ~~Neither of my~~ My cats are philosophers— neither of them ever cries over spilt milk.

Two old crows live in

5: In the ancient folk tale, Bluebeard was a wealthy man whose "chamber" was a locked

room in which he kept the murdered corpses of his many wives.

6: In the published version, "Jigglesqueak" is changed to "Banjo." Montgomery had clipped an article from the Illustrated London News (January 2, 1892) entitled "In Praise of Cats" for her Blue scrapbook (c. 1893–1898). The article was illustrated with a picture of a kitten named Banjo, painted by Henriette Ronner.

7: Montgomery loved cats and her favourite was named Good Luck. A photograph of him was used on postcards to advertise The Blue Castle. Good Luck (or "Lucky" as Montgomery called him) was born in Cavendish, PEI, and Montgomery claimed him while she was visiting there in August 1923. In her journal entry for August 4, 1923, she writes that he is "the most oddly and beautifully marked cat I have ever seen—silvery gray with jet-black marks. The marks on his sides resemble a clover leaf with an M inside it and I said he would bring good luck."

NOTE O9: And I have a demure little tame owl. Name, Leander.[8] I brought him up from a baby & he lives over on the mainland & chuckles to himself o'nights.

8: Leander was the name of Montgomery's uncle, Leander George Macneill (1845–1913).

NOTE P9: where the air was sweet with the incense of the unseen, fragile bells of the linneas[9] that carpeted the banks of the trail.

9: Linneas (spelled "linnæas" in the published version) are small, fragrant woodland plants with tiny, pink, bell-shaped flowers—two to a stem—that bloom in late spring / early summer. They are also called "twinflowers."

10: "There's" is not italicized in the published version.

~

"~~Well, I expected that,~~" said Barney ~~resignedly.~~ "~~But you can't tidy the lean-to. You can't even enter it. The door will be locked and I shall keep the key.~~" NOTE E13 ~~You can do as you like in the rest of the house. There's not much of it = just one big living room and one small bedroom~~ NOTE B15 ~~I have two cats there = Leander and Jigglesqueak~~ ^Jigglesqueak^ ~~& Good Luck. Adorable animals. Jigglesqueak^~~ ~~Leander~~ ^Jigglesqueak^ ~~is a big lush outing gray devil cat = striped, of course ~~^~~ I don't care a hang for any cat that hasn't stripes.~~ NOTE P19 NOTE L19 ~~Jigglesqueak~~ ^Luck^ ~~is a dainty little cat, so lovable that he practically amounts to an obsession~~ ^ NOTE Z14 ^ ~~Two old crows live in~~ a pine[-]tree on the point and are reasonably neighborly. Call 'em Nip and Tuck. ~~NOTE A15~~ NOTE O9 And bats—it's a great place for bats at night. Scared of bats?"

"No[;]~~,~~ I like them."

"So do I. Nice, queer, uncanny[,] mysterious creatures. Coming from nowhere – going nowhere. Swoop! ~~Leander~~ ^Jigglesqueak^ likes 'em, too. Eats 'em. I have a ~~canoe~~ ^canoe^ and a disappearing propeller boat. Went to the Port in it to-day to get my license. ~~Quieter~~ Quieter than Lady Jane."

"I thought you hadn't gone at all – that you <u>had</u> changed your mind," admitted ~~Miranda.~~ Valancy.

Barney laughed—the laugh Miranda Valancy did not like—the little, bitter, cynical laugh.

"I never change my mind," he said shortly.

They went back through Deerwood. ~~A~~ Up the ~~Mistawis~~ Muskoka road. ~~Past~~ ^Past^ Roaring Abel's. Over the rocky, daisied lane. The dark pine=woods swallowed them up. Through the pine woods[,] ~~NOTE C15~~ NOTE P9 ~~in~~ Out to the ~~gle~~ shore of Mistawis. Lady Jane must be left here. They got out[.] = Barney led the way down a little path to the edge of the lake.

"<u>There's</u>[10] our island," he said gloatingly.

~~Miranda~~ Valancy looked – and looked – and looked again. There was a ~~white~~ ^diaphanous, lilac^ mist on the lake, ~~shrouding~~ ^shrouding^ the island. Through it the ~~trees~~ two enormous pine[-]trees that clasped hands over

Barney's shack loomed out ~~darkly~~ like ~~the~~ ^dark^ turrets ~~of a castle~~. Behind them was a sky, still ~~lilac~~ ^rose-^ hued ~~for~~ in the afterlight[,] and a pale young moon.

~~Miranda~~ Valancy shivered like a tree the wind stirs suddenly. Something seemed to sweep over her soul. NOTE J13 NOTE Q9 ~~She trembled~~ ^She found^ ~~Her eyes suddenly filling with tears.~~[12] | NOTE H15

"My Blue Castle!" she said. ^"Oh,^ my Blue Castle!" ~~NOTE D15~~

They got into the canoe and rowed[13] out to it. ~~Barney~~ They left behind the realm of every day[14] and things known and ~~passed~~ ~~reckoning~~ landed on a realm of mystery and enchantment =where anything might happen – anything might be true. Barney lifted ~~Miranda~~ Valancy out of the canoe and swung her to a ~~licken~~ ^lichen-^ covered rock under a young pine[-]tree. His arms were about her and suddenly his lips ~~found~~ ^were on^ hers. ~~Miranda~~ Valancy found herself shivering with the rapture of her first kiss.

"Welcome home, dear," Barney was saying.

NOTE Q9: ~~It hurt her to look at Barney's house yet she liked the hurt.~~[11]

11: This sentence is left out of the published version.

12: This sentence is left out of the published version.

13: "Rowed" is changed to "paddled" in the published version.

14: In the published version, "every day" is spelled "everyday."

.... on a ..... of mysteries
and ..... meet — where anything might happen — anything
might be .... Barney ..... her
..... out of the car and ...
... to a ..... corner of rock under
a young pine tree. She's arms were
.... her and suddenly her
legs ..... her. ..... found
herself shivering with the ....
of her past .....

"Welcome home, dear," Barney was
saying.

XXV

Cousin Georgiana came out down
the lane leading up to her little
house, and turned towards .....
...... She lived half a mile out-
of .... and she wanted to

XXVII

Cousin Georgiana came ~~out of~~ ^down^ the lane leading up to her little house. ~~and turned towards Deerwood.~~ She lived half a mile out of Deerwood and she wanted to go in to Amelia's and find out if ~~Miranda~~ ^Doss^ had come home yet. Cousin Georgiana was anxious to see ~~Miranda~~ ^Doss^. She had something very important to tell her. Something, she was sure, Doss would be delighted to hear. Poor Doss[!]~~:~~ She <u>had</u> had rather a dull life of it. Cousin Georgiana owned to herself that <u>she</u> would not like to live under Amelia's thumb. ~~NOTE G14~~ NOTE R9

And here was Doss herself, coming along the road from Roaring Abel's in such a queer~~,~~green dress and hat. Talk about luck. Cousin Georgiana would have a chance to ~~tell her more~~ impart her wonderful secret right away, with nobody else about to interrupt. It was you might say, a Providence. NOTE S9

~~Miranda Valancy who had been~~ ^NOTE 113?^ ~~living for four days on her enchanted island^ ^married for four days,^~ had decided that she might as well go in to Deerwood and tell her relatives ^that she was married.^ Otherwise, finding that she had disappeared from Roaring Abel's[,] they might get out a search warrant for her. Barney had offered to drive her in[,] but she had preferred to go alone. She smiled very radiantly at Cousin Georgiana[,] who, she remembered, as of some[ ]one known a long time ago, had really been not a bad~~,~~little creature. ~~Miranda~~ Valancy was so happy that she could have smiled at anybody – even Uncle James. She was not averse to Cousin Georgiana's company. Already, since

NOTE R9: But that would be all changed now. Cousin Georgiana felt tremendously important. For the time being[,] she quite forgot to wonder which of them would go next.

NOTE S9: Valancy, who had been living for four days on her enchanted island,

NOTE T9: furtively ~~eyeing~~ eyeing Valancy's dress & wondering if she had <u>any</u> petticoat on at all.

1: wen = a fluid-filled cyst under the skin

2: The second "wen" looks to be a clearer spelling for the typist's benefit.

the houses along the road were becoming numerous, she was conscious that curious eyes were looking at her from every window.

"I suppose you're going home, dear Doss?" said Cousin Georgiana as she shook hands – ~~NOTE K13~~ NOTE T9

"Sooner or later," said ~~Miranda~~ Valancy cryptically.

"Then I'll go along with you. I've been wanting to see you <u>very</u> especially, Doss~~,~~ dear. I've something quite <u>wonderful</u> to tell you."

"Yes?" said ~~Miranda~~ Valancy absently. What on earth was Cousin Georgiana looking so mysterious and important about? But did it matter? No. Nothing mattered but Barney and the Blue Castle up back in Mistawis.

"Who do you suppose called to see me the other day?" asked Cousin Georgiana archly.

~~Miranda~~ Valancy couldn't guess.

"Edward Beck." Cousin Georgiana lowered her voice almost to a whisper. "<u>Edward Beck</u>."

Why the italics? And <u>was</u> Cousin Georgiana blushing?

"Who on earth is Edward Beck?" asked ~~Miranda~~ Valancy indifferently.

Cousin Georgiana stared.

"Surely you remember Edward Beck," she said reproachfully. "~~That~~ "He lives in that lovely house on the Port Laurence road and he comes to our church – regularly. You <u>must</u> remember him."

"Oh, I think I do now," said ~~Miranda~~ Valancy[,] with an effort of memory. "He's that old man with a wen[1] on his forehead and dozens of children who always sits in the pew by the door, isn't he?"

"Not dozens of children, dear – oh, no[,] not dozens. Not even <u>one</u> dozen. Only nine. At least only nine that count. The rest are dead. He <u>isn't</u> old – he's only about forty[-]eight – the prime of life, Doss – and what does it matter about a wen?" wen.[2]

"Nothing, of course," agreed ~~Miranda~~ Valancy quite sincerely. It certainly did not matter to her whether Edward Beck had a wen or a dozen wens or no wen at all. But ~~Miranda~~ Valancy was getting vaguely suspicious.

There was certainly an air of suppressed triumph about Cousin Georgiana. Could it be possible that Cousin G.[3] was ~~going to~~ thinking of marrying ~~Edward Beck~~ ^again[?]~~?~~^ ^Marrying Edward Beck?^ Absurd. Cousin G. was ~~65 sixty~~ sixty[-]five if she was[4] a day ~~NOTE E15~~ NOTE U9 But still –

"My dear," said Cousin ~~G.~~ Georgiana. "Edward Beck wants to marry you."

~~Miranda~~ Valancy stared at Cousin ~~S~~ ^Georgiana^ for a moment. Then she wanted to go off with a peal of laughter. But she only said[:] "Me?"[5]

"Yes, you. He fell in love with you at the funeral. And he came to consult me about it. I was such a friend of his first wife, you know. He is very much in earnest, Dossie. And it's a wonderful chance for you. He's very well off – and you know – you – you "~~are~~" –

"Not[6] so young as I once was," agreed ~~Miranda~~ Valancy. "'To her that hath shall be given.'"[7] Do you really think I would make a good stepmother, Cousin Georgiana?"

~~"I~~ "I'm sure you would. You were always so fond of children[.]"

"But nine is such a family to start with," objected ~~Miranda~~ Valancy gravely."

"The ~~two~~ ^2^ ^two^ oldest are grown-up and the third almost. That leaves only six that really count. And most of them are boys. So much easier to bring up than girls. ~~NOTE E15~~ NOTE V9 Of course I told Mr. Beck that I thought you would – would –"

"Jump at him," supplied ~~Miranda~~ Valancy.

"Oh, no, no, dear. I wouldn't use such an ^indelicate^ expression. I told him I thought you would consider his proposal favorably. And you will, won't you, dearie?"

"There's only one obstacle," said ~~Miranda~~ Valancy dreamily. "You see[,] I'm married already."

"Married!" Cousin Georgiana stopped stock[-]still and stared at ~~Miranda~~ Valancy.

"Married?"[9]

"Yes. I was married to Barney Snaith last Tuesday evening in Port Laurence."

3: In the published version, "Cousin G." is spelled out to read "Cousin Georgiana" each time it appears in the manuscript.

4: In the published version, "was" is corrected to "were."

NOTE U9: and her little anxious face was as closely covered with fine wrinkles as if she had been a hundred.

5: In the published version, "Me?" is on a separate line.

6: In the published version, this line begins "Am not" instead of "Not."

7: This quote is slightly paraphrased from Mark 4:25: "For he that hath, to him shall be given...." Also used in Chapters VIII and XLII.

NOTE V9: There's an excellent book—"[']Health Care of the Growing Child[']"[8] – Gladys has a copy, I think. It would be such a help to you. And there are books about morals. You'd manage nicely[.]

8: Probably The Healthcare of the Growing Child: His Diet -- hygiene -- training -- development and Prevention of Disease by Louis Fischer, first published in 1916 by Funk & Wagnalls Company.

9: In the published version, this line is not a separate paragraph but continues from the previous one.

10: Montgomery neglected to change "women" to "woman" after adding the "a" before "married." It is "woman" in the published version.

NOTE X9:[11] Of course Valancy must be stark mad. But she seemed so happy in her madness that Cousin Georgiana had a momentary conviction that it would be a pity if the clan tried to scold her back to sanity. She had never seen that look in Valancy's eyes before. But what <u>would</u> Amelia say? And Ben? "To marry a man you know nothing about," thought Cousin Georgiana aloud. "I know more about him than I know of Edward Beck," said Valancy. "Edward Beck <u>goes to church</u>," said Cousin Georgiana. Does Bar— does your husband?" "He has promised that he will go with me on fine Sundays," said Valancy.

11: There is no Note W9.

12: "Rose bush" is spelled as one word in the published version.

There was a convenient gate-post hard by. Cousin G. took firm hold of it.

"Doss, dear – I'm an old woman – are you trying to make fun of me?"

"Not at all. I'm only telling you the truth. For heaven[']s sake, Cousin Georgiana" – ~~Miranda~~ Valancy was alarmed by certain symptoms – "don't go crying here on the public road[!]."

Cousin Georgiana choked back the tears and gave a little moan of despair instead.

"Oh, Doss, <u>what</u> have you done? What <u>have</u> you done?"

"I've just been telling you. I've got married," said ~~Miranda~~ Valancy[,] calmly and patiently.

"To that – that – aw – that – <u>Barney Snaith</u>. Why, they say he's had a dozen wives already."

"I'm the only one round at present," said ~~Miranda~~ Valancy.

"What will your poor mother say?" moaned Cousin G.^eorgiana.^

"Come along with me and hear, if you want to know," said ~~Miranda~~ Valancy ~~impatiently~~ ^~~coolly.~~^ "I'm on my way to tell her now."

Cousin G^eorgiana^ let go the gate-post cautiously and found that she could stand alone. She meekly trotted on beside ~~Miranda~~ Valancy – who suddenly seemed quite a different person in her eyes. Cousin G.^eorgiana^ ~~had a tremendous respect for~~ ^had a tremendous respect for ^a^ married women.[10] But it was terrible to think of what the poor girl had done. So rash. So reckless[.] ~~NOTE L15~~ NOTE X9 ~~Yet she looked very happy. Cousin G. had never seen that look in Miranda's eyes before. But what would Amelia say? And Ben?~~

When they turned in at the Stirling gate Miranda gave an exclamation of surprise.

"Look at my rose bush![12] Why, it's blooming[!]."

It was. Covered with blossoms. Great, crimson, velvety blossoms. Fragrant. Glowing. Wonderful.

"My cutting it to pieces must have done it good," said ~~Miranda~~ Valancy, laughing. She gathered a handful of the blossoms ~~NOTE F13~~ NOTE Y9 and went, ~~still~~ still laughing, up the walk, conscious that Olive was standing on the steps, Olive, goddess like in loveliness, looking down ~~condescendingly~~ with a slight frown on her forehead. ~~NOTE Z15 NOTE M13~~ NOTE Z9

So ~~Miranda~~ Valancy had come home.,[13] Thank goodness, ^thought Olive.^ But ~~Miranda~~ Valancy ^this poised, confident thing^ was not looking like a repentant, returned prodigal. This was the cause of Olive's frown. ~~There was something~~ ^She was looking^ triumphant – graceless! – ~~about Miranda~~. That outlandish dress – that queer hat ~~NOTE Q13~~ NOTE A10 Yet there was something about both dress and hat, as Olive instantly felt, that was entirely lacking in her own attire. This deepened the frown. She put out a ~~dignified~~ ^condescending^ hand.

"So you're back, Doss? Very warm day, isn't it? Did you walk in?"

"Yes." Coming in?"

"Oh, no. I've just been in. I've come often to comfort poor Aunty. She's been so lonesome. I'm going to Mrs. Bartlett's ~~XX~~ tea ^next^. ^I have to help pour.^ She's giving it for her cousin from Toronto. Such a charming girl. You'd have loved meeting her, Doss. I think Mrs. Bartlett did send you a card. Perhaps you'll drop in later on."

"No, I don't think so," said ~~Miranda~~ Valancy indifferently. "I'll have to be home to get Barney's supper. We're going for a moonlit canoe ride around Mistawis tonight."

"Barney? Supper?" gasped Olive. "What <u>do</u> you mean, ~~Miranda~~ Valancy Stirling?"

"~~Miranda~~ Valancy Snaith, by the grace of God."

~~Miranda~~ Valancy ~~flashed~~ flaunted her wedding[-]ring in Olive's stricken face. Then she nimbly slipped past her and into the house. Cousin Georgiana followed. She would not miss a moment of the great scene, even though Olive did look as if she were going to faint.

Olive did not faint. She went stupidly down the street to Mrs. Bartlett's. <u>What</u> did Doss mean? She couldn't have – that ring – oh, what fresh scandal was

NOTE Y9: —they would look well on the supper table of the veranda at Mistawis—

NOTE Z9: Olive, beautiful, insolent. Her full form voluptuous in its swathings of rose silk and lace. Her golden-brown hair curling richly under her big, white-frilled hat. Her color ripe and melting.
    "Beautiful," thought Valancy coolly, "but"— as if she suddenly saw her cousin through new eyes—"without the slightest touch of distinction."

13: Montgomery changed a period to a comma here but did not correct the capitalized "Thank" to "thank."

NOTE A10: – those hands full of blood-red roses.

14: "Malice prepense" is a legal term meaning intending to kill or injure someone. It's sometimes expressed as "malice aforethought."

NOTE B10: not humble & deprecating as she should have been. And so oddly, improperly young-looking.

NOTE C10: She could even see a number of good qualities in them that she had never seen before. And she was sorry for them.

NOTE D10: Uncle Benjamin bounced up and sat down again.

that wretched girl bringing on her defenceless family now? She should have been – shut up – long ago.

~~Miranda~~ Valancy opened the ~~parlor~~ ^sitting[-] room^ door and stepped unexpectedly right into a grim assemblage of Stirlings. They had not come together of malice ~~propense~~ prepense.[14] Aunt Wellington and Cousin Gladys and Aunt Mildred ^and Cousin Sarah^ had just called in on their way home from a meeting of the missionary society. ~~to see if~~ Uncle James had dropped in to give Amelia some information regarding a doubtful investment. Uncle Benjamin had called, apparently[,] to tell them it was a hot day and ask them what was the difference between ~~an organist and a man suffering~~ a bee and a donkey. Cousin Stickles had ^been tactless enough to know^ ~~known~~ the answer—"one gets all the honey, the other one all the whacks"—and Uncle Ben^jamin^ was in a bad humor. In all of their minds, unexpressed, was the idea of finding out if ~~Miranda~~ Valancy had yet come home[,] and[,] if not what steps must be taken in the matter.

Well, here was ~~Miranda~~ Valancy at last, ^a poised, confident thing, ~~NOTE J15~~ NOTE B10 She stood in the doorway and looked at them, Cousin Georgiana ~~behind her,~~ timorous, expectant, ^behind her.^

~~Miranda~~ Valancy was so happy she didn't hate her people any more. ~~NOTE Q14~~ NOTE C10 ~~She was just sorry for them.~~ Her pity made her quite gentle.

"Well, mother," she said, pleasantly.

"So you've come home at last[!];" said Mrs. ~~George~~ Frederick, getting out a handkerchief. She dared not be ~~sulky~~ ^outraged[,]^ but she did not mean to be cheated of her tears.

"Well, ~~for an hour or so~~ ^not exactly,^" said ~~Miranda~~ Valancy. She threw her bomb. "I thought I ought to drop in and tell you I was married. Last Tuesday night. To Barney Snaith."
~~NOTE K15~~ NOTE D10

"God bless my soul," ^he^ said ~~Uncle Ben~~ dully. The rest seemed turned to stone. Except Cousin ~~Gladys~~ Gladys, who ~~stepped off the sofa in a~~ ^turned^ faint.

Aunt Mildred and Uncle Wellington had to ~~carry out~~ ^help her out^ to the kitchen. ~~Nobody else followed — not even Cousin Georgiana who was determined~~

"She would have to keep up the Victorian traditions," said ~~Miranda~~ Valancy, with a grin. She sat down, uninvited, on a chair. Cousin Stickles had begun to sob.

"Is there <u>one</u> day in your life that you haven't cried?" asked ~~Miranda~~ Valancy curiously.

"~~Miranda~~ Valancy," said Uncle James, being the first to recover the power of utterance, "did you mean what you said just now?"

"I did."

"Do you mean to say that you have actually gone and married – <u>married</u> – that notorious Barney Snaith – that – that – criminal – that—"

"I have."

"Then," said Uncle James violently, "you are a shameless ~~indecent~~ creature, lost to all sense of ~~decency~~ ^propriety^ and virtue, and I wash my hands entirely of you. I do not want ever to see your face again."

"What have you left to say when I commit ~~murder,~~ ^murder?"^ asked ~~Miranda~~ Valancy ~~coolly~~.

Uncle Ben^jamin^ again appealed to God ~~to bless my^his^ soul.~~ to bless his soul.

"That drunken outlaw – that—"

A dangerous spark appeared in ~~Miranda's~~ Valancy's eyes. They might say what they liked to and of her but they should not abuse Barney.

~~NOTE N13~~ NOTE E10

"<u>You</u> would be more endurable if you got drunk occasionally. Barney is <u>not</u> a ~~drunken~~ drunkard."

"~~I saw him~~ ^He was seen^ drunk in Port Laurence—pickled to the gills," said Uncle Benjamin.

"~~That was the only time he ever was drunk in his life. He told me so. I don't know <u>why</u> he got drunk then but I <u>do know</u>~~ ^"If that is true—and I don't believe it—^ he had a good reason for it. Now, I suggest that you all stop looking tragic and accept the situation. I'm married— you can't undo that. And I'm perfectly happy." ~~NOTE O13~~

NOTE F10

NOTE E10: "Say [']damn['] and you'll feel better," she suggested.

"I ~~cian~~ can express my feelings without blasphemy. And I tell you you have covered yourself with eternal disgrace & infamy by marrying that drunkard[—]"=

NOTE F10: "I suppose we ought to be thankful he has really married her," said Cousin Sarah, by way of trying to look on the bright side.

"If he really has," said Uncle James,

"~~Not if you really are married,~~" said Uncle James, who had just washed his hands of ~~Miranda~~ Valancy. "Who married you?"

"Mr. Towers of Port Laurence."

^"By^ A[15] Free Methodist," groaned Mrs. ~~George~~ Frederick – as if to have been married by an imprisoned Methodist would have been a shade less disgraceful. It was the first thing she had said. Mrs. ~~George~~ Frederick didn't know <u>what</u> to say. The whole thing was too horrible – too ~~nightmarish~~ nightmarish. She was sure she must wake up soon. After all their bright hopes at the funeral!

"It makes me think of those what-d'ye-call-'ems," said Uncle Benjamin helplessly. "Those yarns – you know – of fairies taking babies out of their cradles."

"~~Miranda~~ Valancy could hardly be a changeling at twenty-nine," said Aunt Wellington satirically.

"She was the oddest[-]looking baby I ever saw, anyway," averred Uncle Benjamin. "I said so at the time – you remember, Amelia? I said I had never seen such eyes in a human head."

"~~I'm glad I never had any~~"

"I'm glad <u>I</u> never had any children," said Cousin Sarah. "If they don't break your heart in one way they do it in another."

"Isn't it better to have your heart broken than to have it wither up?" ~~asked Miranda~~ ^queried Valancy^. "Before it could be broken it must have felt something splendid. <u>That</u> would be worth the pain."
~~NOTE J15~~ NOTE G10

~~Miranda~~ "Valancy," said Mrs. ~~George~~ Frederick solemnly, "do you ever pray to be forgiven for disobeying your mother?"

"I <u>should</u> pray to be forgiven for obeying you so long," said ~~Miranda~~ Valancy stubbornly. "But I don't pray about that at all. I just thank God every day for my happiness."

"I would rather," said Mrs. ~~George~~ Frederick, beginning to cry rather belatedly, "see you dead before me than listen to what you have told me to-day."

~~Miranda~~ Valancy looked at her mother and aunts, & wondered if they could ever have known anything of the real meaning of love. She felt sorrier for them than ever. They were so very pitiable. ^And they never suspected it.^

~~"Have you no pride?" demanded Aunt Wellington.~~

~~"Lots of it. For one thing, I'm proud that I have achieved a husband of my own unaided~~

"Barney Snaith is a scoundrel to have ~~induced~~ ^deluded^ you ~~into~~ ^into^ marrying him," said Uncle James violently.

"Oh, I did the ~~inducing.~~ ^deluding.^ I asked him to marry me," said ~~Miranda~~ Valancy, with a wicked smile.

"Have you no pride?" demanded ~~Uncle~~ ^Aunt^ Wellington.

"Lots of it. I am proud that I have achieved a husband by my own unaided efforts. Cousin Georgiana here wanted to help me to Edward Beck."

"Edward Back is worth twenty thousand dollars and has the finest house between here and Port Laurence," said Uncle Ben^jamin^.

"That sounds very fine," said ~~Miranda~~ Valancy scornfully, "but it isn't worth that –" she snapped her fingers – "compared to feeling Barney's arms around me and his cheek against mine."

~~NOTE A14~~ NOTE H10

"~~Miranda~~ Valancy, you need not be indecent~~,~~." ~~said Aunt Wellington.~~

"Why, it surely isn't indecent to like to have your husband put his arm around you? I should think it would be indecent if you didn't."

"Why expect decency from her?" inquired Uncle James ^sarcastically.^ ["]She has cut herself off from decency forevermore. ~~Let he go~~ She has made her bed. Let her lie on it."

"Thanks," said ~~Miranda~~ Valancy ^very^ gratefully ~~NOTE L15~~ NOTE I10 ~~"Mother, may I have those three woolen cushions I worked last winter"~~

~~"Take~~

~~"Now I am~~ must really be getting back. Mother, may I have those three woolen cushions I worked last winter?"

NOTE H10: "Oh, Doss!" said Cousin Stickles. Cousin Sarah said, "Oh, Doss!" Aunt Wellington said,

NOTE I10: "How you would have enjoyed being Torquemada![16] Now, I must really be

16: Tomás de Torquemada (1420–1498), Dominican friar, Grand Inquisitor of the Spanish Inquisition.

NOTE S14: "Doss, dear," said Cousin Georgiana mournfully, "some day you will discover that blood is thicker than water."
"Of course it is. But who wants water to be thick?" parried Valancy. "We want water to be thin – sparkling – crystal-clear." Cousin Stickles groaned.

NOTE K10: ["]My poor, unfortunate girl!"

NOTE L10: "For my part, I believe the man is half Indian. I haven't a doubt they're living in a wigwam."
"If he has married her under the name of Snaith and it isn't his real name wouldn't that make the marriage null & void?" asked Cousin ~~Gladys~~ Stickles hopefully. Uncle James shook his head. "No, it is the man who marries, not the name."

"Take them – take everything," said Mrs. ~~George.~~ Frederick.

"Oh, I don't want everything – or much. I don't want my Blue Castle cluttered. Just the cushions. I'll call for them some day when we motor in."

~~Miranda~~ Valancy rose and went to the door. There she turned. She was sorrier than ever for them all. <u>They</u> had no Blue Castle in the purple solitudes of Mistawis[.] ~~= no calling pine trees. She~~
~~NOTE M15~~ NOTE J10

^❡ ~~Miranda~~ ❡ ~~She~~ Valancy^ would not ask any of them to come and see her—she was afraid they <u>would</u> come out of curiosity. ~~She didn't want~~ But she said,

"Do you mind if I drop in and see you once in a while?[,] Mother?"

"My house will always be open to you," said Mrs. ~~George~~ Frederick, with a mournful dignity.

"You should never recognize her again," said Uncle ~~Be~~ James sternly, as the door closed behind ~~Miranda~~ Valancy.

"I can not quite forget that I am a mother," said Mrs. ~~George~~ Frederick. NOTE K10 ~~"Oh, that~~ ^ "My poor ^ ~~un-fortunate girl! "Who – who – will protect her when I am gone."~~

"I dare[ ]say the marriage isn't legal," said Uncle ~~James,~~^comfortingly.^ "He has probably been married half a dozen times before. But <u>I</u> am through with her. I have done all I could, Amelia. I think you will admit that. Henceforth" – Uncle James was terribly solemn about it – "~~Miranda~~ Valancy is to me as one dead."

"Mrs. Barney Snaith," said Cousin Georgiana, as if trying it out to see how it would sound.

~~"The very idea of a man named ^named^ Snaith," said Cousin Sarah. "Why, his name is enough to con-demn him."~~

"He has a score of aliases, no doubt," said Uncle Benjamin. NOTE L10
~~NOTE S13~~ NOTE L10

"You know," said Cousin Gladys, who had recovered and returned,^but was still shaky.[,]^ "I had a distinct premonition of this at Herbert's ~~our~~ silver dinner—I remarked it at the time. When she was defending Snaith. You remember, of course? It came over me like a revelation. I spoke to David when I went home about it." ~~NOTE R19~~ NOTE M10

"~~Miranda~~ Valancy is so fond of mushrooms," sighed Cousin Georgiana. "I'm afraid she'll get poisoned eating toadstools by mistake, living up back in the woods."

"There are worse things than death," said Uncle James, ~~NOTE B14~~ NOTE N10

~~Miranda,~~ Valancy, hurrying along the dusty road, back to a cool Mistawis and her purple island, had forgotten all about them – just as she had forgotten that she might drop dead at any moment if she hurried.

NOTE M10: "What – what," demanded Aunt Wellington of the universe, "has come over Valancy? Valancy!"

The universe did not answer but Uncle James did.

"Isn't there something coming up of late about secondary personalities cropping out? I don't hold with many of those new-fangled notions[,] but there may be something in this one. It would account for her incomprehensible conduct."

NOTE N10: believing that it was the first time in the world that such a statement had been made.

"Nothing can ever be the same again," sobbed Cousin Stickles.

Valancy 320.

Miranda, hurrying along the
dusty road, back to cool
mistress's and her purple
island, had problem all
along there — just as she
had, problem that she caught
drop dead at any moment.
if she hurried.

XXVI

Summer and autumn passed
by. The Stirling clan had tacitly
agreed to follow Uncle James'
example and look up on ~~Miranda~~ Valancy
as one dead. To be sure, ~~Miranda~~ Valancy
had all ~~her~~ quit ghostly habit of
recurring resurrections, when
she and Barney clattered
through Deerwood and out to

XXVIII

S ummer ~~and autumn~~ passed by. The Stirling clan ~~NOTE U13~~ NOTE O10 had tacitly agreed to follow Uncle James' example and look upon ~~Miranda~~ Valancy as one dead. To be sure, ~~Miranda~~ Valancy had an ~~inconvenient~~ ^unquiet, ghostly^ habit of recurring ~~resurrections,~~when she and Barney clattered through Deerwood and out to the Port in that unspeakable car. ~~Miranda~~ Valancy, bare=headed, ~~and radiant-eyed.~~ ^with stars in her eyes.^ Barney, bare-headed, smoking his pipe. But shaved. Always shaved now, if any of them had noticed it. They even had the audacity to go into Uncle Benjamin's store to buy groceries. Twice Uncle Ben^jamin^ ignored them. Was not ~~Miranda~~ Valancy one of the dead? While Snaith had never existed. But the third time he told Barney he was a scoundrel who should be hung for luring an unfortunate, weak-minded girl away from her home and friends. ~~NOTE S19~~ NOTE P10 | 1

~~"She is happy with me," he ^he^ said Barney coolly," and she was miserable with her friends. So ^that's that." ^ What are you going to do about it?"~~ NOTE S15 NOTE R15

Uncle Benjamin remembered just in time that ~~Miranda~~ Valancy was dead. He turned his back on Barney.

~~Miranda~~ Valancy <u>was</u> happy—gloriously and entirely so. She seemed to be living in a wonderful house of life and every day opened a new mysterious room. ~~NOTE O15~~ NOTE Q10 ❡ The absolute freedom of it all was unbelievable. They could do

---

NOTE O10: —with the insignificant exception of Cousin Georgiana—

NOTE P10: Barney's one straight eyebrow went up.
   ~~"She is happy with me,"~~
^"I have made her happy,"^ he said coolly, "and she was miserable with her friends. So that's that."
   Uncle Benjamin stared. It had never occurred to him that women had to be, or

ought to be, "made happy."
   "You – you pup!" he said.
   "Why be so unoriginal?" queried Barney amiably. "Anybody could call me a pup. Why not think of something worthy of the Stirlings? Besides, I'm not a pup. I'm really quite a middle-aged dog. Thirty[-] five, if you're interested in knowing."

1: NOTE P10 opens as a separate

paragraph in the published version.

NOTE Q10: It was in a world which had nothing in common with the one she had left behind – a world where time was not – which was young with immortal youth – where there was neither past nor future but only the present. She surrendered herself utterly to the charm of it.

177

2: A "Mrs. Grundy" is an extremely judgmental person, overly concerned with propriety, named for a character in *Speed the Plough*, a 1798 play by Thomas Morton.

3: Quoted from the hymn, "Peace, Perfect Peace," written in 1875 by Edward Bickersteth Jr. (1825–1906). Barney's quotation does not begin a new paragraph in the published version but continues the paragraph after "in-laws."

NOTE R10: "And you are really happy, dear?" asked Cousin Georgiana wistfully.
"I really am," said Valancy gravely, her eyes dancing.
"Marriage is such a serious thing," sighed Cousin Georgiana.
"When it's going to last long," agreed Valancy.
Cousin Georgiana did not understand this at all. But it worried her and she lay awake at nights wondering what Valancy meant by it[.]

4: oriel window = a bay window in the main wall of a building that is supported by brackets

NOTE S10: No desecrating gas ^imitation^ log but a real fireplace where you could burn real logs. With a big grizzly-bear skin on the floor before it[,]

5: "Regime" is spelled "régime" in the published version.

exactly as they liked. No Mrs. Grundy.[2] No traditions. No relatives. ^Or in-laws.^

"'Peace, perfect peace with loved ones far away,'"[3] ~~Ba~~ as Barney quoted shamelessly.

~~Miranda~~ Valancy had gone home once and got her cushions. And Cousin Georgiana had given her one of her famous candlewick spreads. ^of most elaborate design.^

"For your spare[-]room bed, dear," she said.

"But I haven't got any spare[-]room," said ~~Miranda~~ Valancy.

Cousin Georgiana looked horrified. A house without a spare[-]room was monstrous to her.

"But it's a lovely spread," said ~~Miranda~~ Valancy, with a kiss, "and I'm so glad to have it. I'll put it on my own bed. Barney's old patch[-]work quilt is getting ragged."

"I don't see how you can be content^ed^ to live ~~back~~ up back," sighed Cousin G^eorgiana^. "It is so out of the world."

"Contented!" ~~Miranda~~ Valancy laughed. What was the use of trying to explain to Cousin Georgiana. "It is," she agreed, "most gloriously and entirely out of the world ~~NOTE V13~~ NOTE R10

~~Miranda~~ Valancy loved her Blue Castle and was completely ~~satisfied~~ satisfied with it. The big living[-]room had three windows, ~~in it~~ all commanding exquisite views of exquisite Mistawis. The one in the end of the room was an oriel window[4] – which Tom McMurray, Barney explained, had got out of some little, old "up back" church that had been sold. It faced the west and when the ~~sunsets~~ flooded it ~~Miranda's~~ Valancy's whole being knelt in prayer as if in some great cathedral. The new moons always looked down through it, the lower pine boughs swayed about the top of it, and all through the nights the soft, "a dim silver of the lake dreamed through it.

There was a ~~big~~ stone fireplace on the other side[.] ~~NOTE T19 NOTE B16~~ NOTE S10 and ~~in front~~ beside it a hideous, red-plush sofa of Tom McMurray's ~~regime~~ regime.[5] But its ugliness was hidden by silver-gray timber wolf skins[,] and ~~Miranda's~~ Valancy's cushions made it gay and comfortable. In a corner a nice, tall, lazy old ~~grandfather~~ clock ticked—the right kind of a clock. One that did not hurry the hours away, but ticked them off deliberately NOTE ~~A16~~ NOTE T10. ❡ There was a big glass case of stuffed owls and several ~~deers~~ deer heads, – likewise of ^the^ Tom McMurray^'s vintage^. Some comfortable old chairs NOTE ~~D14~~ NOTE U10 ^~~and a table, and a big bookcase.~~ ❡ One side of the wall was lined with rough, home-made book-shelves-;filled with books, and between the two side windows hung ~~and~~ an old mirror in a faded gilt frame NOTE ~~V15~~ NOTE V10 A mirror, ~~Miranda~~ Valancy thought, that must ~~have been~~ ^be^ like the fabled mirror into which Venus had once looked and which thereafter reflected as beautiful every woman who looked into it. ~~Miranda~~ Valancy thought she was almost pretty in that mirror. But that may have been because she had shingled her hair.

This was before the day of bobs ~~and was~~ NOTE W10 a ~~drastic innovation. When the news filtered through the Stirling clan that the dead Miranda was running about the~~ and was ~~entirely Miranda's own idea.~~ NOTE U15 ~~Barney cut~~ ^cut the hair^ did it for her, cutting it ^her hair^ ~~square off at the back of her neck and brought~~ ^bringing^ it down in a short black fringe over her forehead. It gave a meaning and a purpose to her ^little, three-cornered^ face that it never had possessed before. Even her nose ceased to irritate her. Her eyes were bright[,] and her sallow skin had cleared ~~up amazingly~~ ^to the hue of creamy ~~old~~ ivory.^ The old family joke had come true—she was really fat at last – anyway, no longer skinny. ~~Miranda could~~ Valancy might never be beautiful[,] but she was of the type that looks its best in the woods – elfin – ~~pron~~ mocking – alluring.

Her heart bothered her very little. When an attack threatened she was generally able to head it off with Dr. Trent's prescription. The only bad one she had was one night when she was temporarily out of medicine. And it <u>was</u> a bad one. For the time being ~~Miranda~~ Valancy realized keenly that death was actually waiting to pounce on her any moment. But ~~she soon contrived to forget again.~~ ^the rest of the time she would not—did not—let herself remember it at all.^

NOTE T10: It was the jolliest looking old clock. A fat, corpulent clock with a great, round[,] man's face painted on it, the hands stretching out of its nose and the hours circling it like a halo.

NOTE U10: that asked to be sat upon. A squat little chair with a cushion was prescriptively Jigglesqueak's. If anybody else dared sit on it Jigglesqueak glared him out of it with his topaz-hued, black-ringed eyes. Jigglesqueak had an adorable habit of hanging over the back of it, trying to catch his own tail. Losing his temper because he couldn't catch it. Giving it a ~~fiece~~ fierce bite for spite when he <u>did</u> catch it. Yowling malignantly with pain. Barney and Valancy laughed at him until they ached. But it was Good Luck they loved. They were both agreed that Good Luck was so lovable that he practically amounted to an obsession.

NOTE V10: with fat cupids gambolling in the panel over the glass[.]

NOTE W10: and was ~~look~~ regarded as a wild, unheard-of proceeding—unless you had typhoid.[6] When Mrs. Frederick heard of it she almost decided to erase Valancy's name from the family Bible. Barney ~~did~~ cut the hair, square of[f] at the back of Valancy's neck-[,]

6: Typhoid is a serious bacterial infection, frequently caused by contaminated food or water. One side effect is hair loss. Sometimes the hair is cut off to cool the patient during the high fever. The first vaccine for typhoid was developed in 1896.

temporarily out of medicine. And
it was a bad one. For the time
being Miranda realised nearly
that death was actually waiting to pounce on her every moment.
But. the rest of the time the
world would not — did not — all nearly
remember it at all.

There is as really very little
work to do. Miranda cooked
their meals on a little coal
oil stove, performing all her
little domestic rites carefully
and even exultingly, and they
ate out on the veranda that
looked over the lake. Before
there mistakens take a scene
only of some fairy tale of old
time.

"What a nice old Tom picked

XXIX

NOTE X10

There was really very little work to do. ~~Miranda~~ ^She^ cooked their meals on a ~~little~~ coal[-]oil stove, performing all her little domestic rites carefully and ~~exiunt~~ exultingly, and they ate out on the veranda that almost overhung the lake. Before them ~~Mistawis lay~~ NOTE U15 NOTE Y10 ~~like a scene out of some fairy tale of old time.~~ NOTE D14 NOTE E14

~~delicate & elusive~~

"What a view old Tom picked out when he built this shack[!];" Barney would say exultantly.
NOTE W13 NOTE Z10

^The^ ~~Tthe~~ faint laughter[2] of winds was always about them and the colors of Mistawis[,] NOTE T15 NOTE A11 ~~under the changing clouds were something that cannot be expressed in wor mere words. Bats swooped about darkly against~~ NOTE W19 ~~the pale western~~ ℭ The cats, with their wise, innocent[,] little faces, would sit on the veranda railing and eat the tid-bits[3] Barney flung them. ~~At the les~~ And how good everything tasted[!]; NOTE Z15 NOTE B11

NOTE X10: Valancy toiled not, neither did she spin.[1]

1: From Matthew 6:28: "Consider the lilies of the field, how they grow; they toil not, neither do they spin."

NOTE Y10: ~~Drowned~~ lay Mistawis, ~~drowned in lilac light incredibly delicate and elusive~~, like a scene out of some fairy[ ]tale of old time. And Barney smiling ~~crookedly~~ ^his twisted, enigmatical smile^ at her across the table.

NOTE Z10: Supper was the meal ~~Miranda~~ Valancy liked best[.]

2: In the published version, "The faint laughter" does not start a new paragraph but follows

from the sentence in NOTE Z10.

NOTE A11: imperial & spiritual, under the changing clouds were something that cannot be expressed in mere words. Shadows, too. Clustering in the pines until a wind shook them out & pursued them over Mistawis. They lay all day along the shores, threaded by ferns & wild blossoms. They stole around the headlands in the glow of the sunset, until twilight wove them all into one great web of dusk.

3: In the published version, "tid-bits" is changed to "titbits."

NOTE B11: Valancy, amid all the romance of Mistawis, never forgot that men had stomachs (Barney paid her no end of compliments on her cookery.)[4]
"After all" he admitted, "there's something to be said for square meals. I've mostly got along by boiling two or three dozen eggs hard at once & eating a few when I got hungry, with a slice of bacon once in a while & a jorum[5] of tea."

4: "Cookery" is changed to "cooking" in the published version.

5: jorum = jug or bowl

Barney paid Miranda no end of complements on her cookery.[6] | NOTE X19 ❰ And she ^Valancy^ poured tea beautifully. It was an art.[7] Out of Barney's little, battered, old pewter teapot of incredible age. She had not even a set of dishes – only Barney's mismatched ^chipped^ bits – and a dear[,] ^big,^ pobby[8] old blue jug of robin's-egg blue.

After the ma meal was over they would sit there and talk for hours – or sit and say nothing, ^in all the languages of the world,^ Barney pulling away at his pipe, Miranda Valancy dreaming idly and deliciously;[.] NOTE C14 NOTE C11 The moonlight would begin to silver the Mistawis dusk. Bats would begin to swoop darkly against the pale, western gold. The little waterfall that came down over[9] the high bank not far away would ^by some whim of the wildwood gods,^ NOTE D11 begin to look like a wonderful, white woman beckoning through the evergreens spicy, fragrant evergreens;[.] the pines ^wo^ at the end of the island ^would begin to look like^ became a group of witches weaving spells by moonlight. NOTE G14 NOTE E11 How sweet it was to sit there and do nothing in the beautiful silence, with Barney at the other side of the table, smoking[!];

There were plenty of other islands in sight, though none were near enough to be troublesome as neighbors. NOTE Y15 NOTE F11 The lights of the houses in them would twinkle ^bloom^ out all over the lake[,] and bonfires would be lighted on their shores, streaming up into the wood shadows and throwing great, blood-red ribbons out over the waters. Music would drift to them alluringly from boats here and there, or from the verandas on the big house of the big millionaire on the biggest island.

"Would you like a house like that, Moonlight?" Barney asked once, waving his hand at it. He had taken to calling her Moonlight[,] and Miranda Valancy loved it. He told her she looked like a gleam of moonlight, though he would not tell her its his reason for it.[10]

"No," said ~~Miranda,~~ Valancy, who had once dreamed of a mountain castle ten times the size of the rich man's "cottage." ^NOTE~~C11~~ NOTE G11^ "~~No. It's too elegant.~~ ^NOTE G16^ ~~It would own me. Possess me, body and soul.~~ ^NOTE G16^ ~~I like a house I can love. And cuddle. And boss. Just like ours here."~~ ^NOTE Y16^

Away down at the far end of the lake they got every night a glimpse of a big[,] ~~transconti~~ transcontinental train ~~passing~~ ^rushing through^ a clearing. ~~Miranda~~ Valancy ~~watched~~ ^~~liked to~~^ ^liked to watch^ its lighted windows flash by and wonder who was on it and what hopes and fears it carried. She ^also^ amused herself by picturing Barney and herself going to the dances and dinners in the houses on the islands[,] but she did not want to go in reality. Once they ~~went~~ ^did go^ to a masquerade dance in the pavilion at one of the ~~big~~ hotels up the lake[,] and had a glorious ~~time~~ ^evening[,]^ but slipped away ^in their canoe[,]^ before unmasking time[,] ~~in their canoe~~ back to the Blue Castle.

"It was lovely – but I don't want to go again," said ~~Miranda.~~ Valancy.

So many hours a day Barney shut himself up in Bluebeard's ~~c~~Chamber. ~~Miranda~~ Valancy never saw the inside of it. ~~From the smells that drifted out sometimes on want~~ From the smells that filtered through at times she concluded he must be conducting chemical experiments—or counterfeiting money. ~~Miranda~~ Valancy supposed there must be smelly processes in making ~~counter~~ counterfeit money. But she did not trouble herself about it. She had no desire to peer into the locked chambers of Barney's house of life. His past and his future concerned her not. Only this rapturous present. Nothing else mattered.

~~Once Three times~~ ^Once^ he went away and stayed away two days and nights. ~~The first time h~~He had asked ~~Miranda~~ Valancy if she would be afraid to stay alone and she had said she would not. He never told her where he had been. ~~nor She was never allowed to see the mail he brought from Port Laurence.~~ She was not afraid to be alone[,] but she was horribly lonely. The sweetest sound

NOTE G11: and now pitied the poor inhabitants of palaces. "No. It's too elegant. I would have to carry it with me everywhere I went. On my back like a snail. It would own me—possess me, body & soul. I like a house I can love & cuddle. And boss.[11] Just like ours here. I don't envy Hamilton Gossard 'the finest summer residence in Canada.' It is magnificent[,] but it isn't my Blue Castle."

11: In the published version, "And boss" is not a new sentence but continues the previous sentence (…"cuddle and boss").

12: Lines from the poem
"Nuns Fret Not at
their Convent's Narrow
Room" (1807) by
William Wordsworth
(1770–1850).

she had ever heard was Lady Jane's clatter through the woods when Barney returned. And then his signal whistle from the shore. ~~NOTE 116~~ She ran down to the landing rock to greet him – to nestle herself into his eager arms – they did seem eager.

"Have you missed me, Moonlight?" Barney was whispering.

"It seems a hundred years since you went away," said ~~Miranda~~ Valancy.

"I won't leave you again."

"You must," protested ~~Miranda~~ Valancy. "If you want to. I'd be miserable if I thought you wanted to go and didn't, because of me. I want you to feel perfectly free."

Barney laughed – a little cynically.

"There is no such thing as freedom on earth," he said. "Only different kinds of bondages." And comparative bondages." ~~I find my present bondage very = bearable."~~ ~~But Miranda~~ You think you are free now because you've escaped from a peculiarly unbearable kind of bondage. But are you? You love me—that's a bondage."

"Who said or wrote that 'the prison into which we doom ourselves no prison is'?"[12] asked ~~Miranda~~ Valancy dreamily, ~~as~~ clinging to his arm as they climbed up the rock steps.

"Ah, now you have it," said Barney. "That's all the freedom we can hope for—the freedom to choose our prison. But, Moonlight"—he stopped at the door of the Blue Castle and looked about him – at the glorious lake, the great, shadowy woods, the bonfires, the twinkling lights [ ] ~~outside = the moonlit oriel —~~ "Moonlight, I'm glad to be home again. When I came down through the woods and saw my home[ ]light[s] – ~~mine~~ mine – gleaming out under the old pines – something I'd never seen before – oh, girl, I was glad – glad!"

But in spite of Barney's ~~decline of freedom~~ ^doctrine of bondage[,]^ ~~Miranda~~ Valancy thought they were splendidly free. ~~They could = and did = do anything they liked, whenever the mo notion took them.~~ It was amazing to be able to ~~stay out all night~~ ^sit up half the night & look at the moon^ if you wanted to. To be late for meals if you wanted to ~~NOTE D16 NOTE E16~~ NOTE H11. Not to come home at all for meals if you wanted to. ~~To s~~Sit on a sun-warm rock and paddle your bare feet in the hot sand if ~~and when~~ you wanted to. ~~in To~~ Just sit and do nothing in the beautiful silence if you wanted to. In short, ~~to~~ do ~~any-thing you liked~~ ^any fool thing you wanted to^ whenever the notion took you. If <u>that</u> wasn't freedom what was?

NOTE H11: —she who had always been rebuked so sharply by her mother & so reproachfully by Cousin Stickles if she were one minute late. Dawdle over meals as long as you wanted to. Leave your crusts ^if you wanted to.^

away, told them[?] 341 you wanted to
you liked whenever the notion
took you. If that wasn't freedom
what was?

<del>XII.</del> XXVIII

They did <del>not spend</del> all their
<del>days</del> on the island. They spend-
 more than half of their wandering
at will through <del>the</del> back. They
explored the <del>Muskoka</del> region on
foot. <del>Barney knew the</del> woods
<del>like</del> <del>a book and to taught</del>
<del>them</del> love <del>of</del> Miranda. She learned
the different fairy-likenesses &
<del>the</del> mosses — the charm and
exquisiteness of woodland blossoms.
She learned to know every bird
at sight and mimic its call —
though never so perfectly as
Barney. She made friends with
every kind of tree. She learned

XXX

They didn't spend all their days on the island. They spent more than half of them wandering at will through ~~up back.~~ ^the enchanted Muskoka country.^ ~~NOTE H16~~ NOTE I11 ~~They explored the Muskoka region on foot. Barney knew the woods like as a book and he taught their lore ^& craft^ to Miranda~~ NOTE F16. ~~She~~ learned the different fairy-likenesses of the mosses – the charm and exquisiteness of woodland blossoms. She learned to know every bird at sight and mimic its call – though never so perfectly as Barney. She made friends with every kind of tree. She learned to row[2] a canoe as well as Barney himself. She liked to be out in the rain and she never caught cold. Sometimes[3] they took a lunch with them and went berrying – strawberries and blueberries[.] ~~NOTE Z13~~ NOTE Z13. How pretty blueberries were—the dainty green of the unripe berries, the glossy pinks and scarlets of the ~~unripe berries~~ half ripes, the misty blue of the fully matured[!][4] | ~~NOTE Z13~~ NOTE J11 ℂ Or they went after water-lilies. Barney knew where to find them in the ~~cruks~~ creeks and bays of Mistawis. Then the Blue Castle was glorious with them. Every receptacle that ~~Miranda~~ Valancy could contrive filled with the exquisite things. ~~If it wasn't~~ NOTE K11

~~Sometimes they went trouting on little hidden woodland nameless rivers. ^ NOTE V19^ where long tracks of~~

Then[9] all they took with them were some raw potatoes and salt. They roasted the potatoes over a fire and Barney showed ~~Miranda~~ Valancy how to cook the trout by wrapping them in leaves, coating them with mud and baking them in a bed of hot coals. Never were such

NOTE I11: ~~where it seemed to Valancy that the ancient gods might be met with in those wild places.~~[1] Barney knew the woods as a book & he taught their lore & craft to Valancy. He could always find trail & haunt of the shy wood people. Valancy

1: The preceding phrase ("where it seemed… in those wild places") is omitted in the published version.

2: In the published version, "row" is changed to "paddle."

3: In the published version, a new paragraph begins with "Sometimes."

4: Montgomery used this passage from her essay "The Woods in Summer": "See how pretty they are—the dainty green of the unripe berries, the glossy pinks and scarlets of the half-ripe, the misty blue of the fully matured."

NOTE J11: And Valancy learned the real flavor of the strawberry in its highest perfection. There was a certain sunlit dell over the banks of Mistawis along which white birches grew on one side & on the other still, changeless ranks of ~~the sp~~ young spruces. *(continued on next page)*

NOTE J11 *continued*: There were long grasses at the roots of the birches, combed down by the winds & wet with morning dew late into the afternoons. Here they found berries ^that might^ ~~fit for~~ have graced the banquets of Lucellus,[5] great ambrosial sweetnesses hanging like rubies to long, rosy stalks. They lifted them by the stalk & ate them from it, uncrushed & virgin, testing each berry by itself with all its wild fragrance ensphered therein. When ~~Miranda~~ Valancy carried any of these berries home that elusive essence escaped & they became nothing more than the common berries of the market[-]place—very kitchenly good indeed[,] but not as they would have been ~~gathered~~ eaten in their birch dell until her fingers were stained as pink as Aurora's[6] eyelids –[7] | NOTE Y14 | 8

5: By "Lucellus" Montgomery means Lucullus (c. 117 BC–57 AD), a Roman general well-known for his extravagant banquets.

6: Aurora = the Roman goddess of the dawn

7: This paragraph, with small changes, appears in Montgomery's essay "The Woods in Summer": "But would you know the real flavour of the strawberry in its highest perfection? Then come with me to a certain sunlit dell, along which white birches grow on one side and on the other the still, changeless ranks of the spruces. There are long grasses here at the roots of the trees, combed down by the winds, and wet with morning dew, long into the afternoon. Here we shall find berries, fit for the gods on high Olympus, great ambrosial sweetnesses, hanging like rubies to long, rosy stalks. Lift them by the stalk and eat them from it while they are uncrushed and virgin, tasting each berry by itself, with all

its wild fragrance ensphered within. If you try to carry it home that elusive essence escapes, and then it is nothing more than a common berry of the fields and sunshine, very kitchenly good, indeed, but not as it should be when gathered and eaten in its uncharted haunts until our fingers are stained as pink as Aurora's eyelids."

NOTE Y14: But they took some strawberries home and Valancy made them up into jam; and sealed it up in lovely little blue-and-white apothecary jars, ~~relics~~ that had come from the drug-store of a dead-and-gone brother of Tom MacMurray's. They had queer names printed on them over which Barney & Valancy had lots of fun.

8: NOTE Y14 is the last note Montgomery added in the Notes section. It is not used in the published version.

NOTE K11: If not water lilies then cardinal flowers, fresh and vivid from the swamps of Mistawis where they burned like ribbons of flame[.]
Sometimes they went trouting on little nameless rivers or hidden brooks on whose banks Naaids might have sunned their white, wet limbs.

9: In the published version, "Then" does not start a new paragraph but continues the previous paragraph after "wet limbs."

delicious meals. ~~Miranda~~ Valancy ~~ate~~ had such an appetite it was no wonder she put flesh on her bones.

Or they just prowled ^& explored^ ~~NOTE Y13~~ NOTE L11 Once or twice[10] night overtook them, too far from their Blue Castle to get back. But Barney made ~~a bed of fern and fir boughs~~ fragrant bed of ~~ferns~~ ^bracken^ and fir boughs and they slept on it dreamlessly, under a ~~ceiling~~ ^ceiling^ of old spruces with ~~long trails of gray-green~~ moss hanging from them~~:~~[,] ~~NOTE G17~~ NOTE M11

~~There were rainy days of course,~~ ~~NOTE P16~~ Then Barney shut himself in Bluebeard[']s Chamber and ~~Miranda~~ Valancy read, or dreamed on the wolf-skins with Good Luck purring beside her and Jigglesqueak watching them suspiciously from his own peculiar chair.[11] On Sunday evenings they rowed[12] across to a point of land and walked from there through the woods to the little Free Methodist church.

NOTE N11 ~~One felt really too happy for Sunday. Miranda had never really liked Sundays before. Found herself really liking Sundays. ^Once, when the organist. For the first time in her life Miranda found herself really liking Sundays. ^~~ ~~NOTE H14 NOTE K14~~

~~Miranda~~ Valancy had taken ~~her 200 dollars~~ ^half of her 200 dollars^ ^some of her two hundred dollars^ out of the bank and spent it in pretty clothes. She had a little smoke-blue chiffon which she always put on when they spent the evening at home—smoke-blue with touches of silver about it. It was after she began wearing it that Barney began calling her Moonlight.

NOTE L11: through woods that always seemed to be expecting something wonderful to happen. At least, that was the way Valancy felt about them. Down the next hollow – over the next hill – you would find it. "We don't know where we're going but isn't it fun to go?" Barney used to say.

10: In the published version, a new paragraph begins here.

NOTE M11: while beyond them moonlight & the murmur of pines blended together so that one could hardly tell

which was light & which was sound.
There were rainy days, of course, when Muskoka was a wet green land. Days when showers drifted across Mistawis like pale ghosts of rain & they never thought of staying in because of it. Days when it rained in right good earnest & they had to stay in[.]

11: In the published version, the sentence that opens with "Then Barney" does not begin a new paragraph but continues after NOTE M11.

12: In the published version, "rowed" is corrected to "paddled."

NOTE N11: One felt really too happy for Sunday. Valancy had never really liked Sundays before.
And always, Sundays & weekdays, she was with Barney. Nothing else really mattered. And what a companion he was! How understanding[!]; On How jolly[!]; on How—how Barney-like! That summed it all up.

"Moonlight and blue twilight—that is what you look like in that dress. I like it. It belongs to you. ~~NOTE J14~~ NOTE O11 ~~Miranda~~ ^She^ had forgotten all the old humiliating things that used to come up against her in the night. ~~The dust pile = the bridesmaid disappointment~~—the injustices and the disappointments.[13] It was as if they had all happened to some other person – not to her, ~~Miranda~~ Valancy Snaith, who had always been happy. ~~NOTE H4~~ NOTE P11 ❦ Holmes speak[s] of grief "staining backward"[14] through the pages of life; but ~~Miranda~~ Valancy found her happiness had stained backwards likewise and flooded with rose[-]color her whole previous drab existence. ~~NOTE H4~~ NOTE Q11 ~~She had her hour now = and her Blue Castle.~~

And her dust pile!

One day ~~Miranda~~ Valancy had heaped up the sand ~~on~~ in the little island cove in a tremendous cone and stuck a gay little Union Jack on top of it.

"What are you celebrating?" Barney wanted to know.

"I'm just exorcising an old ~~memory~~ ^demon^," ~~Miranda~~ Valancy told him.

NOTE O11: You aren't exactly pretty[,] but you have some adorable beauty-spots. Your eyes. And that little, kissable dent just between your collar bones. You have the wrist & ankle of an aristocrat. That little head of yours is beautifully shaped. And when you look backward over your shoulder you're maddening – especially in twilight or moonlight. An elf maiden. A wood sprite. You belong to the woods, Moonlight—you should never be out of them. In spite of your ancestry[,] there is something wild and remote & untamed about you. And you have such a nice, sweet, throaty, summery voice. Such a nice voice for love-making.

"Shure an' ye've kissed the Blarney Stone," scoffed Valancy. But she tasted these compliments for weeks.

She got a pale green bathing-suit, too—a garment which would have given her clan their deaths if they had ever seen her in it. Barney taught her how to swim. Sometimes she put her bathing[-]dress on when she got up & didn't take it off until she went to bed – running down to the water for a plunge whenever she felt like it & sprawling on the sun-warm rocks to dry.

13: In the published version, "She had forgotten" is the start of a new paragraph, and there is no period after "night."

NOTE P11: "I understand now what it means to be born again," she told Barney.

14: From an essay on war by Oliver Wendell Holmes (1809–1894), "Bread and the Newspapers," in The Atlantic, September 1861: "a great calamity…illustrated by the image of a stain spreading backwards."

NOTE Q11: She found it hard to believe that she had ever been lonely & unhappy & afraid.

"When death comes, I shall have lived," thought Valancy. "I shall have had my hour."

~~She had her home now~~ and
her Bear Cattle.

'And her devil-pets'.

Here deep ~~Miranda~~ valiantly had beefed
up the ~~weird~~ in the little
island cove in a tremendous
cone and ~~settle~~ a gay little
lemon-feed ~ top of it.

"What - are you celebrating?"
Barney wanted to know.

"I'm just expressing our sad
~~memory~~ decision" ~~Miranda~~ Valiantly told Barney.
"~~here~~"

<u>III</u> <u>XXIX</u>

Autumn came, late September
with cool nights. They had to
~~smoke~~ the verandah; but
they needed a fire in the
big fireplace and sat before it
with talk and laughter. But

XXXI

Autumn came. Late September with cool nights. They had to forsake the verandah; but they kindled a fire in the big fireplace and sat before it with jest and laughter. ~~But~~ They left the doors open and Jigglesqueak and Good Luck came and went at pleasure; sometimes[1] they sat gravely ^NOTE R11^ ^on the bearskin^ ^~~on the faded Persian rug~~^ ~~between Miranda & Barney~~, sometimes they slunk off into the mystery of the chill night outside. The stars smouldered ~~above the~~ in the horizon mists through the old oriel. ^~~NOTE M14~~ NOTE S11^ The little waves began to make soft, sobbing splashes on the rocks below them in the rising winds. They needed no light but the firelight that sometimes leaped up and revealed them – sometimes shrouded them in shadow. When the night wind rose higher Barney would ~~rise and~~ shut the door and light a lamp and read ~~poetry~~ to her. ^~~NOTE F17~~ NOTE T11^

October – with a gorgeous pageant of colour around ^the great tinted peace of^ Mistawis[,] into which ~~Miranda~~ Valancy plunged her soul. Never had she imagined anything so splendid ^~~NOTE B17~~ NOTE U11^ Long dreamy purple days paddling ~~idlly~~ idly in their canoe along the shores and up the rivers of crimson and gold. ^~~NOTE C17~~^ ^NOTE V11^ Enchanted tempests that stripped the leaves from the trees and heaped them along the shores. Flying shadows of clouds. ^~~NOTE A17 NOTE W~~ NOTE W11^

November. With[3] uncanny witchery in its changed ~~woods~~ ^trees^. With murky, red sunsets flaming in smoky crimson behind the westering ~~woods~~ hills. With dear days when the ^austere^ woods were beautiful and gracious in a dignified serenity of folded hands &

1: In the published version, "sometimes" begins a new sentence.

NOTE R11: on the bearskin rug between Barney & Valancy~~,~~[;]

NOTE S11: The haunting, persistent croon of the pine trees filled the air.

NOTE T11: —poetry & essays & gorgeous, dim chronicles of ancient wars. Barney never would read novels~~,~~[:] he vowed they bored him. But sometimes she read them herself, curled up on the wolf-skins, laughing aloud in peace. For Barney was not one of those aggravating people who can never hear you smiling audibly over something you've read without inquiring blandly, "What is the joke?"

NOTE U11: A great, tinted peace. Blue, wind-winnowed skies. Sunlight sleeping in the glades of that fairy land.[2]

2: In the published version, "fairy land" is spelled as one word.

NOTE V11: A sleepy, red hunter's moon.

NOTE W11: What had all the smug, opulent lands out front to compare with this?

3: In the published version, a dash follows "November" and "With" is not capitalized.

NOTE X11: late, leafless gold of the juniper[-]trees

4: Much of this paragraph was taken from Montgomery's essay, "The Woods in Winter" with a few changes. In the essay it reads: "Of course, there are dear days sometimes, even in November, when the woods are beautiful and gracious in a dignified serenity of folded hands and closed eyes…days full of a fine pale sunshine that sifts through the firs and glimmers in the gray beechwood, lighting up evergreen banks of moss and washing the colonnades of the pines…days with a high-sprung sky of flawless turquoise, shading off into milkiness on the far horizons… days ending for all their mildness and dream in a murky red sunset…." (The ellipses are Montgomery's, for effect.) Other phrases and passages in this chapter were taken from this essay, as well.

NOTE Y11: when there was witch-laughter in the pines & fitful moans among the mainland trees.

NOTE Z11: December. Early snows and Orion. The pale fires of the Milky Way. It was really winter now—wonderful, cold, starry winter. How Valancy had always hated winter! Dull, brief, uneventful days. Long, cold, companionless nights. Cousin Stickles with her back that had to be rubbed continually. Cousin Stickles making weird noises gargling her throat in the mornings. *(continued on next page)*

closed eyes – days full of a fine, pale sunshine that sifted through the ~~pines~~ ^firs^ NOTE N14 NOTE X11 and ~~glim-merd~~ ^glimmered^ among the gray beeches, lighting up evergreen banks of moss and washing the colonnades of the pines. ~~d~~Days with a high-sprung sky of flawless turquoise; ~~shading off into milkiness on the far horizon~~ =.[4] ~~d~~Days when an exquisite melancholy seemed to hang over the landscape and dream about the lake. But days, too, of the wild blackness of great autumn storms, followed by dark, wet, streaming nights ~~NOTE Y16~~ NOTE Y11~~;~~ What cared they? Old Tom had built his roof well[,] and ~~their fire leaped high~~ ^their^ his chimney drew^.

"Warm fire – books – comfort – safety from storm – our cats on the rug. Moonlight," said Barney, "would you be any happier now if you had a million dollars?"

"No – nor half so happy. I'd be bored by conventions and obligations then."

~~"And you are happy?"~~

~~"Happy!" Miranda smiled at him across Good Lucks silver purring flank.~~

~~December~~ ~~NOTE W16 NOTE Z11~~ NOTE Z11 ~~It was winter now really~~ ~~NOTE U16~~ ~~How Miranda had always hated winter. Dull ^brief^ uneventful days. ^Long, ^ cold companionless nights. Cousin Stickles ^with her^ back that had to be^ back to be rubbed continually~~ ~~NOTE E17~~ in snow. The undergrowth along its sides was a little fairy forest out of marble. The shadows cast by the pale sunshine were fine and spiritual.[6]

"Come away," said Barney, turning. "We must not commit the desecration of tramping through there."

One evening they came upon a snowdrift far back in an old clearing which was in the exact likeness of a beautiful woman's profile. Seen too close ~~by~~ the resemblance was lost as in the fairy tale of the Castle of St. John.[7] Seen from behind it was a ~~shapels~~ shapeless oddity. But at just the right distance and angle the outline was so perfect that when they came suddenly upon it, gleaming out against the dark background of spruce in the glow of that winter sunset they both exclaimed in amazement. There was a low, noble brow, a straight, classic nose, lips

NOTE Z11 *continued*: Cousin Stickles whining over the price of coal. Her mother, probing, questioning, ignoring. Endless colds & bronchitis – or the dread of it. ~~Shortre~~ Redfern's Liniment & Purple Pills.

But now she loved winter. Winter was beautiful ["]up back["] – almost intolerably beautiful. Days of clear brilliance. Evenings that were like cups of glamo[u]r – the purest vintage of winter['] s ~~white~~ wine. Nights ~~like white poems~~ with their fire of stars. Cold, exquisite winter sunrises. Lovely ferns of ice all over the windows of the Blue Castle. Moonlight on birches in a silver thaw. Ragged shadows on windy evenings—torn, twisted, fantastic shadows. ~~Snowy twilights.~~ Great silences, austere & searching. Jewelled, barbaric hills. The sun suddenly breaking through gray clouds over long, white Mistawis. Icy-gray twilights, broken by snow[-]squalls, when their cosy living[-]room, with its goblins of firelight & inscrutable cats seemed cosier than ever. Every hour brought a new revelation & wonder.

Barney ran Lady Jane into Roaring Abel's barn and taught Valancy how to snowshoe—Valancy who ought to be laid up with bronchitis. But Valancy had not even a cold. Later on in the winter Barney had a terrible one & ~~Miranda~~ Valancy nursed him through it with a dread of pneumonia in her heart. But Valancy's colds seemed to have gone where old moons go. Which was lucky – for she hadn't even Redfern's Liniment. She had thoughtfully bought a bottle at the Port & Barney had hurled it into frozen Mistawis with a scowl.

"Bring no more of that devilish stuff here," he had ordered briefly. It was the first & last time he had spoken harshly to her.

They went for long tramps through the exquisite reticence of winter woods & the silver jungles of frosted trees[,] & found loveliness everywhere. ~~Valancy thought the hardwoods with their fearlessly displayed nakedness the first finest & rarest of all. And then she would change her mind when they found themselves among young fir trees lightly powdered with new fallen snow as if a veil of aerial lace had been tricksily flung over austere young druid priestesses forsworn to all such frivolities of vain adornment.~~[5] At times they seemed to be walking through a spellbound world of ~~diamond~~ & crystal & pearl, so white & radiant were clearings & lakes & sky. The air was so crisp & clear that it was half intoxicating.

Once they stood in a visitation of ~~ex~~ ecstasy at the entrance of a narrow path between ranks of birches. Every twig & spray was outlined

5: These highlighted lines, which are from Montgomery's essay "The Woods in Winter," do not appear in the published version.

6: From "The Woods in Winter," which reads: "Today I paused at the entrance of a narrow path between upright ranks of beeches. ... Every twig and spray was outlined in snow. The undergrowth along its sides was a little fairy forest cut out of marble. The shadows cast by the honey-tinted winter

sunshine were fine and spirit-like."

7: "Castle of St. John" is from "Bridal of Tremain" by Sir Walter Scott (1771–1832) in which a rock formation looks like a castle (perhaps the Castle of St. John in southwest Scotland) from a certain point but loses the resemblance when viewed from other points. Montgomery and her husband, Ewan Macdonald, visited Castle Rock, said to be the formation Scott wrote about, on their honeymoon in Scotland in 1911.

Montgomery described the phenomenon of the snowdrift in her essay "The Woods in Winter": "I remember coming upon a snowdrift in a clearing far back in the woods which was the exact likeness of a beautiful woman's profile. Seen too close by, the resemblance was lost, as in the fairy tale of the Castle of St. John: seen in front, it was a shapeless oddity; but at just the right distance and angle, the outline was so perfect that when I came suddenly upon it, gleaming out against the dark background of spruce in the glow of a winter sunset, I could hardly convince myself that it was not the work of a human Hand. There was a low, noble brow, a straight, classic nose, lips and chin and cheek curve modelled as if some goddess of old time had sat to the sculptor, and a breast of such cold, swelling purity as the very genius of the winter woods might display.'All the beauty that old Greece and Rome sang, painted, taught' was expressed in it; yet no eyes but mine saw it."

8: In the published version, a new paragraph begins with "'All the beauty.'" Barney's quote (and Montgomery's, in her essay) is slightly paraphrased from the last stanza of a poem by John Greenleaf Whittier (1807–1892), "To ----. After a Summer's Day Excursion" (1851): "The Beauty which old Greece or Rome Sung, painted, wrought, lies close at home; We need but eye and ear In all our daily walks to trace The outlines of incarnate grace, The hymns of gods to hear!"

9: In the published version, "world" is changed to "woods."

10: dingles = wooded valleys

11: incarnadines = reddens

12: This paragraph is from "The Woods in Winter," except that here Montgomery substitutes "tops of hills" for "faraway hill-tops of the south-west"; "world" for "waste places"; "are aware" for "know"; and "moment" for "gleam." She inserts "out" into "redness streams over the snow," and changes "firs" to "pines." She omits the last phrase of the original paragraph: "and over the woods falls the mystic veil of dreamy, haunted winter twilight."

and chin and cheek-curve modelled as if some goddess of old time had sat to the sculptor, and a breast of such cold, swelling purity as the very spirit of the winter woods might display. "'All the beauty that old Greece and Rome, sung, painted, taught,'" quoted Barney.[8]

"And to think no ~~human~~ human eyes save ours have seen or will see it," breathed ~~Miranda~~ Valancy, who felt at times as if she were living in a book by John Foster. As she looked around her she recalled some passages she had marked in the new Foster book Barney had brought her from the Port – with an adjuration not to expect <u>him</u> to read or listen to it.

"'All the tintings for winter woods are extremely delicate and elusive,[']" ~~recalled Miranda~~ ^recalled Valancy.^ "[']When the brief afternoon wanes and the sun just touches the tops of the hills there seems to be all over the world[9] an abundance, not of colour, but of the spirit of colour. There is really nothing but pure white after all, but one has the impression of fairy-like blendings of rose & violet, opal and heliotrope on the slopes – in the dingles[10] and along the curves of the forest[-] land. You feel sure the tint is there but when you look at it directly it is gone. From the corner of your eye you are aware that it is lurking over yonder in a spot where there was nothing but pale purity a moment ago. Only just when the sun is setting is there ~~a moment~~ ^a fleeting ~~space~~ moment^ of real color. Then the redness streams out over the snow and incarnadines[11] the hills and rivers and smites the crest of the pines with flame. Just a few minutes of transfiguration and revelation – and it is gone.'[12]

"I wonder if John Foster ever spent a winter in Mistawis," said ~~Miranda~~ Valancy.

"Not likely," scoffed Barney. "People who write ~~stuff~~ ^tosh^ like that generally write it in a warm house on some smug city street."

"You are too hard on John Foster," said ~~Miranda~~ Valancy severely. "No one could have written that little paragraph I read you last night without having seen it first – you know he couldn't."

"I didn't listen to it," said Barney ~~mosely~~ morosely. "You know I told you I wouldn't."

"Then you've got to listen to it now," persisted ~~Miranda~~ Valancy. She made him stand still on his snow-shoes ~~and listen to it~~ while she repeated it.

"'She is a rare artist, this old mother nature, who works "for the joy of the working"[13] and not in any spirit of vain show. To-day the fir woods are a symphony of greens & grays, so subtle that you cannot tell where one shade begins to be the other. Gray trunks, green bough, gray-green moss above the white, gray-shadowed floor. Yet the old gypsy doesn't like unrelieved monotones. She must have a dash of colour. See it. A broken dead fir bough, of a beautiful red-brown, swinging among the beards of moss.'"[14]

"Good Lord, do you learn all that fellow's books ~~off~~ by heart," was Barney['s] ^disgusted^ reaction, as he strode off.

"John Foster[']s books were all that saved my soul alive the past five years," ~~said Miranda~~ ^ avowed[15] Valancy.^ "Oh, Barney, ~~look~~ look at that exquisite filigree of snow in the furrows of that old elm[-]tree trunk." ~~To think I never noticed.~~

When they came out to the lake they changed from snowshoes to skates and skated home. For a wonder ~~Miranda~~ Valancy had learned, ~~to skate~~ when she was a little schoolgirl, ^to skate^ on the pond behind the Deerwood school. She never had any skates of her own[,] but some of the other girls had lent her their^s^ ~~skates~~ and she seemed to have a natural knack of it. ~~NOTE Z19~~ NOTE A12 She had never skated since she grew up[,] but the old trick came back quickly and glorious ~~which~~ ^were^ the ~~moonlit~~ hours she and Barney spent skimming over the white lakes and past the dark islands ^where the summer cottages were closed & silent.^ To-night they flew down Mistawis before the wind, in an exhilaration that crimsoned ~~Miranda's~~ Valancy's cheeks under her white tam. And at the end was her dear little house[,] ^on the island of pines,^ with a coating of snow on its roof, sparkling in the ~~faint early~~ moonlight. Its windows glinted impishly at her in the stray gleams.

13: A quote from "When Earth's Last Picture is Painted" (1892) by Rudyard Kipling (1865–1936).

14: This paragraph is taken from "The Woods in Winter" except that Montgomery added "gray-shadowed" to the "floor"; substituted "See it" for "And here it is"; and changed "brown" to "red-brown."

15: In the published version, "avowed" is changed to "averred."

NOTE A12: Uncle Benjamin had once promised her a pair of skates for Christmas~~;~~[,] but when Christmas came he had given her rubbers instead[.]

16: In the published version, "Christmas card" is changed to "picture-book."

17: In the published version, "when" is changed to "where."

NOTE B12: Valancy made delightful little tinsel stars & hung them up amid the greenery. She cooked a dinner to which Barney did full justice, while Good Luck & Jigglesqueak picked the bones.

"Looks exactly like ~~an~~ a Christmas card,[16] doesn't it?" said Barney.

They had a lovely Christmas. No rush. No scramble. No niggling attempts to make ends meet. No wild effort to remember whether she hadn't given the same kind of present to the same person ~~in~~ two Christmases before – no mob of last-minute shoppers – no dreary family "reunions" when[17] she sat mute and unimportant. ^No attacks of "nerves."^ They decorated the Blue Castle with pine boughs[,] and ~~NOTE A20~~ NOTE B12 ~~Miranda~~ ^She^ ~~cooked a sp dinner to which Barney did full justice.~~ [B20]

"A land that can produce a goose like that is an admirable land," vowed Barney. "Canada forever[!]~~;~~" And they drank to the Union Jack ~~in~~ a bottle of dandelion wine that Cousin Georgiana had given ~~Miranda~~ Valancy along with the bedspread.

"One never knows," Cousin G.^eorgiana^ had said solemnly[,] "when one may need a little stimulant."

Barney had asked ~~Miranda~~ Valancy what she wanted for a Christmas present.

"Something frivolous and unnecessary," said ~~Miranda~~ Valancy, who had got a pair of galoshes last Christmas and two long-sleeved woollen undervests the year before. And ~~son~~ so on back.

To her delight[,] Barney ~~br~~ gave her a necklace of pearl beads. ~~Miranda~~ Valancy had wanted a string of milky pearl beads—like congealed moonshine—^all her life.^ And these were so pretty. All that worried her was that they were really too good. They must have cost a great deal—fifteen dollars at least. ~~Miranda Valancy was sure~~ Could Barney afford that? She didn't know a thing about his finances. She had refused to let him buy any of her clothes—she had enough for that, she told him, as long as she would ~~need~~ need clothes. In ~~a~~ a round, black jar on the chimney[-]piece Barney put money for their household expenses – always enough. The jar was never ~~absolutely~~ empty[,] though ~~Miranda~~ Valancy never ~~saw~~ ^caught^ him replenishing it. He couldn't have much, of course, and that necklace – but ~~Miranda~~ Valancy tossed care aside. She would wear it and enjoy it. It was the first pretty thing she had ever had.

XXXII

New Year. The old, shabby, inglorious ^outlived^ calendar came down. The new one went up. ~~Aft~~ January was a month of storms. It snowed for three weeks on end. The thermometer went miles below zero and stayed there. But, as Barney & Miranda pointed out to each other, there were no mosquitoes. And the roar and crackle of their big fire drowned the howls of the north wind. Good Luck and Jigglesqueak ~~dozed, one~~ waxed fat and developed resplendent coats of thick, silky fur. Nip and Tuck had gone.

"But they'll come back in spring," promised Barney.

~~NOTE N17 NOTE I17~~ NOTE C12

It was easier now for the Stirlings to believe ~~Miranda~~ Valancy of the dead. Not even dim rumors of her having seen[6] at the Port, ~~whether she and Barney used to skate~~ came to trouble them[,] ~~NOTE K17~~ NOTE D12 Presumably ~~th~~ none of ~~them~~

NOTE C12: There was no monotony. Sometimes they had dramatic little private spats that never even thought of becoming quarrels. Sometimes Roaring Abel dropped in—for an evening or a whole day—with his old tartan cap and his long red beard coated with snow. He generally brought his fiddle & played for them[,] ═to the delight of all except Jigglesqueak[,] who would go temporarily insane & retreat under Valancy's bed. Sometimes Abel & Barney talked while Valancy made candy for them; sometimes they sat & smoked in silence a̲ l̲a̲ Tennyson & Carlyle[1], until the Blue Castle reeked & Valancy fled to the open. Sometimes Barney & Abel[2]

played checkers fiercely & silently the whole night through. Sometimes they all ate the russet apples Abel had brought while the jolly old clock ticked the delightful minutes away.[3]

"A plate of apples, an open fire, and a jolly goode booke wheron to looke"[4] are a fair substitute for heaven," vowed Barney. "Any[ ]one can have the streets of gold. Let's have another whack at Carman."[5]

1: Tennyson & Carlyle: English poet Alfred Lord Tennyson (1809–1892) and Scottish essayist Thomas Carlyle (1795–1881)

2: In the published version, "Barney & Abel" is changed to "they."

3: Montgomery seemed to forget about Roaring Abel after Cissy died and adds this scene in NOTE C12 to bring him back into the story.

4: From a poem by John Wilson (1785–1854): "Oh, for a book and a shady nook"

5: Bliss Carman: Canadian poet (1861–1929)

6: In the published version, "seen" is changed to "over."

NOTE D12: though she & Barney used to skate there occasionally to see a movie & eat hot dogs shamelessly at the corner stand afterwards.

NOTE E12: ~~But Jiggle~~ It was very nice to feel a little Lucky cat jump up on your bed in the darkness & snuggle down at your feet, purring; but Jigglesqueak would be sitting dourly by himself out in front of the fire like a brooding demon. At such moments Jigglesqueak was anything but canny, but Valancy loved her uncanniness.[7]

7: Although Jigglesqueak is a male cat, Montgomery used the feminine pronoun here. In the published version, "her" is changed to "his."

8: In the published version, "in" is omitted.

9: empery = empire

10: "Given over to the empery of silence" is a phrase from Montgomery's essay "The Woods in Winter."

^the Stirlings ever^ thought about her—except Cousin Georgiana, who used to lie awake ~~at nights~~ worrying about poor Doss. ~~Was she warm enough at nights~~ Did she have enough to eat? Was that dreadful ~~cra~~ creature good to her? Was she warm enough at nights?

~~Miranda~~ Valancy was quite warm at nights. She used to wake up and revel silently in the cosiness of those winter nights on that little island in the frozen lake. The ~~winter~~ nights of other winters had been so cold and long. ~~Miranda~~ Valancy had hated to wake up in them and think about the bleakness ^and emptiness^ of the day that had passed and the bleakness ^and emptiness^ of the day that would come. Now she almost counted that night lost on which she didn't wake up and lie awake for half an hour just being happy, while Barney's regular breathing went on beside her[,] and through the open door the smouldering brands in the fireplace winked at her in the gloom. ~~NOTE O14~~ NOTE E12

The ^side of the^ bed had to be right against the window. There was no other place for it ^in the tiny room.^ ~~Miranda~~ Valancy, lying there, could look out of the window, through the big pine boughs that actually touched it, away up Mistawis, white and ~~shining in the moonlight~~ ^lustrous as a pavement of pearl[,] in[8]^ ~~NOTE L17~~ or dark and terrible in the storm. Sometimes the pine boughs tapped against the panes with friendly signals. Sometimes she heard the little hissing whisper of snow against them ~~all through the~~ right at her side. Some~~times~~ ^nights^ the whole, ^outer^ world ~~outside~~ seemed given over to the empery[9] of silence[10] ; then ~~there would be~~ ^came^ nights when there would be a majestic sweep of wind in the pines; nights ~~when~~ of ~~cl~~dear starlight when it whistled freakishly and joyously around the Blue Castle~~;~~; brooding nights before storm when it crept along the flow of the lake with a low, wailing cry ~~that~~ of boding and mystery. ~~Miranda~~ Valancy wasted many perfectly good sleeping hours in these delightful communings. But she could sleep as long in the morning as she wanted to. Nobody cared. Barney cooked his own breakfast of bacon and eggs and then shut himself up in

Bluebeard's chamber[11] till ~~evening~~ ^supper time^. Then they had an evening of reading and talk. They talked about everything in this world and a good many things in other worlds. They laughed over their own jokes until the Blue Castle re-echoed. ~~NOTE P14~~ NOTE G12 ❡ It struck ~~Miranda~~ Valancy ^more than^ once that Barney ^himself^ laughed a great deal oftener than he used to and that his laugh had changed. ~~She heard~~ It had become wholesome. She rarely heard the little cynical note in it now. Could a man laugh like that who had crimes on his conscience? Yet Barney <u>must</u> have done something. ~~Miranda~~ Valancy had indifferently made up her mind as to what he had done. She concluded he was a defaulting bank cashier. She had found in one of Barney's books ~~when reading it a yellow~~ ^an^ old clipping cut from a Montreal paper in which a ^vanished,^ defaulting cashier ~~who had skipped out after~~ was described. The description applied to Barney—as well as to half a dozen other men ~~Miranda~~ Valancy knew—and from some casual remarks he had dropped from time to time she concluded he knew Montreal rather well. ~~Miranda~~ Valancy had it all figured out in ^the back^ [of] her mind. Barney had been in a bank. He was tempted to take some money to speculate—meaning, of course, to put it back. He had got ~~it~~ in deeper and deeper, ~~until~~ until he found there was nothing for it but flight. It had happened so to scores of men. He had, ~~Miranda~~ Valancy was absolutely certain, never meant to do wrong. Of course, the name of the man in the clipping was ~~Alan~~ ^Bernard^ Craig. But ~~Miranda~~ Valancy had always thought ~~Bar~~ Snaith was an alias. ~~She did not care. It was the man she had married, not the name.~~ ^Not that it mattered.^

~~Miranda~~ Valancy had only one unhappy night that winter. It came in ^late^ March when most of the snow had gone and Nip and Tuck had returned. NOTE H12 ~~Barney had gone~~ ^ NOTE Q14 ^ ~~off in the afternoon, ^saying he would^ promising to be back by dark ^if all went well^. And Barney Soon after he had gone it had begun to snow. The wind rose and presently Mistawis was in the grip of one of the worst storms of the winter.~~

11: In the published version, "chamber" is upper case.

NOTE G12: "You <u>do</u> laugh beautifully," Barney told her once. "It makes me want to laugh just to hear you laugh. There's a trick about your laugh – as if there were so much more fun back of it that you wouldn't let out. Did you laugh like that before you came to Mistawis, Moonlight?"
  "I never laughed at all – really. I used to giggle foolishly when I felt I was expected to. But now – the laugh just <u>comes</u>."

NOTE H12: Barney had gone off in the afternoon ^for a long woodland tramp,^ saying he would be back by dark if all went well. Soon after he had gone it had begun to snow. The wind rose & presently Mistawis was in the grip of one of the worst storms of the winter. It tore up the lake & struck at the little house. The dark angry woods ~~sco~~ on the mainland scowled at Valancy, ~~mean~~ menace in the toss of their boughs, threats in their windy gloom, terror in the roar of their heart[s]. The trees on the island crouched in fear.

NOTE I12: slender & black against the glistening white world. She did not run to meet him. Something happened to her knees & she dropped down on Jigglesqueak's chair. Luckily Jigglesqueak got out from under in time, his whiskers bristling with indignation.

12: In the published version, "Muskosh" is changed to "Muskoka."

NOTE H20 NOTE M17. Miranda Valancy spent the night huddled on the rug before the fire, her face buried in her hands, when she was not vainly peering from the oriel in a futile effort to see through the frenzy ^furious white smoke^ of wind and snow ^that had once been Mistawis blue-dimpled Mistawis.^ Where was Barney? Lost in the ^on^ the merciless lakes? Sinking exhausted in the drifts ^of the pathless woods?^ Miranda Valancy died a hundred deaths that night and paid in full for all the happiness of the her Blue Castle. When morning came the storm broke and cleared; the sun shone gloriously over Mistawis; and at noon Barney came home. Miranda Valancy saw him from the oriel as he came around a point wooded point NOTE F20 NOTE I12 She did not run to meet him. NOTE G20 Instead she ran dropped on her knees by the couch. Barney found her there, her head buried in the wolfskins. her hands her hands[.]

"Barney, I thought you were dead," she whispered.

Barney hooted.

"After two years of the Klondike did you think a little baby storm like this could get me? I spent the night in that old lumber shanty up the Green River over in ^by^ Muskosh.[12] A bit cold but snug enough. I thought you were My dear girl. ^Little goose!^ Your eyes look like burnt holes in a blanket. Did you sit up here all night worrying over an old woodsman ^woodsman^ like me?"

"Yes," said Miranda Valancy. "I—couldn't help it. The storm seemed so wild. Anybody might have been lost in it. When – I saw you – come round the point – there – something happened to me. I don't know what It was as if I had died and come and come back to life. I can't describe it any other way."

...... the point — then —
something happened to me. I don't
know what. It was as if I had
died and come — and come back
to life. I can't describe it any
other way."

XXXI

I'm going to climb mountains
and bury treasure in the
faces of the earth.

Spring. Mistassini black and
sullen for a week or two, then
flaming in turquoise, again,
sapphire and rose again, and
laughing through the oriel, caressing
its ..... amethyst islands, ...
frogs, little, green, wizards of
swamp and pool, singing
everywhere in the long twilight.

XXXIII

<del>I'm going to climb mountains and hunt treasure in the bazaars of the east</del>

Spring. Mistawis black and sullen for a week or two, then ^flaming in^ sapphire and turquoise, <del>again,</del> ^lilac and rose again,^ laughing through the oriel, caressing its <del>fringe</del> amethyst islands[,] <del>NOTE X17</del> NOTE J12<del>.</del> Frogs, little, green wizards of swamp and pool, singing everywhere in the long twilights and long into the nights; islands fairylike in a green <del>mist</del> ^haze^ ^haze;^ the <del>incredible</del> ^evanescent^ beauty of wild young trees in early leaf[;] <del>NOTE Q17</del> NOTE K12; (the woods <del>wakening up</del> putting on a fashion of spring flowers—dainty, spirit fine[1] things akin to the soul of the wilderness; <del>NOTE F17</del> red mist on the maples;)[2] <del>golden tassels on the pines.</del> <del>NOTE R14</del> NOTE S17 | 3

"Think how many thousands of springs have been here on Mistawis—and all of them beautiful," said <del>Miranda</del> Valancy. "Oh, Barney, <del>will you please</del> look at that <del>flowering</del> wild plum[!]<del>.</del> <del>NOTE W17</del> NOTE L12 <del>And here's a patch of dandelions.</del> "Dandelions[6] shouldn't grow in the woods[,] though. They haven't any sense of the fitness of things at all. They are too cheerful and <del>ste</del> self-satisfied. <del>for the woods.</del> They haven't any of the mystery and reserve of the real wood-flowers.

"In short, they've no secrets," said Barney. "But wait a bit. The woods will have their own way even with those <del>obvous</del> obvious dandelions. In a little while all that obtrusive yellowness and complacency will be gone and we'll find here misty, phantom-like globes <del>hoving</del> hovering over those long grasses in full harmony with the traditions of the forest."[7]

NOTE J12: rippling under-winds soft as silk.

NOTE K12: frost-like loveliness of the new foliage of juniper trees; the woods putting on a fashion of spring flowers, dainty spiritual things akin to the soul of the wilderness; red mist on the maples; <del>white birches hung over with golden tassels;</del> willows decked out with glossy silver pussies; all the forgotten violets of Mistawis blooming again; lure of April moons.

1: In the published version, "spirit fine" is changed to "spiritual" as in NOTE K12.

2: Pencilled parentheses around these phrases are perhaps made by the typist since they are repeated in NOTE K12.

3: Much of this paragraph, including the passage in NOTE K12, is from Montgomery's essay "Spring in the Woods," with a few alterations. The essay portion reads: "The spring woods have a fashion of flowers—dainty, spirit-fine things akin to the soul of the wilderness.... The willows are decked with glossy silver catkins; the maples are mistily red-budded, and that cluster of white birches, a meet home for a dryad, is hung over with golden tassels."

NOTE L12: "I will – I must quote from John Foster. There's a passage in one of his books – I've re-read it a hundred times. He must have written it before a tree just like that: "'Behold this young wild plum[-]tree which has adorned herself after immemorial fashion in a wedding[-] veil of fine lace.[4] The fingers of wood pixies must have woven it[,] for nothing like it ever came from an earthly loom. I vow the tree is conscious of its loveliness. It is bridling before our very eyes – as if its beauty were not the most ephemeral thing in the woods, as it is the rarest & most exceeding, for to-day it is & to-morrow it is not. Every south wind purring through the boughs will winnow away a shower of slender petals. But what matter? To-day it is queen of the wild places & it is always to-day in the woods.'"[5]

"I'm sure you feel much better since you've got that out of your system," said Barney heartlessly.

"Here's a patch of dandelions," said Valancy, unsubdued.

4: Anne Shirley compared a blossoming wild plum tree to "a bride all in white with a lovely misty veil" in Chapter 2 of *Anne of Green Gables*.

5: Most of this paragraph is lifted from Montgomery's essay "Spring in the Woods." She substitutes a "young wild plum tree" here for "a young wild pear" in the essay: "and will you please look at that young wild pear which has adorned herself after immemorial fashion as a bride for her husband, in a wedding veil of fine lace. The fingers of wood pixies must have woven it for nothing like it ever came from an earthly loom. I vow

the tree is conscious of its own loveliness; it is trembling and bridling before our very eyes – as if its beauty were not the most ephemeral thing in the woods, as it is the rarest and most exceeding, for to-day it is and to-morrow it is not. Every south wind purring gently through the boughs will winnow away a shower of slender petals. But what matter? To-day it is queen of the wild places, and it is always to-day in the woods, where there is neither past nor future but only the prescience of immortality."

6: In the published version, "Dandelions" does not start a new paragraph but continues the previous one after "unsubdued."

7: Montgomery again lifts from her essay, "Spring in the Woods": "Of course, there are dandelions in the woods, because there are dandelions everywhere. They have no sense of the fitness of things at all; they are a cheerful, self-satisfied folk, firmly believing that they are welcome wherever grass can grow and sunshine beckon. But they are alien to the ancient wood. They are too obvious and frank; they possess none of the mystery and reserve and allurement of the real wood flowers; in short, have no secrets. Still, nothing, not even the smug dandelion, can live long in or near the woods without some sort of psychic transformation coming over it; and presently all the obtrusive yellowness and complacency are gone, and we have instead misty, phantom-like globes that hover over the long grasses in full harmony with the traditions of the forests."

"That sounds John Fosterish," teased ~~Miranda.~~ Valancy[.]

"What have I done that deserved a slam like that?" complained Barney.

One of the earliest signs of spring was the renaissance of Lady Jane. Barney put her on roads that no other car would look at[,] and they went through Deerwood in mud to the axles. They passed several Stirlings[,] who groaned and reflected that now spring was come they would encounter that shameless pair everywhere. ~~Miranda~~ Valancy, prowling about Deerwood shops, met Uncle Benjamin on the street, but he did not realize until he had gone two blocks further on that the girl ~~in scarlet tam and~~ ^in the^ scarlet-collared blanket coat, with cheeks reddened in the sharp April air and the fringe of black hair over laughing, slanted eyes, was ~~Miranda~~ Valancy. When he did realize it[,] Uncle Benjamin was indignant. What business had ~~Miranda~~ Valancy to look like ~~that~~ – like – like a young girl? The way of the transgressor was hard.[8] Had to be. ~~The Bible said so.~~ ^Scriptural and proper.^ Yet ~~Miranda's~~ Valancy's path couldn't be hard. She wouldn't look like that if it were. There was something wrong. It was almost enough to make a man turn modernist.

Barney and ~~Miranda~~ Valancy ~~clattered~~ clanged on to the Port, so that it was dark when they went through Deerwood again. At her old home ~~Miranda~~ Valancy, seized with a sudden impulse, got out, opened the little gate and tiptoed around to the ~~dining~~ ^sitting^ room window. There sat her mother and Cousin Stickles drearily, ^grimly^ knitting. ~~NOTE T17~~ NOTE M12 If they had looked the least bit lonesome ~~Miranda~~ Valancy would have gone in. But they did not. ~~Miranda~~ Valancy would not disturb them for worlds.

8: From Proverbs 13:15: "Good understanding giveth favour: but the way of transgressors is hard."

NOTE M12: Baffling & inhuman as ever.

XXXIV

NOTE N12: ⁋Valancy
had two wonder[ful]
moments that spring.
One day, coming home
through the woods, with
her arms full of trailing
arbutus[1] & creeping
spruce, she met a man
whom she knew must
be Allan Tierney. Allan
Tierney, the celebrated
painter of beautiful
women. He lived in
New York ~~winters~~ in
winter[,] but he owned
an island cottage at
the northern end of
Mistawis to which he
always came the minute
the ice was out of the
lake. He was reputed
to be a lonely, eccentric
man. He never flattered
his sitters. There was no
need to[,] for he would
not paint any[ ]one
who required flattery.
To be painted by ~~Job~~
Allan Tierney was all
the cachet of beauty a
woman could desire.
Valancy had heard so
much about him that
she couldn't help turn-
ing her head back over
her shoulder for another
shy, curious look at him.
A shaft of pale spring
sunlight fell through a
great pine athwart her
bare black head and her
slanted eyes.
(continued on next page)

NOTE N12

^Her second wonder moment came^ one evening in May. ~~Miranda knew~~ ^She realized^
that Barney ~~really~~ ^actually ^ liked her. She had always
hoped he did, but sometimes she had a little, disagreeable, haunting dread that he was just kind and nice and
charming[4] out of pity; knowing that she hadn't long to
live and determined she should have a good time as long
as she did live; but away back in his mind rather ~~desirous
of~~ ^looking forward to^ freedom again, with no intrusive
woman creature in his island fastness and no chattering
thing beside him in his woodland prowls.

She knew[5] he could never love her. She did not even
want him to. If he loved her he would be unhappy when
she died – ~~Miranda~~ Valancy never flinched from the
plain word. No "passing away" for her. And she did not
want him to be the least unhappy. But neither did she
want him to be glad – or relieved. She ~~wanted~~ ^wanted^
him to like her and miss her as a good chum. But she had
never been sure until this night that he did.

~~They had walked over the hills in the sunset;~~[.] ~~they
had drunk together~~ ^from it^ ~~out of a birch bark cup
from a little spring in a ferny hollow;~~ NOTE Z17 NOTE O12
they had come to an old[-]tumble[-]down, rail fence and
sat on it for a long time. They didn't talk much[,] but
~~Miranda~~ Valancy had a curious sense of ~~one ness~~ one-
ness. She knew that ~~they~~ ^she^ couldn't have ~~been silent
together so long~~ ^felt that^ if he hadn't liked her.

"You nice, little thing," said Barney suddenly. "~~Oh,~~
^Oh,^ you nice little thing! Sometimes I feel you're too
nice to be real – that I'm just dreaming you."

NOTE N12 *continued*: She wore a pale green sweater and had bound a fillet[2] of linnea vine about her ~~hea~~ hair. The feathery fountain of trailing spruce overflowed her arms & fell around her. Allan Tierney's eyes lighted up.

"I've had a caller," said Barney the next afternoon, when Valancy had returned from another flower quest.

"Who?" Valancy was surprised but indifferent. She began filling a basket with arbutus.

"Allan ~~Tierney~~ Tierney. He wants to paint you, Moonlight."

"Me!" Valancy dropped her basket & her arbutus. "You're laughing at me, Barney."

"I'm not. That's what Tierney came for. To ask my permission to paint my wife – as the Spirit of Muskoka, or something like that."

"But – but – " stammered Valancy, "Allan Tierney never paints any but – any but – "

"Beautiful women," finished Barney. "Conceded. Q.E.D.,[3] Mistress Barney Snaith is a beautiful woman."

"Nonsense," said Valancy stooping to retrieve her arbutus. "You know that's nonsense, Barney. I know I'm a heap better-looking than I was a year ago[,] but I'm not beautiful."

"Allan Tierney never makes a mistake," said Barney. "You forget, Moonlight, that there are different kinds of beauty. Your imagination is obsessed by the very obvious type of your cousin Olive. Oh, I've seen her—she's a ~~stummer~~ ^stunner^—but you'd never catch Allan Tierney wanting to paint her. In the horrible but expressive slang phrase[,] she keeps all her goods in the shop window. But in your subconscious mind you have a conviction that

nobody can be beautiful who doesn't look like Olive. Also, you remember your face as it was in the days when your soul was not allowed to shine through it. Tierney said something about the curve of your cheek as you looked back over your shoulder. You know I've often told you it was distracting. And he's quite batty about your eyes. If I wasn't absolutely sure it was solely professional— he's really a crabbed old bachelor, you know—I'd be jealous."

"Well, I don't want to be painted," said Valancy. "I hope you told him that."

"I couldn't tell him that. I didn't know what *you* wanted. But I told him *I* didn't want my wife painted – hung up in a salon for the mob to stare at. Belonging to another man. For of course I couldn't buy the picture. So even if you had wanted to be painted, Moonlight, your tyrannous husband would not have permitted it. Tierney was a bit squiffy. He isn't used to being turned down like that. His requests are almost like royalty's."

"But we are outlaws," laughed Valancy. "We bow to no decrees – we acknowledge no sovereignty."

In her heart she thought unashamedly,

"I wish Olive could know that Allan ~~Tierney~~ Tierney wanted to paint me. *Me!* Little-old-maid-Valancy[-] Stirling-that-was."

Her second wonder-moment came

1: trailing arbutus = mayflowers

2: fillet = circlet or garland

3: Q.E.D. stands for the Latin phrase "quod erat demonstratum," meaning "which was to be demonstrated (or proven)."

4: In the published version, "charming" is changed to "chummy."

5: In the published version, "She knew..." does not begin a new paragraph but continues the previous one.

NOTE O12: They had the delight of discovering a virgin spring in a ~~fern of~~ ferny hollow & had drunk together from it out of a birch bark [cup;][6]

6: Montgomery had struck out "cup" in the preceding passage but neglected to add it in NOTE O12.

NOTE P12: But[,] some-
how[,] she had always
counted on living out
her year[.]

7: After finishing this page
(#386 in the manu-
script), Montgomery
leaves a page blank (and
unnumbered), then
starts the next chapter
on the page she num-
bers 387.

"Why can't I die now – this very minute – when I am so happy?" thought ~~Miranda~~ Valancy.

Well, it couldn't be so very long now[.]‡ Somehow ~~Miranda~~ Valancy had always felt she would live out the year Dr. Trent had allotted. She had not been careful – she had never tried to be. ~~NOTE P17~~ NOTE P12 She had not let herself think about it at all. But now, sitting here beside Barney, with her hand in his, a sudden realization came to her. She had not had a heart attack for a long while— two months at least. The last one she had had was ~~the one the nig~~ two or three nights before Barney was out in the storm. Since then she had not remembered she had a heart. Well, no doubt[,] it betokened the nearness of the end. Nature had given up the struggle. There would be no more pain.

"~~I think~~ ^I'm afraid^ heaven will be very dull after this past year," thought ~~Miranda~~ Valancy. But perhaps one will not remember? Would that be – nice? No, no. I don't want to forget Barney. I'd rather be miserable in heaven remembering him than happy forgetting him. And I'll always remember =through all eternity – that he really <u>really</u> liked me."[7]

XXXV

Thirty seconds can be very long sometimes. Long enough to work a miracle or a revolution. In thirty seconds life changed wholly for Barney and ~~Miranda~~ Valancy Snaith.

They had gone around the lake one June evening in ~~the~~ their ~~little motor boat~~ ^disappearing propeller^, ~~left it in a creek~~ fished for an hour in a little creek, left their boat there, and walked up through the woods to Port Laurence, two miles away. ~~They did a little shopping and Miranda~~ Valancy prowled a bit in the ~~bookshops~~ ^shops^ and got herself a new pair of sensible shoes. Her old pair had suddenly and completely given out[,] and this evening she had been compelled to put on the little fancy pair of patent[-]leather with rather high, slender heels, which she had bought in a fit of folly one day in the winter ~~and wore evenings in the blue castle~~ because of their beauty and because she wanted to make one foolish, extravagant purchase in her life. ~~This was~~ She sometimes put them on of an evening in the Blue Castle[,] but this was the first time she had worn them outside. She had not found it any too easy walking up through the woods ~~for them~~ in them[,] and Barney guyed her unmercifully about them. But in spite of the inconvenience[,] ~~Miranda~~ Valancy secretly rather liked the look of her trim ankles and high instep above those pretty[,] ^foolish^ shoes and did not change them in the shop as she might have done.

The sun was hanging low above the pines when they left Port Laurence. To the north of it the woods closed around the town quite suddenly. ~~About Miranda~~ Valancy always had a sense of stepping from one world to another—from reality to fairyland—when she ~~left the~~ went out of Port Laurence and in a twinkling found it shut off behind her by the armies of the pines.

A mile and a half from Port Laurence there was a small railroad ~~junction~~ ^station^ with a little station[-]house which at this hour of the day was deserted, since no local train was due. Not a soul was in sight when Barney and ~~Miranda~~ Valancy emerged from the woods ~~and crossed the track at the switch~~. Off to the left a sudden curve in the track hid it from view[,] but over the tree[-]tops beyond[,] the ~~trail of~~ long plume of smoke betokened the approach of a through train. The rails were vibrating to its thunder as Barney stepped across the switch. ~~Miranda~~ Valancy was a few steps behind him, loitering to gather ~~Jun~~ June-bells along the little, winding path. But there was plenty of time to get across before the train came. She stepped unconcernedly over the first rail.

She could never tell how it happened. The ensuing thirty seconds always seemed in her recollection like a ~~terrible~~ chaotic nightmare in which she endured the agony of a thousand life=times. ℂ The heel of her pretty, foolish shoe caught in a crevice of the switch. She could not pull it loose.

"Barney – Barney," she called in alarm.

Barney ~~turned – saw her predicament~~ – saw her ashen face – dashed back. He tried to pull her clear – he tried to wrench her foot from the prisoning hold. In vain. In a moment the train would sweep around the curve – would be on them.

"Go – go – quick – you'll be killed, Barney," shrieked ~~Miranda~~ Valancy, trying to push him away.

Barney dropped on his knees, ~~white to the lips~~ ^ghost-white^, frantically tearing at her shoe-lace. The knot defied his trembling fingers. He snatched a knife from his pocket and ~~en~~ slashed at it. ~~Miranda~~ Valancy

^still^ strove ^blindly^ to push him away. Her mind ~~"Barney = go = go = for God's sake = go.~~ was full of the hideous thought that Barney was going to be killed. She had no thought for her own danger.

"Barney – go – go – for God's sake – go[!]"

"Never[!]" muttered Barney between his set teeth. He ~~was tearing madly~~ ^gave one mad wrench^ at the lace. As the train thundered around the curve he sprang up and caught ~~Miranda~~ Valancy – dragging her clear, leaving the shoe behind her. The wind from the train as it swept by turned to icy cold the streaming perspiration on his face.

^"Thank God[!]" he breathed.^

For a moment they stood stupidly staring at each other, two white, shaken wild-eyed creatures. Then they stumbled over to the little seat at the end of the station[-]house and dropped on it. Barney buried his face in his hands and said not a word. ~~Miranda~~ Valancy sat, staring straight ahead of her with unseeing eyes at the great pine woods, the stumps of the clearing, the long, gleaming rails. There was only one thought in her dazed mind, ~~and it was not of her escape from death~~—a thought that seemed to burn it as a shaving of fire might burn her body.

Dr. Trent had told her over a year ago that she had a serious form of heart disease – that any excitement might be fatal. ⟨ If that were so[,] why was she not dead now? This very minute? ~~In thirty seconds s~~She had ~~lived through as much exci~~ just experienced as much ^and as terrible^ excitement as most people experience in a lifetime[,] crowded into that endless thirty seconds. Yet she had not died of it. She was not an ~~io iota~~ iota the worse of[1] it. A little ~~shaky,~~ ^wobbly at the knees[,]^ as any[ ] one would have been; a quicker heart-beat[,] as any[ ] one would have; nothing ~~like the old palpitation.~~ more.

Why!

Was it possible Dr. Trent had made a mistake?

~~Miranda~~ Valancy shivered as if a cold wind had suddenly chilled her to the soul. She looked at Barney, hunched up beside her. ~~How strange he was acting!~~ ^

1: In the published version, "of" is changed to "for."

His silence was very eloquent.^ Had the same thought occurred to him? Did he suddenly find himself confronted by the appalling suspicion that he was married, not for a few months or a year, but for good and all to a woman he did not love and who had foisted herself upon him by some trick or lie? ~~Miranda~~ Valancy turned sick before the horror of it. It could not be. It would be too cruel – too devilish. Dr. Trent <u>couldn't</u> have made a mistake. Impossible. He was one of the best heart specialists in Ontario. She was foolish – unnerved by the recent horror. ~~She would not think about it.~~ She remembered some of the hideous spasms of pain she had had. There must be something serious the matter with her heart to account for them. ~~But~~

But she had not had any for nearly three months. Why?

Presently Barney bestirred himself. He stood up, without looking at ~~Miranda~~ Valancy, and said casually,

"I suppose we'd better be ~~getting~~ ^hiking^ back. Sun's getting low. Are you good for the rest of the road?"

"I think so," said ~~Miranda~~ Valancy miserably.

Barney went across the clearing and picked up the parcel he had dropped—the parcel containing her new shoes. He brought it to her and let her take out the shoes and put them on without any assistance, while he stood with his back to her and looked out over the pines.

They walked in silence down the shadowy trail to the lake. In silence Barney steered his boat into the sunset miracle that was Mistawis. In silence they went around feathery headland[s] and across ~~fairy~~ ^coral^ bays ~~NOTE A18~~ NOTE Q12 In silence drew up at the landing place below the Blue Castle.

~~Miranda~~ Valancy went up the rock steps and into the house. She dropped miserably on the ~~wolfskins~~ ^first chair she came to^ and sat there staring through the oriel, oblivious of Good Luck's frantic purrs of joy and Jigglesqueak[']s savage glares of protest at her occupancy of his chair.

Barney came ~~gently~~ in a few minutes later. He did not come near her[,] but he ^stood behind her and^

asked gently if she felt any the worse for her experience. ~~Miranda~~ Valancy would have given her year of ~~the Blue~~ happiness to have been able honestly to answer "Yes."

"No," she said flatly.
~~NOTE B18~~ NOTE R12

And an hour ago – only an hour ago – she had been so happy! ~~prancing in her foolish pretty shoes through~~

NOTE R12: Barney went into Bluebeard's chamber[2] & shut the door. She heard him pacing up & down – up & down. He had never paced like that before[.]

2: In the published version, "chamber" is capitalized.

~~XXXV~~ ~~XXXVI~~

Finally ~~Miranda~~ Valancy went to
bed ~~CK~~ & she pretended she was asleep
when Barney came in. Barney
pretended to go to sleep. ~~Real~~-
~~Miranda~~ Valancy knew perfectly well
he wasn't sleeping anyway. ~~there was~~
quieting that. When Barney was
really ~~asleep~~ he ~~sighed and~~
~~squirmed and tossed and~~
~~muttered~~ ~~an occasional~~ through his teeth word
~~now and then~~. She knew he was
lying there, staring through the
darkness. Thinking of what? Typing
of ~~all~~ what—?

~~Miranda~~ Valancy, who had ~~slept~~ so
many happy ~~sleepy~~ ~~waking~~ hours of night
lying by that window, now faced the

XXXVI

Finally, ~~Miranda~~ Valancy went to bed. ~~NOTE C18~~ NOTE S12 She pretended to be asleep when Barney came in. Barney pretended to go to sleep. But ~~Miranda~~ Valancy knew perfectly well he ~~was not~~ ^wasn't^ sleeping ^any more than she was.^ ~~He was too quiet for that. When Barney was really asleep he sighed and squirmed and tossed and muttered ^through his teeth^ an occasional word now and then.~~ She knew he was lying there, staring through the darkness. Thinking of what? Trying to face – what?

~~Miranda~~ Valancy, who had spent so many happy ~~waking~~ ^wakeful^ hours of night lying by that window, now paid the price of them all in this one night of misery. A horrible, portentous fact was slowly looming out before her from the nebula of surmise and fear. She could not shut her eyes to it – push it away – ignore it.

There could be nothing seriously wrong with her heart, no matter what Dr. Trent had said. If there had been those thirty seconds would have killed her. It was no use to recall Dr. Trent's letter and reputation. The greatest specialists made mistakes sometime. Dr. Trent had made one.

~~And divorce was so hard to get in Canada! So expensive! And Barney was poor.~~

Towards morning ~~Miranda~~ Valancy fell into a fitful dose[1] with ~~crazy~~ ^absurd^ ^ridiculous^ dreams. One of them was of Barney taunting her with having tricked him. In her dream she lost her temper and struck him violently on the head with her rolling[-]pin. He proved to be made of glass and shivered into splinters all over the floor.

NOTE S12: Before she went she re-read Dr. Trent's letter. It comforted her a little. So positive. So assured. The writing so black and steady. Not the writing of a man who didn't know what he was writing about. But she could not sleep.

1: In the published version, "dose" is changed to "doze."

217

She woke with a cry of horror – a gasp of relief – a short laugh over the absurdity of her dream – a miserable sickening recollection of what had happened.

Barney was gone. ~~Miranda~~ Valancy knew, as people sometimes know things—inescapably, without being told—that he was not in the house or in Bluebeard's Chamber either. ~~She dressed and~~ There was a curious silence in the living[-]room. ~~NOTE F8~~ NOTE T12 The old clock had stopped. Barney must have forgotten to wind it up, ~~salem the~~ something he had never done before. The room without it was dead, though the ~~sunlight~~ ^sunshine^ streamed in through the oriel and ~~beams~~ ^dimples of light^ from the dancing waves beyond quivered over the walls.

The canoe was gone but Lady Jane was under the mainland trees. So Barney ~~was gone~~ ^had betaken himself^ to the wilds. He would not return till night—perhaps not even then. He must be angry with her. That furious silence of his must mean anger—cold, deep, justifiable resentment. Well, ~~Miranda~~ Valancy knew what she must do first. She was not suffering very keenly now. Yet the curious numbness that pervaded her being was in a way worse than pain ~~NOTE K20~~ NOTE U12. She forced herself to cook and eat a little breakfast. ~~She~~ ^Mechanically she^ put the Blue Castle in perfect order. Then she put on her ~~suit~~ ^hat and coat,^ locked the door and hid the key in the hollow of the old pine and crossed to the mainland in the motor boat. She was going in to[2] Deerwood to see Dr. Trent. She must know.

to see Dr. Trent. She must <u>know</u>.

XIX

Dr. Trent looked at her blankly and did not ~~recognize her at~~ all. fumbled seeing his recollections.

"Er — miss — miss —

"Miss Snaith", said ~~Miranda~~ Valancy quietly. "I was miss ~~Miranda~~ Valancy Stirling when I came to you last May — over a year ago. I wanted to consult you about my heart."

Dr. Trent's face cleared.

"Oh, of course. I remember her now. But ~~you~~ I'm really not to deceive you not knowing you. You've changed — splendidly. And ~~married~~ ~~warned~~. Well, well, it does

XXXVII

D r. Trent looked at her blankly and ~~did not recognize her at all.~~ fumbled among his recollections.

"Er – Miss – Miss – ["]

"Mrs. Snaith," said ~~Miranda~~ Valancy quietly. "I was Miss ~~Miranda~~ Valancy Stirling when I came to you last May—over a year ago. I wanted to consult you about my heart."

Dr. Trent's face cleared.

"Oh, of course. I remember now. ~~But you really~~ I'm really not to blame for not knowing you. You've changed – splendidly. And ~~married.~~ ^married.^ Well, well, it has agreed with you. You don't look much like an invalid now, hey? I remember that day. I was badly upset. Hearing about poor ~~Fred~~ ^Ned^ bowled me over. But ~~Fred's~~ ^Ned's^ as good as new and you, too, evidently. I told you so you know – told you ~~you had~~ ^there was^ nothing to worry over."

~~A little nervous affect~~ ^Valancy looked at him.^

"You told me, ^in your letter[,]^ ~~said Miranda~~ ^she said^ slowly ~~NOTE 120~~ NOTE V12 "that I had angina pectoris – in the last stages – complicated with an ~~aneurism.~~ ^an-eurism.^ That I might die any minute – that I couldn't live longer than a year."

Dr. Trent stared at her.

"Impossible," he said blankly. "I couldn't have told you that."

~~Miranda~~ Valancy took his letter from her bag and handed it to him.

"Miss Miranda Stirling," he read. "Yes – yes. Of course I wrote you – on the train – that night. But I <u>told</u> you there was nothing serious."

NOTE V12: with a curious feeling that some[ ]one else was talking through her lips,

NOTE W12: He jumped to his feet & strode agitatedly about the room.

1: In the published version, a new paragraph begins with "I can never."

"Read your letter," insisted ~~Miranda.~~ Valancy.

Dr. Trent took it out – unfolded it – glanced over it. A dismayed look came into his face. ~~NOTE D18~~ NOTE W12

"Good heavens! This is the letter I meant for old Miss Jane Sterling. From Port Laurence. She was here that day, too. ~~I we~~ I sent you the wrong letter. What unpardonable carelessness! But I was beside myself that night. My God, and you believed that – you've believed – but you didn't – you went to another doctor –"

~~Miranda~~ Valancy stood up, turned round, looked foolishly about her and sat down again.

"I believed it," she said faintly. "I didn't go to any other doctor. I – I – it would take too long to explain. But I believed I was going to die soon."

Dr. Trent halted before her. "I can never[1] forgive myself. What a year you must have had! But you don't look— I can't understand."

"Never mind," said ~~Miranda~~ Valancy dully. "And ^so^ there's nothing the matter with my heart?"

"Well, nothing serious. You had what is called pseudo-angina. It's never fatal – passes away completely with proper treatment. Or sometimes with a shock of joy. Have you been troubled much with it?"

"Not at all since ~~Marsh~~ March," answered ~~Miranda~~ Valancy. She remembered the marvelous feeling ^of re-creation^ she had had when she saw Barney coming home safe after the storm. Had that "shock of joy" cured her?

"Then likely you're all right. I told you what to do in the letter you should have got. <u>And</u> of course I supposed you'd go to another doctor. Child, why didn't you?"

"I didn't want anybody to know."

"Idiot[,]," said Dr. Trent bluntly. "I can't understand such folly. And poor old Miss Sterling. She must have got your letter – telling her there was nothing ~~serious~~ ^serious^ the matter. Well, well, it couldn't have made any difference. Her case was hopeless. Nothing that she could have done or left undone could have made ~~much~~ ^any^ difference. I was surprised she lived as long as she did—two months. She was here that day – not long before you. I hated to tell her the truth = ~~she was so anxious to live~~. You think I'm a blunt old curmudgeon – and my letters <u>are</u> blunt enough. I can't soften things. But I'm a snivelling coward when it comes to telling a woman ^face to face that^ she's got to die soon. I told her I'd look up some features of the case I wasn't quite sure of and let her know ~~later on~~. next day. But you got her letter – look here 'Dear Miss S-t-e̲-r-l-i-n-g.'

"Yes, I noticed that. But I thought it a mistake. I didn't know there were any Sterlings in Port Laurence."

"She was the only one. A lonely old soul. Lived ~~by herself~~ with a[2] ~~cou married cousin there~~. ^by herself with only a little home girl.^ She died two months after she was here—died in her sleep. ~~The~~ My mistake couldn't have made any difference to her. But you! ~~Why, you've got years before you, girl. And you look as if you'd live to be a hundred.~~ I can't forgive myself for inflicting a year's misery on you. It's time I retired[,] all right[,] when I do things like that – even if my son was supposed to be fatally injured. Can you ever forgive me?["]

A year of misery! ~~Miranda~~ Valancy smiled a tortured smile as she thought of all the happiness Dr. Trent's mistake had bought her. But she was paying for it now—oh, she was paying. If to ~~very~~ feel was to live she was living with a vengeance.

She let Dr. Trent examine her and answered all his questions. When he told her she was fit as a fiddle and would probably live to be a hundred, she got up and went away silently ~~NOTE E15~~ NOTE X12 Dr. Trent thought she was odd. Anybody would have thought, from her ~~woe-be-gone~~ ^hopeless^ eyes and woe-begone face, that he had given her a sentence of death instead of life. Snaith? Snaith? Who the devil had she married? He had never heard of Snaiths in Deerwood. And she had been such a sallow, faded, little old maid. God, but marriage <u>had</u> made a difference in her, anyhow, whoever Snaith was. Snaith? Dr. Trent remembered. That rapscallion ["]up back["]! Had ~~Miranda~~ Valancy Stirling married <u>him</u>? And her clan had let her! Well, probably that solved the mystery. She had married in haste and repented

2: Montgomery did not strike out "with a" here even though she included it in her replacement phrase.

NOTE X12: She knew that there were a great many horrible things outside waiting to be thought over.

NOTE Y12: Married! To God knew whom! Or what! Jail[-]bird? Defaulter? Fugitive from justice?

at leisure[,] and that was why she wasn't overjoyed at learning she was a good insurance prospect after all. ~~NOTE G18~~ NOTE Y12 ~~Tied for life to~~ It must be pretty bad if she ^had^ looked to death as a release, poor girl. But why were women such fools? Dr. Trent dismissed ~~Miranda~~ Valancy from his mind, though to the day of his death he was ashamed of ~~the mistake he had~~ putting those letters into the wrong envelopes.

he had putting these letters into
the wrong envelopes.

XIX XXXII

Miranda walked quickly
through the back streets and
through Lovers Lane. She did
not want to meet anyone
she knew. She didn't want to
meet even the people she didn't
know. She hated to be seen. Her
mind was so confused, so torn,
so messy. She felt that her
appearance must be the same.
She drew a sobbing breath of
relief as she left the village
behind and found herself
on the up back road. There
was little fear of meeting anyone
she knew here. The cars that

XXXVIII

~~Miranda~~ Valancy walked quickly through the back streets and through Lover[']s Lane. She did not want to meet any[ ]one she knew. She didn't want to meet even ~~th~~ people she didn't know. She hated to be seen. Her mind was so confused, so torn, so messy. She felt that her appearance must be the same. She drew a sobbing breath of relief as she left the village behind and found herself on the ~~Deer~~ ["]up back["] road. There was little fear of meeting any[ ]one she knew here. The cars that fled by her with rauc[o]us shrieks were filled with strangers. One of them was packed with young people who whirled past her singing uproariously.

~~"Oh, my wife has the fever~~
~~I hope it won't leave her~~
~~For I want to be single again."~~
~~NOTE J20~~ NOTE Z12

~~Miranda~~ ^~~Mirands~~^ ^Valancy^ flinched as if one of them had leaned from the car and cut her across the face with a whip.

~~She had trapped Barney. Trapped him into marrying her.~~ She had made a covenant ~~of~~ ^with^ death and death had cheated her. Now life stood ~~grinning at~~ ^mocking^ her. She had trapped Barney. Trapped him into marrying her. And divorce was so hard to get in Ontario. So ~~E~~expensive. And Barney was poor.

With life, fear had come back into her heart. Sickening fear. Fear of what Barney would think. Would say. Fear of the future that must be lived without him. ~~Oh, how could anyone bear an unbearable thing?~~ ^Fear of her insulted, repudiated clan.^

NOTE Z12: "My wife has the fever, O, then,
  My wife has the fever, O, then,
  My wife has the fever,
Oh, I hope it won't leave her,
For I want to be single again!"[1]

1: From "I Wish I Was Single Again," a folk song by J. C. Beckel (1811–1880), written in 1871.

2: Even though the "A" is
struck out in the manu-
script, it appears in the
published version.

3: Vere de Vere = aristoc-
racy. From Tennyson's
poem "Lady Claire Vere
de Vere," c. 1842.

4: tonneau = rear seat of
an automobile

She had had one draught from a divine cup and
now it was dashed from her lips. With no kind, friendly death to rescue her. She must ~~live an~~ go on living
and longing for it. Everything was spoiled, smirched,
defaced. Even that year in the Blue Castle. Even her
~~unshamed~~ ^unashamed^ love for Barney. It had been
beautiful because death waited. Now it was only sordid
because death was gone. How could any[ ]one bear an
unbearable thing?

She must go back and tell him. Make him believe
she had not meant to trick him—she <u>must</u> make him
believe that. She must say good-bye to her Blue Castle
and ~~go back~~ ^return^ to the brick house on Elm Street.
Back to everything she had thought left behind forever.
The old bondage – the old fears. But that did not matter.
All that mattered now was that Barney must somehow
be made to believe she had not consciously tricked him.

When ~~Miranda~~ Valancy reached the pines by the
lake she ~~came~~ ^was brought^ out of her daze of pain by a
startling sight. ~~Old~~ There, ~~drawn up by~~ ^parked by the^
side of old, battered, ~~ragged~~ Lady Jane, was another car.
A wonderful car. A purple car.[2] Not a dark, royal purple
but a blatant, screaming purple. It shone like a mirror
and its interior plainly indicated the car caste of Vere de
Vere.[3] On the driver[']s seat sat a haughty chauffeur in
livery. And in the tonneau[4] sat a man who opened the
door and bounced out nimbly as ~~Miranda~~ Valancy came
down the path to the landing place. He stood under the
~~pines waiting for her~~ and ~~Miranda~~ Valancy took in every
detail of him.

A stout[,] ^short[,]^ pudgy ~~little~~ man with a broad,
rubicund, good-humored face – a clean-shaven face,
though an unparalyzed little imp at the back of ~~Mirandas~~
Valancy's paralyzed mind suggested the thought, "Such
a face should have a fringe of white whisker around it."
~~Great tortoise shell~~ ^Old-fashioned, steel-rimmed^
spectacles on prominent blue eyes. A purs[e]y mouth;
a little round knobby nose. Where – where – where,
groped ~~Miranda~~ Valancy, had she seen that face before?
It seemed as familiar to her as her own.

The stranger wore a ^green hat and a^ light fawn overcoat over a suit of a loud check pattern. ^~~and a green hat.~~^ His tie was a brilliant green ^of lighter shade[;]^ ~~and~~ on the plump hand he outstretched to intercept ~~Miranda~~ Valancy an enormous diamond ~~blinked~~ winked at her. ~~He spoke in a pleasant voice that impressed her more fav.~~ But he had a pleasant, fatherly smile[,] and ~~in~~ [in] his hearty, unmodulated voice was a ring of something that attracted her.

"Can you tell me, miss,[5] if that house yonder ~~is~~ belongs to a Mr. ~~Shortreed~~ ^Redfern^? And if so[,] how can I get to it?"

~~Shortreed!~~ ^Redfern!^ A ~~vi~~ vision of bottles seemed to dance before ~~Miranda's~~ Valancy's eyes—long bottles of ~~hair tonic~~ ^bitters^ – round bottles of hair tonic – square bottles of liniments – short, corpulent little bottles of ^purple^ pills—and all of them bearing that very prosperous, beaming moon-face and steel-rimmed spectacles on the label.

Dr. ~~Shortreed!~~ ^Redfern!^

"No," said ~~Miranda~~ Valancy faintly[.] =^"no[6]^ – that house belongs to ~~a~~ Mr. Snaith."

Dr. ~~Shortreed~~ ^Redfern^ nodded.

"Yes, I understand Bernie's been calling himself Snaith. Well, it's his middle name—was his poor mother[']s. Bernard Snaith ~~Shortreed~~ ^Redfern^—that's him. And now, miss, can you tell me how to get over to that island? Nobody ^~~Miranda had already~~^ seems to be home there. I've done some waving and yelling. ~~Henry~~ Henry[,] there[,] wouldn't yell. He's a one-job man. But old Doc. ~~Shortreed~~ ^Redfern^ can yell with the best of them yet[,] and ain[']t above doing it. Raised nothing but a couple of crows. Guess Bernie's out for the day."

"He was away when I left this morning," said ~~Miranda~~ Valancy. "I suppose he hasn't come home yet."

She spoke flatly and tonelessly. This last shock had ~~left her for the~~ temporarily bereft her of whatever little ~~spirit~~ ^power of reasoning^ had been left her by Dr. Trent's revelation. In the back of her mind the aforesaid little imp was jeeringly repeating a silly old proverb.

5: In the published version, "miss" is capitalized, here and throughout.

6: In the published version, "no" is upper case.

7: Montgomery has Dr. Redfern call him "Bernie" in other parts of the conversation but apparently writes "Barney" here and elsewhere out of habit. It also appears as "Barney" in these few places in the published version.

"It never rains but it pours." But she was not trying to think. What was the use?

Dr. ~~Shortreed~~ ^Redfern^ was gazing at her in perplexity.

"When you left this morning? Do you live – over there?"

He ~~pointed to the~~ waved his diamond at the Blue Castle.

"Of course," said ~~Miranda~~ Valancy stupidly. "I'm his wife."

Dr. ~~Shortreed~~ ^Redfern^ took out a yellow silk handkerchief, removed his hat and mopped his brow. He was very bald[,] and ~~Miranda's~~ Valancy's imp whispered[,] "Why ~~not~~ be bald? Why lose your manly beauty? Try ~~Shortreed's~~ ^Redfern's^ Hair Vigor. It keeps you young."

"Excuse me," said Dr. ~~Shortreed~~ ^Redfern.^ "This is a bit of a shock."

"Shocks seem to be in the air this morning." The imp said this out loud before ~~Miranda~~ Valancy could prevent it.

"I didn't know Bernie was – married. I didn't think he would have got married without telling his old dad."

Were Dr. ~~Shortreeds~~ ^Redfern's^ eyes misty? Amid her own dull ache of misery and fear and dread[,] ~~Miranda~~ Valancy felt a pang of pity for him.

"Don't blame him," she said hurriedly. "It – it wasn't his fault. It – was all my doing[.]~~?~~"

"You didn't ask him to marry you, I suppose," twinkled Dr. ~~Shortreed~~ ^Redfern.^ "He might have let me know. ~~Por~~ I'd have got acquainted with my daughter-in-law before this if he had. But I'm glad to meet you now, my dear,—very glad. You look like a sensible young woman. I used to sorter fear Barney'd[7] pick out some pretty bit of fluff just because she was good-looking. They were all after him, of course. Wanted his money. ~~Ha, ha.~~ ^Eh?^ Didn't like the pills and the ~~lini~~ bitters but liked the dollars. Eh? Wanted to dip their pretty little fingers in old Doc's millions. Eh?"

"Millions!" said ~~Miranda~~ Valancy faintly. She wished she could sit down somewhere – she wished she could have a chance to think – she wished she and the Blue Castle could sink to the bottom of Mistawis and vanish from human sight forever more.[8]

"Millions," said Dr. ~~Shortreed~~ ^Redfern^ complacently. "And Bernie chucks them for – that." Again he shook the diamond ~~rather~~ contemptuously at the Blue Castle. "Wouldn't you think he'd have more sense? And all on account of a white bit of a girl. He must have got over <u>that</u> foolery,[9] anyhow, since he's married. You must persuade him to come back to civilization.[10] All nonsense wasting his life like this. Ain't you going to take me over to your house, my dear? I suppose you've some way of getting there.[″]

"Of course," said ~~Miranda~~ Valancy stupidly. She led the way down to the little cove where the disappearing propeller boat was snuggled.

"Does ~~your man~~ your – your man want to come, too?"

"Who? Henry? Not he. Look at him sitting there disapproving. Disapproves of the whole expedition. That[11] trail up from the road nearly gave him a conniption. Well, it <u>was</u> a devilish road to put a car on. Whose old bus is that up there?"

"Barney's.," ~~said Miranda.~~

"Good Lord! Does Bernie ~~Shortreed~~ ^Redfern^ ride in a thing like that? It looks like the great-great-grandmother of all the Fords."

"It isn't a Ford. It's a ~~Grey~~ Grey-Slosson," said ~~Miranda~~ Valancy spiritedly. For some occult reason[,] Dr. ~~Shortreed's~~ ^Redfern's^ good-humored ridicule of dear old Lady Jane stung her to life. A life that was all pain but still <u>life</u>. Better than the horrible half-dead-and-half-aliveness of the past few minutes—or years. She waved Dr. ~~Shortreed~~ ^Redfern^ curtly into the boat and took him over to the Blue Castle. The key was still in the old pine – the house still silent and deserted. ~~Miranda~~ Valancy took the doctor through the living[-]room to the western veranda. She must at least be out where there was air. ~~NOTE K18~~ NOTE A13 The doctor dropped with a gasp on ~~the~~ a rustic chair and mopped his brow again.

8: "Forever more" is written as one word in the published version.

9: In the published version, "foolery," is changed to "feeling."

10: In the published version, "civilization" is spelled "civilisation."

11: In the published version, "That" is changed to "The."

NOTE A13: It was still sunny[,] but in the southwest a great thundercloud, with white crests & gorges of purple shadow, was slowly rising over Mistawis[.]

12: "Puss. Puss." is changed to "Puss, puss!" in the published version.

"Warm, eh? Lord, what a view! Wonder if it would soften Henry if he could see it."

"Have you had dinner?" asked ~~Miranda~~ Valancy.

"Yes, my dear – had it before we left Port Laurence. Didn't know what sort of wild ~~hermit's hollow~~ hermit's hollow we were coming to, you see. Hadn't any idea I was going to find a nice little daughter-in-law here all ready to toss me up a meal. Cats, eh? Puss. Puss.[12] See that. Cats love me. Bernie was always fond of cats. It is about the only thing he took from me. He's his poor mother[']s boy."

~~Miranda~~ Valancy had been thinking idly that Barney must resemble his mother. She had remained standing by the steps[,] but Dr. ~~Shortreed~~ ^Redfern^ waved her to the swing seat.

"Sit down, dear. Never stand when you can sit. I want to get a good look at Barney's wife. Well, well, I like your face. No beauty – you don't mind my saying that – you've sense enough to know it, I reckon. Sit down."

~~Miranda~~ Valancy sat down. To be obliged to sit still when mental agony urges us to stride up and down is the refinement of torture. Every nerve in her ~~body~~ being was crying out to be alone – ~~to look all this in the face~~ ^to be hidden^. But she had to sit and listen to Dr. ~~Shortreed~~ ^Redfern[,]^ ~~who didn't mind talking~~ ^who didn't mind talking^ at all.

"When do you think Bernie will be back?"

"I don't know – not before night probably."

"Where did he go?"

"~~I don't know that either. Likely to the woods – up~~ back."

"So he doesn't tell you all his comings and goings, either? Bernie was always a secretive young ~~devil~~ ^devil^. Never ~~understood~~ ^understood^ him. Just like his poor mother. But I thought a lot of him. It hurt me when he disappeared as he did. ~~Ten~~ ^Eleven^ ^Eleven^ years ago. I haven't seen my boy for ~~ten~~ ^eleven^ years."

"~~Ten~~ ^Eleven^ years." ~~Miranda~~ Valancy was surprised. "It's only six – since he came here."

"Oh, he was in the Klondike before that – and all over the world. He used to drop me a line now and then

– never give any clue to where he was but just a line to say he was all right. I s'pose he's told you all about it."

"No, ~~He~~ I know nothing of his past life,"[13] said ~~Miranda~~ Valancy with sudden eagerness. She wanted to know – she must know now. It hadn't mattered before. Now she must know all. And she could never hear it ~~again~~ from Barney. ~~now~~ She might never even see him again. If she did it would not be to talk of his past.

"What happened? Why did he leave his home? Tell me." Tell me."

"Well, it ain't much of a story. Just a young fool gone mad because of a quarrel with his girl. Only Bernie was a stubborn fool. Always stubborn. You never could make that boy do anything he didn't want to do. ~~Yet~~ From the day he was born. Yet he was always a quiet, gentle little chap, too. Good as gold. ~~We were poor enough when he was born – me and his mother up there in that little Quebec village~~ His poor mother died when he was only ~~three~~ ^two^ years old. I'd just begun to make money with my Hair Vigor ~~then.~~ ~~NOTE J18~~ NOTE B13 . ~~It rolled in.~~ Bernie had everything he wanted. I sent him to the best schools—private schools. I meant to make a gentleman of him. Never had any chance myself. Meant he should have every chance. He went ~~through~~ ^through^ McGill.[14] Got honors and all that. I wanted him to go in for law. He hankered after journalism and stuff like that. Wanted me to buy a paper for him – or back him in publishing what he called a 'real, worthwhile, honest-to-goodness Canadian magazine.'[15] I s'pose I'd have done it—I always did what he wanted me to do. Wasn't he all I had to live for? I wanted him to be happy. And he never was happy. Can you believe it? Not that he said so. But I'd always a feeling that he wasn't happy. Everything he wanted—all the money he could ~~want~~ ^spend^ – his own bank account – travel – seeing the world—but he wasn't happy. Not till he fell in love with Ethel ~~Traverse~~ ^Traverse^. Then he was happy for a little while." ~~NOTE L18~~ NOTE C13

"Yes," ~~said Miranda~~ ^she said,^ with painful eagerness, though every word was cutting her to the heart. "What – was – she – like?"

13: It's not true that Valancy knows nothing of his past life. She heard Barney tell tales from his past life—such as searching for gold in the Yukon, taking a cattle boat to England, spending two years in the Klondike—when he and Roaring Abel were talking. Those tales were written in NOTE Y6 in Chapter XVIII, probably after Montgomery had written this scene.

NOTE B13: I'd dreamed the formula for it, you see. Some dream that. The cash rolled in.

14: McGill University, founded in 1821 in Montreal, Quebec.

15: In the published version, "magazine" is capitalized. (Coincidentally, perhaps, *Canadian Magazine* is the magazine in which Montgomery's essays on the seasons were published.)

NOTE C13: ❦ The cloud had reached the sun and a great, chill, purple shadow came swiftly over Mistawis. It touched the Blue Castle – rolled over it. Valancy shivered.

NOTE D13: Don't wonder
Bernie fell for her. And
brains as well. <u>She</u>
wasn't a bit of fluff. B. A.
from McGill[.]

16: "Bank" is lower case in
the published version.

"Prettiest girl in Montreal," said Dr. ~~Shortreed~~
^Redfern^. "Oh, she was a looker all right. Eh? Gold
hair – shiny as silk – great, big, soft, black eyes – skin
like milk and roses ~~NOTE H18~~ NOTE D13 A thoroughbred, too.
One of the best families. But a bit lean in the purse. Eh!
~~Bernie w~~ Bernie was mad about her. Happiest young
fool you ever saw~~.~~ ~~Came out of his shell.~~ ^Then – the
bust-up."^

"What happened?" ~~Miranda~~ Valancy had taken off
her hat and was absently thrusting a pin in and out of
it. Good Luck was purring beside her. Jigglesqueak was
regarding Dr. ~~Shortreed~~ ^Redfern^ with suspicion. Nip
and Tuck were lazily cawing in the pines. Mistawis was
beckoning. Everything was the same. Nothing was the
same. It was a hundred years since yesterday. Yesterday
at this time[,] she and Barney had been eating a belated
dinner here with laughter. Laughter? ~~Miranda~~ Valancy
felt that she had done with laughter forever. And with
tears[,] for that matter. She had no further use for either
of them.

"Blest if I know, my dear. Some fool quarrel I suppose. Bernie just lit out—disappeared. He wrote me
from the Yukon. Said his engagement was broken and
he wasn't coming back. And not to try to hunt him up
because he was never coming back. I didn't. What was
the use? I knew Bernie. I went on piling up money because there wasn't anything else to do. But I was mighty
lonely. All I lived for was them little notes now and then
from Bernie – Klondike – England – South Africa –
China – everywhere. I thought maybe he'd come back
some day to his lonesome old dad. Then six years ago
even the letters stopped. I didn't hear a word of or from
him till last Christmas."

"Did he write?"

"No. But he drew a check for fifteen thousand dollars on his back account. The Bank[16] manager is a friend
of mine—~~has shares in the Purple Pills company~~ ^has
shares in one^ ^one of my biggest shareholders.^ He'd
always promised me he'd let me know if Bernie drew
any checks. Bernie had ~~$50,000~~ ^fifty thousand^ there.

And he'd never touched a cent of it till last Christmas. The check was ~~drawn on~~ ^made out to^ Aynsleys, Toronto[—]" ~~=the big jewelry firm there."~~

"Aynsley's?" ~~Miranda~~ Valancy heard herself saying. Aynsleys! She had a box ~~in her~~ on her dressing[-]table with the Aynsley trade-mark.

"Yes. The big jewel[le]ry house there. ~~I got busy then. I wanted to~~ ^After I'd thought it over a[ ]while[,] I got busy[17]. I wanted to^ locate Bernie. Had a special reason for it. It was time he gave up his fool hoboing and come to his senses. Drawing that fifteen told me there was something in the wind. ~~I put a private detective on the case. Found out~~ The manager ~~got~~ communicated with the ~~Anysleys~~ Aynsleys—his wife was an Aynsley—and found out that Bernard ~~Shortreed~~ ^Redfern^ had bought a pearl necklace there. His address was given as ^Box 444^ Port Laurence, Muskoka[,] Ont. First I thought I'd write. Then I ~~had pneumonia and mighty near passed out.~~ thought I'd wait till ~~car seas~~ the open season for cars and come down myself. Ain[']t no hand at writing. ~~W~~ I've ~~not~~ motored from Montreal. Got to Port Laurence yesterday. Enquired at the Post Office.[18] Told me they knew nothing of any ~~Shortreed~~ ^Bernard Snaith ~~Shortreed~~ Redfern[,]^ but there was a Barney Snaith had a P.O. box there. Lived on an island out here[,] they said. So here I am. And where's Barney?"

~~Miranda~~ Valancy was fingering her necklace. She was wearing fifteen thousand dollars around her neck. And she had worried lest Barney had paid ~~$18~~ ^fifteen^ for it and couldn't afford it. Suddenly she laughed in Dr. ~~Shortreed's~~ ^Redfern's^ face.

"Excuse me. It's so – amusing," said poor ~~Miranda.~~ Valancy.

"Isn't it?" said Dr. ~~S~~ ^Redfern,^ seeing a joke – but not exactly hers. "Now, you seem like a sensible young woman[,] and I daresay you've lots of influence over Bernie. Can't you get him to come back to civilization and live like other people? I've a house up there. Big as a castle. Furnished like a palace. I want company in it – Barney's wife – Barney's children."[19]

17: In the published version, "busy" is changed to "brisk."

18: "Post Office" is in lower case and hyphenated in the published version.

19: In the published version, both instances of "Barney" in this sentence are changed to "Bernie."

"Did Ethel Travers ever marry?" queried ~~Miranda~~ Valancy irrelevantly.

"~~Beless~~ "Bless you, yes. Two years after Bernie le-vanted.[20] But she's a widow now. Pretty as ever. ^To be frank[,]^ ~~T~~that was my special reason for wanting to find Bernie. I thought they'd make it up[,] maybe. But[,] of course[,] that's all off now. Doesn't matter. Bernie's choice of a wife is good enough for me. It's my boy I want. Think he'll soon be back?"

"I don't know. But I don't think he'll come before night. Quite late perhaps. And perhaps not till tomorrow. But I can put you up comfortably. He'll certainly be back tomorrow."

Dr. ~~Shortreed~~ ^Redfern^ shook his head.

"Too damp. ~~I'm afraid of rheumatism.~~ ^I'll take no chances with rheumatism."^

"'Why suffer that ~~beastless~~ ^ceaseless^ anguish? Why not try ~~Shortreed's~~ ^Redfern's^ Liniment?'" quoted the imp in the back of ~~Miranda's~~ Valancy's mind.

"~~That~~

"I must get back to Port Laurence before rain starts. Henry goes quite mad when he gets mud on the car. But I'll come back tomorrow. Meanwhile~~,~~ you talk Barney into reason."

He shook her hand and patted her kindly on the shoulder. ~~NOTE 118~~ NOTE E13 He was ~~very~~ ^rather^ dreadful and loud – and – and – dreadful. But there was something about him she liked. She ~~did not think she would have minded~~ ^thought dully that she might have liked^ being his daughter-in-law if he had not been a millionaire. A score of times over. And Barney was his son—and heir.

She took him over in the motor boat and watched the lordly purple car roll away ~~over the boulders~~ through the woods with Henry at the wheel looking things not lawful to be uttered. Then she went back to the Blue Castle. What she had to do must be done quickly. Barney might return at any moment. And it was certainly going to rain. She was thankful she no longer felt very bad~~ly~~. When you are bludgeoned on the head repeatedly[,] you naturally and ~~mercerfully~~ ^mercifully^ become more or less ~~insen rest~~ insensible and stupid.

~~"At anyrate," thought Miranda Valancy wanly, "Barney isn't poor. He will be able to afford a divorce quite nicely." Standing by the fireplace and looking down at the white ashes of the last fire she and Barney had sat by together, "Barney isn't poor. He will be able to afford a divorce quite nicely."~~

She stood briefly like a faded flower bitten by frost, by the hearth, looking down on the ~~ash~~ white ashes of the last fire that had blazed in the Blue Castle.

"At any[ ]rate," she thought wearily, "Barney isn't poor. He will be able to afford a divorce. Quite nicely."

NOTE F13: Chemical exper-
iments probably, she
reflected dully.

She must write a note. The imp in the back of her mind laughed. In every story she had ever read when a runaway wife ~~left her~~ ^decamped from^ home she left a note, generally on the pincushion. ~~Bu~~ It was not a very original idea. But one had to leave something intelligible. What was there to do but write a note? She looked vaguely about her for something to write with. Ink? There was none. ~~Miranda~~ Valancy had never written anything since she had come to the Blue Castle, save memoranda of household necessaries for Barney. A pencil sufficed for them, but now the pencil was not to be found. ~~Miranda~~ Valancy absently crossed to the door of Bluebeard's Chamber and tried it. She vaguely expected to find it locked[,] but it opened unresistingly. She had never tried it before[,] and did ~~not~~ not know whether Barney habitually kept it locked or not. If he did[,] he must have been badly upset to leave it unlocked. She ~~was~~ ^did^ not realize that she was doing something he had told her not to do, She was only looking for something to write with. All her faculties were concentrated on deciding just what she would say and how she would say it. There was not the slightest curiosity in her as she went into the lean-to. ⁋ There were no beautiful women hanging by their hair on the walls. ~~The~~ It seemed a very harmless apartment with a commonplace little sheet-iron stove in the middle of it, its pipe sticking out through the roof. At one end was a table or counter crowded with odd-looking ~~int~~ utensils. Used no doubt by Barney in his smelly operations. ~~chem clim~~ ~~NOTE L20~~ NOTE F13 At the other end was a big writing desk and swivel[-]chair. The side walls were lined with books.

~~Miranda~~ Valancy went blindly to the desk. There she stood,~~looking down for~~ motionless for a few minutes, looking down at ~~two things~~ ^something^ that lay on it. ~~One was a neat little pile of typewritten manuscript entitled"~~

~~"In the upper left hand corner was the address.~~
~~Bernard Snaith~~
~~Box 444~~
~~Port Laurence~~
~~Muskoka~~
~~Ont.~~

~~Below the title were the words "by John Foster.~~
~~The other was a~~ ^A^ bundle[1] of galley proofs. The page on top bore the title ^"Wild Honey"^[2] and under the title were the words "by John Foster."

The opening sentence – "Pines are the trees of myth and legend. ~~NOTE M20~~ NOTE G13 she had heard Barney say that one day when they walked under them.

So Barney was John Foster!

~~Miranda~~ Valancy was not ~~at all~~ excited. She had absorbed all the shocks and sensations that she could compass for one day. This affected her neither one way ~~on~~ or the other. She only thought,

"So this explains it."

"It" was a small matter that had, somehow, stuck in her mind more persistently than its importance seemed to justify. Soon after Barney had ~~giv~~ brought her John Foster[']s latest book she had been in a Port Laurence bookshop and heard a customer ask the ~~clerk~~ ^proprietor^ for John Foster[']s new book. The ~~clerk~~ ^proprietor^ had said curtly, "Not out yet. Won't be out till next week."

~~Miranda~~ Valancy had opened her lips to say, "Oh, yes, it _is_ out" but closed them again. After all, it was none of her business. She supposed the proprietor wanted to cover up his negligence in not getting the book in promptly. Now she knew. The book Barney had given her had been one of the author[']s complimentary copies, sent in advance. ~~of~~

1: In the published version, "A bundle" does not begin a new paragraph but continues after "lay on it" in the lines above.

2: "Wild Honey" is in italics in the published version with no quotation marks.

NOTE G13: They strike their roots deep into the traditions of an older world[,] but wind and star love their lofty tops. What music when old Aeolus[3] draws his bow across the branches of the pines." –[4]

3: Aeolus is the Greek god of the winds.

4: Montgomery wrote this passage in her essay, "The Woods in Summer": "Pines are the trees of myth and legend. They strike their roots deep into the traditions of an older world, but wind and star love their lofty tops. What music when old Aeolus draws his bow across the branches of a pine!"

5: "Won't be a sufficient?" is omitted in the published version.

NOTE H13: Is desertion a ~~gou~~ ground for divorce in Canada? Of course if there is anything I can do to help or hasten it I will do it gladly, if your lawyer will let me know. I thank you for all your kindness to me.

6: The postscript was first signed with an "M" for Miranda, then changed to a "V" for Valancy. In the published version, the postscript is not signed.

NOTE I13: On it she laid the string of pearls. If they had been the beads she believed them she would have kept them in memory of that wonderful year. But she could not keep the fifteen thousand dollar gift of a man who had married her out of pity & whom she was now leaving. It hurt her to give up her pretty bauble. That was an odd ~~fact;~~ ^thing,^ she reflected. The fact that she was leaving Barney did not hurt her – yet. It lay at her heart like a cold, insensible thing. If it came to life – Valancy shuddered & went out[—]
She put on her hat & mechanically fed Good Luck & Jigglesqueak. She locked the door and carefully hid the key in the old pine.

Well! ~~Miranda~~ Valancy pushed the proofs indifferently aside and sat down in the swivel chair. She took up Barney's pen—and a vile one it was—pulled a sheet of paper to her and began to write. She could not think of anything to say except bald facts.

"Dear Barney: –

I went to Dr. Trent this morning and found out he had sent me the wrong letter by mistake. ~~I am quite well~~ ^There never was^ anything serious the matter with my heart and I am quite well now.

I did not mean to trick you. Please believe that. I could not bear it if you ~~tho~~ did not believe that. I am very sorry for the mistake. But ~~I think~~ ^surely^ you can get a divorce if I leave you. ^~~Will~~ (Won't be a suffi-cient?)^5 | NOTE H13 ~~Desertion is a ground for divorce even in Canada? Isn't it? ^And of course if there is anything I can do to help or hasten it I will gladly do it if your^~~

~~Thank you very I thank you for all your kindness to me.~~ I shall never forget it. Think as kindly of me as you can because I did not mean to trap you. Good-bye.

~~Yours~~

Yours gratefully

~~Miranda~~ Valancy."

It was very cold and stiff, she knew. But to try to say anything else would be dangerous – like tearing away a dam. She didn't know what ^torrent of^ wild incoherences and passionate anguish might pour out. In a postscript she added,

"Your father was here to-day. ^He is coming back tomorrow.^ He told me everything. I think you should go back to him. He is very lonely for you."

~~M.~~ V. 6

She put the letter in an envelope, ~~addressed~~ wrote "Barney" across it, and left it on the desk NOTE M18 NOTE I13. ~~She went to her room and put on her hat and mechanically fed Good Luck and Jigglesqueak~~ ^NOTE N18^. Then she crossed to the mainland in the disappearing propeller. She stood for a moment on the bank[,] looking at her Blue Castle. The rain had not yet come[,] but the sky was dark, and Mistawis gray and sullen. The little house under the pines looked very pathetic – a casket rifled of its jewels – a lamp with its flame blown out.

"I shall never again hear the wind in those old pines at night,"[7] thought ~~Miranda~~ Valancy. This hurt her, too. She could have laughed to think that such a trifle could hurt her at such a time.

[7]: In the published version, this sentence reads: "I shall never again hear the wind crying over Mistawis at night."

looking at her Blue Castle. The rain had not yet come but the sky was dark, and ... were grey and sullen. The little house under the pines looked very pathetic — a casket rifled of its jewels — a lamp with its flame blown out.

"I shall never again read the wind in those old pines at night," thought Valancy. This hurt her, too. She could have laughed to think that such a trifle could devastate her at such a time.

XXXIV   XXXVII

Valancy paused a moment — on the porch of the brick house

XL

Miranda Valancy paused a moment on the ~~verandah~~ porch of the brick house in Elm Street. She felt that she ought to knock like a stranger. ~~NOTE N20~~ NOTE J13 ~~A momentary horror overcame her. ^--^ a horror of the existence to which she was going back.^ So back to~~ that. ~~Then she opened the door and walked in.~~ ~~NOTE S20~~

Mrs. ~~George~~ Frederick and Cousin Stickles were in the sitting[-]room. Uncle Benjamin was there, too. They looked blankly at ~~Miranda~~ Valancy, realizing at once that something was wrong. This was not the saucy, impudent thing who had laughed at them in this very room last summer. This was a ~~white~~ ^gray-^ faced woman with the eyes of a creature who had been stricken by a mortal blow. ~~NOTE P18~~ NOTE K13

NOTE J13: Her rosebush, she idly noticed, was loaded with buds. The rubber[-]plant stood beside the prim door. A momentary horror overcame her – a horror of the existence to which she was returning. Then she opened the door & walked in[.]

"I wonder if the Prodigal Son ever felt really at home again," she thought[.]

NOTE K13: Valancy looked indifferently around the room. She had changed so much – and it had changed so little. The same pictures hung on the walls, the little orphan who knelt at her never-finished prayer by the bed whereon reposed the black kitten that never grew up into a cat.[1] The gray "steel engraving" of Quatre Bras, where the British regiment forever stood at bay.[2] The crayon enlargement of the boyish father she had never known. There they all hung in the same places. The green cascade of "Wandering Jew"[3] still tumbled out of the old granite saucepan on the window[-]stand. The same elaborate, never-used ~~pic~~ pitchers stood at the same angle on the sideboard shelf. The blue and gilt vases that had been ~~her~~ among her mother's wedding present[s] still primly adorned the mantel piece, flanking the china clock of berosed & besprayed ware that never went. The chairs in exactly the same places. Her mother & Cousins Stickles, likewise unchanged, regarding her with stony unwelcome.

1: Prints of "The Orphan's Prayer" were offered as a supplement to the *Family Herald and Weekly Star*, a newspaper published in Montreal, Quebec (date unconfirmed). It was also offered as a supplement to the *North American Sunday* paper on October 31, 1915. The artist is unknown. Coincidentally, this print hangs in the parlour at Green Gables house in Cavendish, Prince Edward Island.

The *Family Herald and Weekly Star* published at least twenty-nine stories and one poem by L. M. Montgomery.

2: The Battle of Quatre Bras (1815), fought two days before the Battle of Waterloo.

3: Wandering Jew = tradescandia, a tropical plant with trailing stems; a houseplant in northern climes.

~~Miranda~~ Valancy had to speak first.

"I've come home, mother," she said tiredly.

"So I see." Mrs. ~~George's~~ Frederick's voice was very icy. She had resigned herself to ~~Miranda's~~ Valancy's desertion. She had almost succeeded in forgetting there was a ~~Miranda~~ Valancy. She had rearranged and organized her systematic life without any reference to an ungrateful, rebellious child. She had taken her place again in a society which ignored the fact that she had ever had a daughter and pitied her, if it pitied her at all, only in discreet whispers and asides. The plain truth was that[,] by this time[,] Mrs. ~~George~~ Frederick did not want ~~Miranda~~ Valancy to come back – did not want ever to see or hear of her again.

And now, of course, ~~Miranda~~ Valancy was here. With tragedy and disgrace and scandal trailing after her visibly.

"So I see," said Mrs. ~~George~~ Frederick. "May I ask why[?]."

"Because – I'm – not going to die," said ~~Miranda~~ Valancy huskily.

"God bless my soul," said Uncle Benjamin, "who said you were going to die?"

"I suppose[,]" said Cousin Stickles shrewishly— Cousin Stickles did not want ~~Miranda~~ Valancy back either—"I suppose you've found out he has another wife – as we've been sure ~~along~~ all along."

"No. I only wish he had," said ~~Miranda~~ Valancy. ~~duly~~ She was not suffering particularly but she was very tired. If only the explanations were all over and she were were upstairs in her old, ugly room – alone. Just alone! The rattle of the beads on her mother's sleeves, as they swung on the arms of the reed chair, ^almost^ drove her crazy. Nothing else was worrying her, but all at once it seemed that she simply could not endure that thin, insistent rattle.

"My home, as I told you, is always open to you," said Mrs. ~~George~~ Frederick stonily, "but I can never forgive you."

~~Miranda~~ Valancy gave a mirthless ~~little~~ laugh.

"I'd care very little for that if I could only forgive myself," she said.

"Come, come," said Uncle Benjamin testily. But rather enjoying himself. He felt he had ~~Miranda~~ Valancy under his thumb again. "We've had enough of mystery. What has happened? Why have you left that fellow? No doubt there's reason enough – but what ~~is it?~~ ^particular reason is it?^"

~~Miranda~~ Valancy began to speak mechanically. She told her tale bluntly and barely.

"A year ago Dr. Trent told me I had angina pectoris and could not live long. I wanted to have some – life – before I died. That's why I went away. Why I married Barney. And now I've found it is all a mistake. There is nothing wrong with my heart. I've got to live – and ~~I tricked~~ Barney only married me out of pity. So I have to leave him – free."

"~~Unc Uncle Benjamin again appealed to God to bless his soul.~~ ^"God bless me," said Uncle Benjamin.^ Cousin Stickles began to cry.

"~~Miranda,~~ Valancy, if you'd only had confidence in your own mother—"

"Yes, yes, I know," said ~~Miranda~~ Valancy impatiently. "What's the use of going into that now? I can't undo this year. God knows I wish I could. I've tricked Barney into marrying me – and he's really Bernard ~~Shortreed~~ ^Redfern.^ Dr. ~~Shortreed's~~ ^Redfern's^ son[,] of Montreal. And his father wants him to go back to him."

Uncle Benjamin's mouth fell open and stayed open.[4] Cousin Stickles took her ^black-bordered^ handkerchief away from her eyes and stared at ~~Miranda~~ Valancy. A queer gleam suddenly shot into ~~Mrs. George's~~ Mrs. Frederick's stone-gray ~~eyes.~~ ^orbs.^

"Dr. ~~Shortreed~~ ^Redfern^ – not the Purple Pills man?" she said.

"~~Yes Miranda~~ Valancy nodded.
~~NOTE O18~~ NOTE L13

~~"But – but –" Mrs. George was visibly agitated – "Dr. Shortreed is a millionaire."~~

4: In the published version, this sentence reads "Uncle Benjamin made a queer sound."

NOTE L13: "He's John Foster,[5] too – the writer of those nature books."
"But – but –" Mrs. Frederick was visibly agitated, though not over the thought that she was the mother-in-law of John Foster – "Dr. Redfern is a millionaire!"

5: In the published version, "He's John Foster" does not start a new paragraph but continues on after "Valancy nodded."

NOTE M13: ~~How amaz-~~
~~ingly paternal Uncle~~
~~Benjamin was!~~ --

NOTE T14: Tell me this,
Dossie. Have you been
happy up back? Was
Sn— Mr. Redfern good
to you?"
    "I have been very
happy & Barney was
very good to me," said
Valancy, as if reciting a
lesson. She remembered
that when she studied
grammar at school she
had disliked the past
and perfect tenses. They
had always seemed so
pathetic. "I have been"—
it was all over & done
with.
    "Then don't worry,
little girl." How amaz-
ingly paternal Uncle
Benjamin was!

Uncle Benjamin shut his mouth with a snap.

"Ten times over," he said.

~~Miranda~~ Valancy nodded.

"Yes. Barney left home years ago – because of – of some trouble. ^– some – disappointment.^ Now he will likely go back. So you see – I had to come home. He doesn't love me. I can't hold him to a bond he was tricked into."

Uncle Benjamin looked incredibly sly.

"Did he say so? Does he want to get rid of you?"

"No. I haven't seen him since I found out. But I tell you – he only married me out of pity – ~~because~~ ^because^ I asked him to – because ~~cause~~ he thought it would only be for a little while."

Mrs. ~~George~~ Frederick and Cousin Stickles both tried to speak[,] but Uncle Benjamin waved a ~~pudgly~~ pudgy hand at them and frowned portentously.

"Let _me_ handle this," wave and frown seemed to say. ~~He went to~~ To ~~Miranda~~ Valancy,[:]

"Well, well, dear, we'll talk it all over later. You see, we don't quite understand everything yet. As Cousin Stickles says you should have confided in us before. Later on – I daresay we can find a way out of this."

"You think Barney can easily get a divorce, don't you?" said ~~Miranda~~ Valancy eagerly.

Uncle Benjamin silenced with another wave the exclamation of ~~hur~~ horror he knew was trembling on Mrs. ~~George's lips~~ ^Frederick's lips.^

"Trust to me, ~~Miranda~~ Valancy. Everything will arrange itself." ~~NOTE H8 NOTE M13 NOTE T14~~ D~~on't worry, little girl.~~ Your family will stand behind you. We'll see what can be done."

"Thank you," said ~~Miranda~~ Valancy dully. Really, it was quite decent of Uncle Benjamin. "Can I go and lie down a little while? I'm – I'm – tired."

"Of course you're tired." Uncle Benjamin patted her ~~kindly on the shoulder~~ ^hand gently – very gently.^

"All worn out ^and nervous.^ Go and lie down[,] by all means. ~~Get a good sleep.~~ You'll see things in quite a different light after you've had a good sleep."

He held the door open. As she went through he whispered, "What is the best way to keep a man's love?"

~~Miranda~~ Valancy smiled ~~wanly~~ wanly. But she had come back to the old life – the old shackles. "What?" she ~~said~~ asked ^as^ ~~meekly,~~ ^as of yore.^

"Not to return it," ~~whispered~~ ^said^ Uncle Benjamin with a chuckle. He shut the door and rubbed his hands. Nodded & smiled mysteriously round the room.

"Poor little Doss," he said pathetically.

"Do you really suppose that – Snaith – can ~~really~~ ^actually^ be Dr. ~~Shortreed's~~ ^Redfern's^ son?" gasped Mrs. ~~George.~~ Frederick.

"I see no reason for doubting it. She says Dr. ~~Shortreed~~ ^Redfern^ has been there. Why, the man is rich as wedding[-]cake. ~~Didn't I always~~ Amelia, I've always believed there was more in Doss than most people thought. You kept her down too much – repressed her. She never had a chance to show what was in her. And now she's landed a millionaire for a husband."

"But" – hesitated Mrs. ~~George~~ Frederick "he – he— they told terrible tales about him."

"All gossip and invention – all gossip and invention ~~NOTE P20~~ NOTE N13. Just because he didn't choose to mix up with everybody people resented it. I was surprised to find what a decent fellow he seemed to be that time he came into my store with ~~Miranda~~ Valancy. I discounted all the yarns ~~right off~~ ^then & there.^"

"But he was seen dead drunk in Port Laurence once," said Cousin Stickles. Doubtfully, yet as one very willing to be convinced to the contrary.

"Who saw him?" ~~demanded~~ demanded Uncle Benjamin ~~trucantly~~ truculently. "Who saw him? Old ~~Jemmy~~ ^Jemmy^ Strang <u>said</u> he saw him. I wouldn't take old Jemmy Strang's word on oath. He's too drunk himself half the time to see straight. He said he saw him lying drunk on a bench in the Park. Pshaw! ~~Shortreed's~~ ^Redfern's^ been asleep there. Don't worry over <u>that</u>."

"But his clothes – and that awful old car –[,]" said Mrs. ~~George~~ Frederick uncertainly.

NOTE N13: It's always been a mystery to me why people should be so ready to invent & circulate slanders about other people they know absolutely nothing about. I can't understand why you paid so much attention to gossip & surmise.

6: In the published version, "Uncle B." is changed to "Uncle Benjamin."

NOTE O13: This whole affair has been bungled from start to finish. If you had put yourself to a little trouble years ago, Amelia, she would not have bolted over the traces as she did[.]

7: Montgomery neglected to strike out this phrase even though she rewrote it in NOTE P13.

NOTE P13: When ~~tea was~~ supper was . ready she went up & asked Valancy if she wouldn't like a cup of tea. Valancy, lying on her bed, declined. She just wanted to be left alone for awhile. Mrs. Frederick left her alone. She did not even remind Valancy that her plight was the outcome of her own lack of daughterly respect and obedience. One could not – exactly – say things like that to the daughter[-in-law] of a millionaire.

"Eccentricities of genius," declared Uncle B^enjamin^. "You heard Doss say he was John Foster. I'm not up in literature myself[,] but I heard ~~Mr. Stalling~~ ^a lecturer from Toronto^ say that John Foster's books had put Canada on the literary map of the world."

"I – suppose – we must forgive her," ~~said Mrs.~~ yielded Mrs. ~~George~~ Frederick.

"Forgive her!" Uncle B.[6] snorted. Really, Amelia was an incredibly stupid woman. No wonder poor Doss had gone sick and tired of living with her. "Well, yes, I think you'd better forgive her! The question is – will Snaith forgive us!"

"What if she persists in leaving him? You've no idea how stubborn she can be," said Mrs. ~~George~~ Frederick.

"Leave it all to me, Amelia. Leave it all to me. You women have muddled it enough ~~NOTE R20~~ NOTE O13 Just let ~~Doss~~ ^her^ alone – don't worry her ~~till~~ with advice or questions till she's ready to talk. ~~Snaith~~ She's evidently run away in a panic because she's afraid he'd be angry with her for fooling him. Most extraordinary thing of Trent to tell her such a yarn! That's what comes of going to strange doctors. Well, well, we mustn't blame her too harshly, poor child. ~~Snaith~~ ^Shortreed^ ^Redfern^ will come after her. If he doesn't[,] I'll hunt him up and talk to him as man to man. He may be a millionaire[,] but ~~Miranda~~ Valancy is a Stirling. He can't repudiate her just because she was mistaken about her heart disease. Not likely he'll want to. Doss is a little overstrung. Bless me, I must get in the habit of calling her ~~Miranda~~ Valancy. She ~~never liked Doss~~ ^isn't^ a baby any longer. Now remember, Amelia. Be very kind and sympathetic."

It was something of a large order to expect Mrs. ~~George~~ Frederick to be kind and sympathetic. But she did her best. ~~She left Miranda alone till tea-time. Then~~ ^When tea ~~time~~ was ready^[7] ~~she went up and asked her~~ ^Miranda^ ~~if she wouldn't like a cup of tea. Miranda, lying on her bed, sa declined. She just wanted to be left alone for awhile. Mrs. George left her alone.~~ ~~NOTE T18~~ NOTE P13

XLI

~~Miranda~~ Valancy looked dully about her old room. It ~~was~~ ^, too, was^ so exactly the same that it seemed almost impossible to believe in the changes that had come to her since she had last slept in it. It seemed ^– somehow –^ indecent that it should be so much the same. There was Queen Louise everlastingly coming down the ~~storeway~~ stairway[,] and nobody had let the forlorn puppy in out of the rain ~~NOTE R18~~ NOTE Q13 ❦Here the old life waited for her, like some grim ~~inc giant~~ ^ogre^ that bided his time ^and licked his chops.^ A monstrous horror of it suddenly possessed her. When night fell and she had undressed and got into bed, the merciful numbness passed away and she lay in anguish and thought of her island under the stars. The camp[-]fires ~~=Barney frying bacon~~ – ~~NOTE T20~~ NOTE R13 the lights agleam on the fairy islands – canoes skimming over Mistawis in the magic of morning – white birches shining among the dark spruces like beautiful women's bodies – winter snows and rosered sunset fires – ^lakes drunken with moonshine –^ all the delights of her lost paradise. ~~NOTE V20~~ NOTE S13

~~And Barney.~~ She ached[1] for him. She wanted his arms around her – his face against hers – his whispers in her ear. She recalled all his friendly looks & quips & jests – his little complements[2] – ~~his tenderness~~ =his caresses. She counted them all over as a woman might count her jewels – not one did she miss from the first day they had met. These memories were all she could have now. She shut her eyes and prayed.

"Let me remember every ~~moment~~ ^one^, God. Let me never forget one of them."

NOTE Q13: Here was the purple paper blind & the greenish mirror. ~~Yonder was the station with its derelicts & flirtatious flappers = The~~ ^Outside, the^ old carriage[-]shop with its blatant advertisements. Beyond it, the station with the same derelicts & flirtatious flappers.

NOTE R13: – all their little household jokes & phrases & catch words – their furry, beautiful cats –

NOTE S13: She would not let herself think of Barney. Only of these lesser things. She could not endure to think of Barney.
Then she thought of him inescapably.

1: In the published version, "She ached" does not start a new paragraph but continues after "inescapably."

2: In the published version, "complements" is corrected to "compliments."

NOTE T13: Hadn't he told her he never changed his mind?

NOTE U13: Barney would marry her, of course, when he got his divorce. How Valancy hated her! And envied her! NOTE U14

Yet, "She can never have those hours in the Blue Castle. They are <u>mine!</u>" thought Valancy savagely. Ethel would never make strawberry jam or dance to old Abel's fiddle or fry bacon for Barney over a camp fire. She would never come to the little Mistawis shack at all.

~~But~~
~~NOTE V13~~

❲What was ~~he~~ ^Barney^ doing – thinking – feeling now? Had he come home & found her letter? Was he still angry with her? Or a little pitiful. Was he lying on their bed looking out on stormy Mistawis & listening to the rain streaming down on the roof? Or was he still wandering in the wilderness, raging at the predicament in which he found himself? Hating her? Pain took her & wrung her like some great, pitiless giant. ~~NOTE V2 NOTE V13~~

3: Parentheses were pencilled around this phrase in the manuscript; Montgomery neglected to cross it out even though she rewrote it ~~in NOTE U13~~.

NOTE U14: Barney had said, "I love you" to <u>her</u>. Valancy wondered what tone Barney would say "I love you" in – how his dark-blue eyes would look when he said it. Ethel Traverse knew. Valancy hated her for the knowledge—hated and envied her.[4]

4: At this point, after "hated and envied her," the story resumes in NOTE U13.

Yet it would be better to forget. This agony of ~~lonsg~~ longing and loneliness ~~might~~ ^would^ not be so terrible if one could forget. And Ethel Traverse. That shimmering witch woman with her white skin and black eyes and shining hair. The woman Barney had loved. The woman whom ~~still~~ he still loved NOTE Q20 NOTE T13. Who was waiting for him in Montreal. Who was the right wife for a rich and famous man. NOTE Y20 NOTE U13 ~~How Miranda hated her. And envied her.~~ ~~NOTE X20~~ ~~Barney had said "I love you" to her. Miranda~~ ~~Valancy wondered what tone Barney would say "I love you in"~~ – (how his dark blue eyes would look when he said it).[3] | NOTE W1 NOTE Q18 NOTE U13 ~~Miranda~~ ^She^ got up and walked the floor. Would morning never come to end this hideous night? And yet what could morning bring her? The old life without the old ~~peace~~ stagnation that was at least bearable. The old life with the new memories, the new longings, the new anguish.

NOTE V20

"Oh, why can't I die?" moaned ~~Miranda.~~ Valancy.

XXXIX

It was not until early afternoon the next day that a
dreadful old car clanked up
Sleen street and stopped at the
in front of the brick house. A ~~was~~
hatless ~~man in~~ sprang
from it and rushed up the steps.
The bell, ~~was~~ rang as if it had
never been rung before — vehemently,
~~deen~~ intensely. The ringer was
demanding entrance, not asking
it. Uncle Benjamin chuckled as
he turned to the door. Uncle Ben-
had "just dropped in" to ~~inquire~~
how dear ~~Hassie~~ was — ~~because~~
was. dear Doss — ~~Tuesday~~, he had

XLII

It was not until early afternoon the next day that a dreadful old car clanked up Elm Street and stopped ~~at the~~ in front of the brick house. A ~~man~~ hatless man ~~in overalls~~ sprang from it and rushed up the steps. The bell ^was^ ~~rang~~ rung as ~~if~~ it had never been rung before—vehemently, ~~dema~~ intensely. The ringer was demanding entrance, not asking it. Uncle Benjamin chuckled as he hurried to the door. Uncle B^enjamin^ had "just dropped in" to inquire how dear ~~Dossie~~ Doss – ~~Miranda~~ Valancy was. Dear Doss – ~~Miranda~~ Valancy, he had been informed, was just the same. She had come down for breakfast – which she didn't eat – gone back to her room, come down for dinner – which she didn't eat – gone back to her room. That was all. She had not talked. And she had been let, kindly, considerately alone.

"Very good. ~~Shortreed~~ ^Redfern^ will be here to-day," said ~~Uncle B~~ ^Uncle ~~Beyamin~~ Benjamin^.

And now Uncle B's ^enjamin's^ reputation as a prophet was made. ~~Shortreed~~ ^Redfern^ was here—unmistakeably so.

"Is my wife here?" he demanded of Uncle B^enjamin^ without preface.

Uncle B^enjamin^ smiled expressively. "~~She is.~~ Mr. ~~Shortreed~~ ^Redfern^, I believe? Very glad to meet you, sir. Yes, that naughty little girl of yours is here. We have been—"

"I must see her," Barney cut Uncle B^enjamin^ ruthlessly short.

"Certainly, Mr. ~~Shortreed Sh Shortreed~~ ^Redfern.^ Just step in here. ~~Miranda~~ Valancy will be down in a minute."

He ushered Barney into the parlor and betook himself to the sitting[-]room and Mrs. ~~George~~ Frederick.

253

"Go up and ~~ask~~ ^tell^ ~~Miranda~~ Valancy to come down. Her husband is here."

But so dubious was Uncle B^enjamin^ as to whether ~~Miranda~~ Valancy would really come down in a minute—or at all—that he followed Mrs. ~~George~~ Frederick on tiptoe up the stairs and listened in the hall.

"~~Miranda~~ Valancy, dear," said Mrs. ~~George~~ Frederick tenderly, "your husband is in the parlor, asking for you."

"Oh, mother."[1] ~~Miranda~~ Valancy got up from the window and wrung her hands. "I cannot see him—I cannot. Tell him to go away – <u>ask</u> him to go away. I can't see him."

~~"But you~~

"Tell her," hissed Uncle Ben^jamin^ through the keyhole, "that ~~Shortreed~~ ^Redfern^ says he won't go away until he <u>has</u> seen her."

~~Shortreed~~ ^Redfern^ had not said anything of the ~~sort~~ ^kind[,]^ but Uncle B^enjamin^ thought he was that sort of a fellow. ~~Miranda~~ Valancy knew he was. She understood that she ~~must go down.~~ might as well go down first as last.

She did not even look at Uncle B^enjamin^, as she passed him on the landing. Uncle B^enjamin^ did not mind. Rubbing his hands and chuckling[,] he retreated to the kitchen[,] where he genially demanded of Cousin Stickles~~,~~[:]

"Why are good husbands like bread?"

Cousin Stickles asked why.

"Because women need them," beamed Uncle B^enjamin^. ~~He was already thinking that he would call in his lawyer and alter his will again – making Doss his sole legatee. To her that hath ^had^ ought to be given.~~

~~Miranda~~ Valancy was looking anything but beautiful when she entered the parlor. ~~A sleepless tearful~~ ^Her white^ night had played fearful havoc with her face. She wore an ugly old brown-and-blue gingham, having left all her pretty dresses in the Blue Castle. But Barney dashed across the room and caught her in his arms.

"~~Miranda~~ Valancy, darling – oh, you darling little idiot! Whatever possessed you to ~~runaway~~ ^run away^

like that? When I came home last night and found your letter,I went quite mad. It was twelve o'clock—I knew it was too late to come here then. I walked the floor all night. Then this morning dad[2] came – I couldn't get away till now. ~~Miranda~~ Valancy, what ever got into you? Divorce, forsooth! Don't you know—"

"I know you only married me out of pity," said ~~Miranda~~ Valancy, brushing him away feebly. "I know you don't love ~~you~~ me – I know—"

"You've been lying awake at three o'clock ^too long,^" said Barney, shaking her. "That's all that's the matter with you. Love you. Oh, don't I love you! My girl, when I saw that train coming down on you I knew whether I loved you or not[!]."

"Oh, I ~~knew~~ ^was afraid^ you would try to make me think you cared," said ~~Miranda~~ Valancy passionately. "Don't – don't. I know. I know all about Ethel Traverse— your father told me ^everything^. Oh, Barney, don't torture me. I can never go back to you^!"^ ~~because~~

Barney released her ~~and~~ ^and^ looked at her for a moment. Something in her pallid, resolute face spoke more convincingly than words of her determination.

"~~Miranda~~ Valancy," he said quietly. "~~let's just sit down here.~~ Father couldn't have told you everything because he didn't know it. Will you let _me_ tell you – everything?"

"Yes," said ~~Miranda~~ Valancy wearily. Oh, how dear he was! How she longed to throw herself into his arms! As he put her gently down in a chair[,] she could have kissed the slender, brown hands that touched her arms. She could not look up as he stood before her. ~~If he saw into her eyes he would~~ She dared not meet his eyes. For his sake she must be brave. She knew him – kind, unselfish. Of course he would pretend he did not want his freedom – she might have known he would pretend that, once the first shock of realization was over. He was so sorry for her – he understood her terrible position. When had he ever failed to understand? But she would never accept his sacrifice. Never!

"You've seen ~~father~~ dad and you know I'm Bernard ~~Shortreed~~ ^Redfern^. And I suppose you've guessed

2: In the published version, "dad" is capitalized, here and throughout.

that I'm John Foster – since I found your letter by my proofs." you went

"Yes. But into Bluebeard's chamber."

"Yes. But I didn't go in out of curiosity. I forgot you had told me not to go in – I forgot—"

"Never mind. I'm not going to kill you and hang you up on the wall[,] so there['] s no need to call for Sister Anne.[3] I'm only going to tell you my story from the beginning. I came back last night intending to do it. Yes, I'm 'old Doc. Shortreed's ^Redfern's^ son'—of Purple Bitters Pills and Bitters fame. Oh, don't I know it? Wasn't it rubbed into me for years?"

Barney laughed bitterly and strode up and down the room a few times. Uncle B.^enjamin, ^ tiptoeing through the hall, heard the laugh and frowned. Surely Doss wasn't going to be a stubborn little fool.

Barney threw himself into a chair before Miranda Valancy.[4]

"Yes. When I was born dad wasn't a millionaire. He wasn't even a doctor = isn't yet. He was veterinary and a failure at it. We lived in a little village up in Quebec.

"As long as I can remember[5] I've been a millionaire's son. But when I was born dad wasn't a millionaire. He wasn't even a doctor – isn't yet. He was a veterinary and a failure at it. We He and mother[6] lived in a little village up in Quebec and were abominably poor. I don't remember mother. ^Haven't even a picture of her[.]^ She died when I was a ^two^ year^s^ old. She was fifteen years younger than father – a little school teacher. When she died dad moved into Montreal and started making ^formed a company to sell^ his hair tonic. He'd dreamed the prescription one night, it seems. Well, it caught on. Money began to flow in. Dad invented – or dreamed – the other things, too – Pills, Bitters, Liniment and so on. = and formed a company. He was a millionaire by the time I was ten. NOTE V20 NOTE W13 I had every toy a boy could wish for ^ –given tutors^ and I was the loneliest little devil in the world. I remember only one afternoon happy day in my childhood, Miranda Valancy. Only one. Even you were better off than that. Dad had gone out to see an old friend in the country and took me along. I was turned loose in the barnyard and I spent the whole day hammering nails in a block of wood. I had ~~the time of my life~~ ^a glorious day^. When I had to go back to my ~~only~~ roomful of playthings in the big house in Montreal I cried. But I didn't tell ~~for~~ dad why. I never told him anything. It's always been a hard thing ~~to tell~~ for me to tell things, ~~Miranda~~ Valancy – anything that went deep. And most things went deep with me. I was a sensitive child and I was even more sensitive as a boy. No one ever knew what I suffered. Dad never dreamed of it. When[7] he sent me to a private school ^– I was only eleven –^ the boys ducked me in the swimming[-]tank until I stood on a table and read aloud ~~the~~ all the advertisements of father's[8] patent abominations. I did it – then"—Barney clenched his fists—"I was frightened and half drowned and all my world was against me. But when I went to college and the sophs tried the same stunt I didn't do it." Barney smiled grimly. "They couldn't make me do it. But they could – and did – make my life miserable. I never heard the last of the Pills and the Bitters and the Hair Tonic.~~"~~[']After ~~Taking~~ ^Using[']~~"~~^[9] was my nickname—you see I'd always such a thick thatch. My four college years were a nightmare. You know—or you don't know—what merciless beasts boys can be when they get a victim like me. I had few friends—there was always some barrier between me and the kind of people I cared for. ~~Old Doc Shortreed's son.~~ And the other kind—who would have been very willing to be intimate with rich old Doc. ~~Shortreed's~~ ^Redfern's^ son—I didn't care for. But I had one friend – or thought I had. A clever, bookish chap – a bit of a writer. That was a bond between us—I had some secret aspirations along that line. He was older than I was – I looked up to him and worshipped him. ~~Then~~ For a year I was happier than I'd ever been. Then – a ^burlesque^ sketch came out in the college magazine – a mordant thing, ridiculing dad's remedies. ~~No~~ The names were changed, of course[,] but everybody knew what and who was meant. Oh, it was clever—damnably so—and witty. McGill rocked with laughter over it. I found out <u>he</u> had written it.

7: In the published version, a new paragraph begins here.

8: In the published version, "father's" is capitalized.

9: In the published version, "Using" is lower case.

NOTE V14: And he added a gratuitous thrust. 'You know, Redfern, there are some things ~~money~~ money won't buy. For instance – it won't buy you a grandfather[.]'‡

NOTE X13: The proverbial fate of the eavesdropper overtook me.

10: These two crossed-out words are difficult to read in the manuscript; I have attempted to write them as they look, even though they seem nonsensical.

"Oh, were you sure?" ~~Miranda~~ Valancy's dull eyes flamed with indignation.

"Yes. He admitted it when I ~~faced him and~~ asked him. Said a good idea was worth more to him than a friend any time. NOTE V14 ~~I went away, cut to the heart. No more friendship for me~~ Well, it was a nasty slam. I was young enough to feel cut up. And it destroyed a lot of my ideals and illusions, which was the worst thing about it. I was a young misanthrope after that. Didn't want to be friends with any[ ]one. And then – the year after I left college – I ~~went~~ met Ethel Traverse."

~~Miranda~~ Valancy shivered. Barney, his hands stuck in his ~~overalls~~ pockets, was regarding the floor moodily and didn't notice it.

"Dad told you about her, I suppose. She was very beautiful. And I loved her. Oh, yes I loved her. I won't deny it or belittle it now. It was a ~~boy's love = romantic~~ lonely, romantic boy's ^first passionate^ love ~~but~~ ^and^ it was very real. And I thought she loved me. I was fool enough to think that. I was wildly happy when she promised to marry me. For a few months. Then – I found out she didn't. ~~Never~~ I was an involuntary eavesdropper on a certain occasion for a moment. That moment was enough. ~~NOTE Y18~~ NOTE X13 A ~~chum~~ ^girl friend^ of hers ~~was as asked~~ ^was asking^ her how she could stomach Doc. ~~Shortreed's~~ ^Redfern's^ son and the patent medicine background.

"[']His money will gild the Pills and sweeten the Bitters,[']" said Ethel, with a laugh. "[']Mother told me to catch him if I·could. We're on the rocks. But pah! I smell ~~the liniment~~ ^turpentine^ whenever he comes near me.[']"

"Oh, Barney," cried ~~Miranda~~ Valancy, wrung with pity for him. She had forgotten all about herself and was filled with compassion for Barney and rage against Ethel Traverse. How dared she?

"Well[,];"[—]Barney got up and began pacing round the room;[—]"That finished me. Completely. I left ~~Montreal~~ ^civilization^ and those accursed ~~und ... one decenes...~~[10] ^dopes^ behind me and went to the Yukon.

For five years I knocked about the world; ^– in all sorts of outlandish places^ I earned enough to live on—I wouldn't touch a cent of dad's money. Then one day I woke up to the fact that I no longer cared a hang about Ethel, one way or another. She was somebody I'd known in another world – that was all. But I had no hankering to go back to the old life. None of that for me. I was free and I meant to keep so. I came to Mistawis – saw Tom MacMurray's island. ~~You know the rest.~~ My first book had been published the year before – ^and made a hit; [–]^ I had a bit of money from my royalties. I bought my island. ~~You know the rest.~~ But I kept away from people. I had no faith in anybody. I didn't believe there was such a thing as real friendship or true love in the world—not for me anyhow; ^– the son of Purple Pills.^ ~~Then you came. Oh, yes, I had to believe you loved me. There was no other reason~~ I used to revel in all the wild yarns they told of me. In fact, I'm afraid I suggested a few of them myself. By mysterious remarks which people interpreted in the light of their own prepossessions. Then[11] – you came. I <u>had</u> to believe you loved me – really loved <u>me</u> – not my father's millions. There was no other reasons why you should want to marry a penniless devil with my supposed record. And I was sorry for you. Oh, yes, I don't deny I married you because I was sorry for you. And then,[–] I found you the best and jolliest and dearest little pal and chum a fellow ever had ~~NOTE Q15~~ NOTE Z13 I'd have been willing to go on forever just as we were.[12] | NOTE O19 |[13] But[14] I didn't realize what you ^actually^ meant to me till that moment at the switch. Then it came ~~light~~ like a lightning flash. NOTE A14 I admit it bowled me over – knocked me silly. I couldn't get my bearings for awhile. That's why I acted like a mule. But the thought that drove me to the tall timber was the awful one that you were going to die. I'd always hated the thought of it – but I supposed there wasn't any chance for you[,] so I put it out of my mind. Now I had to face it—you were under sentence of death and I couldn't live without you. When I came home last night I had made up my mind that I'd take you to all the specialists in the world – that something surely could

11: In the published version, a new paragraph begins here.

NOTE Z13: Witty – loyal – sweet. You made me believe again in the reality of friendship & love. The world was good again just because you were in it, honey. I'd have been willing to go on forever just as we were. I knew that the night I came home & saw my homelight shining out from the island for the first time. And knew you were there waiting for me. After being homeless all my life it was beautiful to have a home. To come home hungry at night & know there was a good supper & a cheery fire – and <u>you</u>.

12: Montgomery neglected to strike this sentence even though she rewrote it into NOTE Z13. This is corrected in the published version.

13: There is no NOTE O19. It likely was one of Montgomery's old notations that she neglected to strike out in the manuscript.

14: In the published version, a new paragraph begins here.

NOTE A14: I knew I couldn't live without you – that if I couldn't pull you loose in time I'd have to die with you.

NOTE B14: Was she, Valancy, being called "darling?"

15: In the published version, a new paragraph begins with "Valancy looked up."

NOTE C14: in the silk-smooth voice of ultimate rage. "You're tired of me. You want to get out of it – free from me. ~~Jus~~ You're ashamed of the Pills & the ~~Luna~~ Liniment, just as she was. Your Stirling pride can't stomach them.

16: In the published version, "doc" is capitalized.

be done for you. I felt sure you couldn't be as bad as Dr. Trent thought when those moments on the track hadn't even hurt you. And I found your note – and went mad with happiness – and a little terror for fear you didn't care much ^for^ me[,] after all[,] and had gone away to get rid of me. But now, it's all right isn't it, ~~sweetheart?~~ ^darling?"^ ^NOTE B14^

"I <u>can't</u> believe you care for me," ^she^ said ~~Miranda~~ helplessly. "I <u>know</u> you can't. What's the use, Barney? Of course, you're sorry for me – of course you want to do the best you can to straighten out the mess. But it can't be straightened out that way. You couldn't love me – <u>me</u>[.]" She ~~rose~~ stood up and pointed tragically to the mirror over the mantel. Certainly, not even ~~John~~ ^Allan^ Tierney could have seen beauty in the ~~pale~~ ^woeful,^ haggard little face reflected there. ~~B~~

Barney didn't look at the mirror. He looked at ~~Miranda~~ Valancy as if he would like to snatch her—or beat her.

"Love you. Girl, you're in the very core of my heart. I hold you there like a jewel. Didn't I promise you I'd never tell you a lie? Love you! I love you with all there is of me to love. Heart, soul, brain. Every fibre of body & spirit thrilling to the sweetness of you. There's ~~simply~~ nobody in the world for me but you, ~~Miranda."~~ Valancy."

"You're – a good actor, Barney," said ~~Miranda~~ Valancy with a wan little smile.

Barney looked at her.

"So you don't believe me – yet?"

"I – can't."

"Oh – damn!" said Barney violently. ~~Miranda~~ Valancy looked up[15] startled. She had never seen <u>this</u> Barney. Scowling! Eyes black with anger. ~~Lips sneering.~~ ^Sneering lips. Dead white face.^

"You don't want to believe it," said Barney ~~furiously.~~ ~~NOTE Z18~~ NOTE C14 "~~You're tired of me. You want to get out of it = free from me. You're ashamed of the pills and the liniment just as she was~~ ^NOTE A19^: It was all right as long as you thought you hadn't long to live. A good lark – you could put up with me. But a lifetime with old doc[16]

~~Shortreed's~~ ^Redfern's^ son is a different thing. Oh, I understand – perfectly. I've been very dense – but I understand at last."

~~Miranda~~ Valancy stood up. She stared into his furious face. Then – she suddenly laughed.

"You darling!" she said. "You do mean it[!]~~;~~ You do really love me[!]~~;~~ You wouldn't be so enraged if you didn't." ~~Everything is all right."~~

Barney stared at her for a moment. Then he caught her in his arms with the little~~,~~low~~,~~laugh of the triumphant lover.

Uncle Benjamin, who had been frozen with horror at the keyhole, suddenly thawed out and tiptoed back to ~~the~~ Mrs. ~~George~~ Frederick and Cousin Stickles.

"Everything is all right," he announced jubilantly.

Dear little Doss! He would send for his lawyer right away and ~~allen~~ alter his will again. Doss should be his sole heiress. To her that had should certainly be given.[17] | ~~NOTE~~
~~X20~~ NOTE D14

17: A paraphrase of Mark 4:25: "For he that hath, to him shall be given"; also used in Chapters VIII and XXVII.

NOTE D14: Mrs. Frederick, returning to her comfortable belief in an overruling Providence, got out the Family Bible & made an entry under "Marriages."

of the triumphant lover.

Uncle Benjamin, who had been frozen with horror at the keyhole, suddenly (turned out and whirled back to the Mrs Frederick and Cousin Stickles.

"Everything is all right," he announced jubilantly.

Dear little Doss! He would send for his lawyer right away and alter his will again. Doss showed he his sole heiress. To her that had should certainly be given. D/Y

~~XXX~~ ~~XXXIII~~ XI

"But Barney," protested Valancy after a few minutes, "your father — somehow — gave me to understand that you still loved her."

XLIII

"But Barney," protested ~~Miranda~~ Valancy after a few minutes, "your father – somehow – gave me to understand that you <u>still</u> loved <u>her</u>."

"He would. Dad's ~~got a champion reas~~ ^holds the^ championship for ~~saying~~ ^making^ blunders. NOTE B19 NOTE E14 But he isn't a bad old soul, ~~Miranda~~ Valancy. You'll like him."

"I do, now."

"And his money isn't tainted money. He made it honestly. ^~~And~~ His medicines are quite harmless.^ ~~Really,~~ ^Even^ his Purple Pills do people whole heaps of good when they believe in them."

"But – I'm not fit for your life," sighed ~~Miranda~~ Valancy. "I'm not – clever – or well-educated – or—"

"My life is in Mistawis – and all the wild places of the world. I'm not going ~~back to~~ to ask you to live the life of a society woman. Of course[,] we must spend a bit of the time with dad—he's lonely and old—"

"But not in that big house of his," pleaded ~~Miranda~~ Valancy. "I can't live in a palace."

"Can't come down to that after your Blue Castle," grinned Barney. "Don't worry, sweet. ~~NOTE Y20~~ NOTE F14 ~~We'll get a little house somewhere outside of Montreal – in the real country. And we'll near enough to see dad often.~~ NOTE Z20 But we'll spend our summers in Mistawis. And our autumns ~~in~~ travelling. I want ~~to show you~~ ^you to see^ the Alhambra—[1] it's the nearest thing to the Blue Castle of your dreams I can think of. And there's an old[-]world garden in Italy where I want to show you the moon rising over Rome through the dark cypress[-]trees."

NOTE E14: If there's a thing that's better left unsaid you can trust him to say it[.]

NOTE F14: I couldn't live in that house myself. It has a white marble stairway with gilt bannisters & looks like a furniture shop with the labels off. Likewise it's the pride of dad's heart. We'll get a little house somewhere outside of Montreal – in the real country – near enough to see dad often. I think we'll build one for ourselves. A house you build for yourself is so much nicer than a hand-me-down.

1: The Alhambra is a palace built in the thirteenth and fourteenth centuries by Islamic rulers in Granada, Andalusia, Spain. It is now a UNESCO World Heritage Site. See the chapter "My Castle in Spain" in Elizabeth Epperly's *Through Lover's Lane* for more on the Alhambra as it relates to *The Blue Castle*.

NOTE G14: Valancy, before this year you've spent all your life in ugliness. You know nothing of the beauty of the world. We'll ~~sp~~ climb mountains – hunt for treasures in the bazaars of ~~Somar~~ Samarcand[2] – search out the magic of east & west – run hand in hand to the rim of the world[.] ~~"You sound like John Foster~~

2: Samarcand, also spelled Samarkand or Samarqand, is an ancient city on the Silk Road, located in south-eastern Uzbekistan.

"Will that be any lovelier than the moon rising over Mistawis?" ~~ask~~

"Not lovelier. But a different kind of loveliness. There are so many kinds of loveliness[,] ~~in the world~~ ~~NOTE B21~~ NOTE G14 I want to show you ~~them~~ ^it^ all – ~~to~~ see ~~them~~ ^it^ again through your eyes. ~~NOTE B21~~ ~~We'll spend our summers in the Blue Castle and our autumns in Montreal but the rest of the time we'll tramp. Climb mountains – hunt for treasure in the bazaars~~ ~~NOTE A21~~ ~~of the east.~~ – Girl, there are a million things I want to show you – do with you – say to you. It will take a lifetime. ^And we must see about that picture by Tierney[,] after all."^

"Will you promise me one thing?" asked ~~Miranda~~ Valancy solemnly.

"Anything," said Barney recklessly.

"Only one thing. You are never, under any circumstances or under any provocation, to cast it up to me that I asked you to marry me.["]

5.11

a show you — do with you — say
to you. It will take a lifetime. And
up, Miriel — see about that picture by Tierney.
"I'll after all promise me one thing?"
asked Miranda solemnly.

"Anything," said Barney recklessly.

"Only me thing. You are never,
under any circumstances or
under any provocation, to cast
it up to me that I asked you
to marry me.

———— XXVIII XLII

(Extract from letter written by
Miss Anne _____ to Mr. Cecil Price)

"It's really disgusting that
Ross's crazy adventures should
have turned out — like this. It really
makes one feel that there is

XLIV

(Extract from letter written by Miss Olive Stirling to Mr. Cecil Price}

"It's really disgusting that Doss's crazy adventures should have turned out like this. It really makes one feel that there is no use in behaving properly.

I'm <u>sure</u> her mind was unbalanced when she left home. What she said about a dust-pile showed that. ~~Of cou, She~~ Of course I don't think there was ever a thing the matter with her heart. Or perhaps Snaith or ~~Shortreed~~ ^Redfern^ or whatever his name really is fed Purple Pills to her back in that Mistawis hut & cured her. It would make quite a testimonial for the family ads, wouldn't it?

He's such an insignificant[-]looking creature[,] ~~with mismated eyebrows and flying jibs jibs.~~ I mentioned this to Doss but all she said was, "I don't like collar ad men." NOTE E19 NOTE H14

He also claims[,] I believe[,] to be John Foster. We can believe <u>that</u> or not[,] as we like, I suppose.

Old Doc ~~Shortreed~~ ^Redfern^ has given them two millions for a wedding present NOTE E21 NOTE I14 ~~They're going to spend the fall in Italy, & the winter on the Riviera and motor through Normandy in apple blossom time.~~ ^~~Not in that old dreadful old Lizzie of theirs, though.~~^ ~~Well, I think I'll run away too and disgrace myself, too. It seems to pay.~~

~~Uncle Ben is a scream~~ NOTE F21: The fuss they all make over Doss now is absolutely sickening. To hear Aunt Amelia talking of ="[']my-son-in-law, Bernard ~~Shortreed~~ ^Redfern[']"=^ and

NOTE H14: Well, he's certainly no collar ad=[ ] man. Though I must say there is something rather distinguished about him, now that he has cut his hair & put on decent clothes. I really think, Cecil, you should exercise more. It doesn't do to get too fleshy.

NOTE I14: Evidently the Purple Pills are money-makers.[1] They're going to spend the fall in Italy & the winter in Egypt and motor through Normandy in apple-blossom time. <u>Not</u> in that dreadful old Lizzie, though. Redfern has got a wonderful new car.

Well, I think I'll run away, too, & disgrace myself. It seems to pay.

Uncle Ben is a scream. Likewise Uncle James.

1: In the published version, "are money-makers" is changed to "bring in the bacon."

267

NOTE J14: 'my daughter,
Mrs. Bernard Redfern.'
Mother & father[2] are as
bad as the rest. And they
can't see that Valancy is
just laughing at them all
in her sleeve."

2: In the published version,
"father" is capitalized.

NOTE J14

"~~my daughter Mrs. Bernard Shortreed~~" ^Re^!
^~~Mother and father are as bad as the rest.~~ ^ ~~And they
can't see that Miranda Doss is laughing at them all, in
her sleeve."~~

J.14.   5-14

"My people ... has been ... Be-Shadu-
reed"! And they ... All
... as the rest —
that ... class is laughing
at — cheese all, it her please."

XXIII
III XXXVII

Miranda and Barney ... drifted
into the canoe and turned under
the mainland pines, ... a farewell
look at — the Blue castle, beyond
... The West were
... delicately delicate and
elusive. The Fortunate Islands, over
the roof of the little house ...
... suggestion of gray-blue
... hip and such
were coming eagerly in the ...
pines. Good Luck and ...

XLV

~~Miranda~~ Valancy and Barney ~~stepped into the canoe and~~ turned under the mainland pines ^in the cool dusk of the September night =^ for a farewell look at the Blue Castle. ~~Beyond them Mira The~~ Mistawis was ~~drowned in suml sunset~~ ^drowned in sunset^ lilac ~~lake~~ ^light,^ incredibly delicate and elusive. ~~The Fortunate Isles. Over the roof of the little house was still a subtle suggestion of gray-blue chimney smoke.~~ Nip and Tuck were cawing lazily in the old pines. Good Luck and Jigglesqueak were mewed and mewing in separate ~~baskets~~ baskets in Barney's new dark-green car. <del>NOTE C21</del> NOTE K14 ~~Miranda~~ Valancy was in tears.

"Don't cry, ~~darling~~ ^honeysweet Moonlight^. We'll be back next summer. And now we're off for a real honeymoon."

~~Miranda~~ Valancy smiled through her tears. She was so happy that her happiness ~~terrified~~ ^terrified^ her. ~~And she~~ But despite the delights before her – 'the glory that was Greece & and the grandeur that was Rome'[1] – lure of the ageless Nile – ^mosque^ – glamor of the Riviera, <del>NOTE P21</del> NOTE L14 ~~sorcery of the Alhambra = she knew that her 'real honeymoon' had been the one~~ she knew perfectly well ^that^ no spot or place or home in the world could ever ~~be so dear to her as her Blue Castle.~~ ^possess the magic of her ^ ^possess the sorcery of her Blue Castle.^

The End

NOTE K14: <u>en route</u> to Cousin Georgiana's. Cousin Georgiana was going to take care of them until Barney & Valancy came back. Aunt Wellington and Cousin Sarah and Aunt Alberta had also entreated the privilege of looking after them but to Cousin Georgiana was it given[.]

1: From "To Helen" (1831), a poem by Edgar Allan Poe (1809–1849).

NOTE L14: – mosque & palm & minaret –

For Further Reading

Bolger, F. W. P. and Elizabeth Epperly, eds. *My Dear Mr. M.: Letters to G. B. MacMillan from L. M. Montgomery.* Toronto: Oxford University Press, 1992.

Cavert, Mary Beth. "*The Blue Castle*: How to Identify Early and Later Printings." *The Shining Scroll*, 2022, https://lmmontgomeryliterarysociety.weebly.com/uploads/2/2/6/5/226525/the_shiningscroll2022.pdf.

———. "Why is *The Blue Castle* About a Castle and Why is it Blue?" *The Shining Scroll*, 2018, https://lmmontgomeryliterarysociety.weebly.com/uploads/2/2/6/5/226525/the_shiningscroll2018.pdf.

Collins, Carolyn Strom, ed. *After Many Years: Twenty-one "Long-Lost" Stories by L. M. Montgomery.* Halifax: Nimbus Publishing, 2017.

———, ed. *Anne of Green Gables: The Original Manuscript.* Halifax: Nimbus Publishing, 2019.

———, ed. *An Annotated Bibliography of L. M. Montgomery's Stories and Poems.* Charlottetown, PEI: University of Prince Edward Island Press, 2016.

———. "Cutting and Pasting: What L. M. Montgomery's Island Scrapbooks Reveal about her Reading." Presentation to the L. M. Montgomery International Conference on Reading, 2018, https://journalof lmmontgomerystudies.ca/reading/Collins/-Cutting-and-Pasting

Epperly, Elizabeth Rollins. "Approaching the Montgomery Manuscripts." In Mary Rubio, ed. *Harvesting Thistles: The Textual Garden of L. M. Montgomery.* Guelph, ON: Canadian Children's Press, 1994.

———. *The Fragrance of Sweet-Grass: L. M. Montgomery's Heroines and the Pursuit of Romance.* Toronto: University of Toronto Press, 1992.

———. *Imagining Anne: L. M. Montgomery's Island Scrapbooks*. Halifax: Nimbus Publishing, 2019. First published 2008 by Penguin Canada (Toronto).

———. *Through Lover's Lane: L. M. Montgomery's Photography and Visual Imagination*. Toronto: University of Toronto Press, 2007.

Hutton, Jack and Linda Jackson-Hutton. *Lucy Maud Montgomery and Bala*. Bala, ON: Bala Museum with Memories of Lucy Maud Montgomery, 1998. Reprinted 2022.

Lefebvre, Benjamin. "How Fair the Realm Literary Allusions Open to the View." https://lmmonline.org/blog/2022/11/how-fair-the-realm-literary-allusions-open-to-the-view/, November 22, 2022.

———, ed. *The L. M. Montgomery Reader: Volume One: A Life in Print*. Toronto: University of Toronto Press, 2013.

———, ed. *The L. M. Montgomery Reader: Volume Three: A Legacy in Review*. Toronto: University of Toronto Press, 2015.

Montgomery, L. M. *Anne of Green Gables*. Boston: L. C. Page and Co., 1908.

———. *The Blue Castle*. Toronto: McClelland and Stewart, 1926.

———. *Rainbow Valley*. New York: Stokes, 1919.

———. "Spring in the Woods." *Canadian Magazine*, May 1911.

———. "The Woods in Summer." *Canadian Magazine*, September 1911.

———. "The Woods in Winter." *Canadian Magazine*, December 1911.

Rubio, Mary. *Lucy Maud Montgomery: The Gift of Wings*. Doubleday Canada, 2008.

———. "Subverting the Trite: L. M. Montgomery's Room of Her Own." In Benjamin Lefebvre, ed., *L. M. Montgomery Reader: Volume Two: A Critical Heritage*. Toronto: University of Toronto Press, 2014.

Rubio, Mary and Elizabeth Waterston, eds. *The Selected Journals of L. M. Montgomery*. Volumes I (1890–1910), II (1910–1921), III (1921–1929), and IV (1929–1935). Toronto: Oxford University Press, 1985; 1987; 1992; 1998.

Russell, Ruth Weber, D. W. Weber, and Rea Wilmshurst. *Lucy Maud Montgomery: A Preliminary Bibliography*. Waterloo, ON: University of Waterloo Library, 1986.

Tiessen, Hildi Froese and Paul Gerard Tiessen, eds. *After Green Gables: L. M. Montgomery's Letters to Ephraim Weber, 1916–1941*. Toronto: University of Toronto Press, 2006.

Waterston, Elizabeth. *Magic Island: The Fictions of L. M. Montgomery*. Toronto: Oxford University Press, 2008.

Acknowledgements

The Confederation Centre of the Arts in Charlottetown, Prince Edward Island, holds fifteen of L. M. Montgomery's original manuscripts, including *Anne of Green Gables* and *The Blue Castle*. Kathleen MacKinnon, Registrar, in the Confederation Centre Art Gallery, graciously made both manuscripts available to me so that I could photograph each page in preparation for transcribing them and for studying Montgomery's writing and editing methods. *Anne of Green Gables: The Original Manuscript* was published by Nimbus in 2019. And now, *The Blue Castle: The Original Manuscript* is available for Montgomery admirers to study.

My thanks to Mary Beth Cavert, Bernadeta Milewski, Benjamin Lefebvre, Jack Hutton, Linda Jackson-Hutton, Sandra Wagner, and Linda Boutilier for their continued encouragement and clarification of some of the questions I have had along the way. Also, thanks to my editor, Marianne Ward, and the team at Nimbus Publishing—editors Claire Bennet and Whitney Moran, as well as General Manager Terrilee Bulger—for their invaluable support for the works of L. M. Montgomery.

And to my husband, Andrew, I owe much appreciation for his patience and understanding of the long hours I've spent at the computer and buried in dozens of books while preparing *The Blue Castle: The Original Manuscript* for publication.

– CSC